Asian Americans in the United States

Volume 1

Alexander Yamato
Soo-Young Chin
Wendy L. Ng
Joel Franks

San Jose State University

KENDALL/HUNT PUBLISHING COMPANY
2460 Kerper Boulevard P.O. Box 539 Dubuque, Iowa 52004-0539

Contents

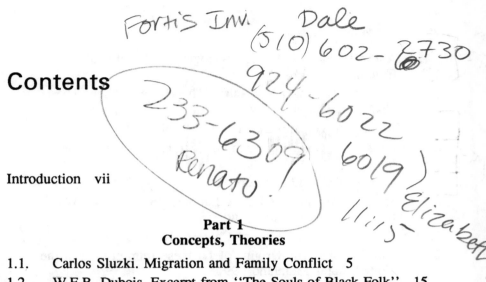

Introduction vii

Part 1
Concepts, Theories

1.1. Carlos Sluzki. Migration and Family Conflict 5

1.2. W.E.B. Dubois. Excerpt from "The Souls of Black Folk" 15

1.3. Robert Ezra Park. Excerpt from "Our Racial Frontier on the Pacific" 16

1.4. Milton M. Gordon. Excerpt from "Assimilation in American Life" 17

1.5. Robert Blauner. Excerpt from "Colonized and Immigrant Minorities" 19

1.6. Edna Bonacich. Excerpt from "A Theory of Ethnic Antagonism: The Split Labor Market" 21

1.7. Benjamin B. Ringer. Excerpt from "We the People" and Others 22

1.8. Multiple Consciousness 25

Part 2
International Relations Between Asia and the United States: Immigration

2.1. The First Naturalization Act of 1790 31

2.2. Oscar Handlin. The Uprooted 32

2.3. Eric C. Wolf. International Capitalism and Labor on the Move 33

2.4. Herbert Gutman. Immigrant Culture and Social Change in Industrializing America 35

2.5. Denett Tyler. "The American Share in the Opium Trade" 37

2.6. John Quincy Adams. Lecture on the War with China 39

2.7.   Aaron H. Palmer. Memoir: Geographical, Political, and Commercial   53

2.8.   Harley Farnsworth MacNair: ''The Chinese Alien: The Contract Laborer,''   59

2.9.   Alexander Yamato. Labor in California   67

2.10.   Ping Chiu. Changing Economic Structure and Chinese Immigration, 1865–1880   71

2.11.   Chinese Railroad Workers   83

2.12.   John R. Commons. Chinese Laborers in Post-Civil War Massachusetts and the South   85

2.13.   Fraudulent Importation of Chinese, 1886   91

2.14.   Yuji Ichioka. The Origins of Japanese Immigration to the United States Mainland   99

2.15.   Immigration to Hawaii   101

Part 3
Work, Occupation, Community

3.1.   Joel Franks. The Chinese Laundry and the Chinese Restaurant   111

3.2.   California Trade Unions and the Anti-Chinese Movement   113

3.3.   Joel Franks. Ping Chiu's Chinese Labor in California 1850–1880   117

3.4.   James H. Okahata (Ed). Excerpt from *A History of Japanese in Hawaii*   125

3.5.   John A. Whitney. Excerpt from *The Chinese and the Chinese Question*   131

3.6.   Joel Franks. Chinese Shoemakers in Industrializing San Francisco   137

Part 4
Discrimination and Anti-Asian Movements

4.1.   Joel Franks. Republicanism, Producerism, and the Origins of the Anti-Asian Movement in the United States   145

4.2.   Joel Franks. The Democratic Party and the Anti-Chinese Movement in California   149

4.3.   Alexander Yamato. Institutionalized Discrimination in California   151

4.4.   The United States Constitution and Slavery   161

4.5.   Thomas Benton. Oregon Question   163

4.6.   Robert F. Heizer and Alan F. Alkmquist. Making California a White Man's Paradise: 1849 California Constitutional Convention   167

4.7.   Native American during the Early Years of California Statehood   169

4.8.   John Bigler. To the Senate and Assembly of the State of California, 1852   173

4.9.   Foreign Miner's Tax, California, 1853   181

4.10.   Report of the Committee on Mines and Mining Interests, 1853   185

4.11.   Supreme Court of the State of California: People v Hall, 1854   189

4.12.   Robert F. Heizer and Alan F. Almquist. The Mexican Californian and the New State: 1855   195

4.13.   Dred Scott v. Sandford, 1856   197

4.14.   Report of Joint Select Committee Relative to the Chinese Population of the State of California, 1862   205

4.15.   San Francisco, Cubic Air Ordinance, 1870   213

4.16.   An Address to the People of the United States Upon the Evils of Chinese Immigration, 1877   215

4.17.   Constitution of the State of California, Article XIX, 1879   229

4.18.   Henry George. Henry George and the Workingmen's Party of California   231

4.19.   Chinese Exclusion Act of 1882   235

Part 5
Responses to Anti-Asian Sentiment

5.1.   Lai Chun-Chuen. Remarks of the Chinese Merchants of San Francisco upon Governor Bigler's Address, 1855   245

5.2.   Norman Asing. To His Excellency Governor Bigler   247

5.3.   Reverend William Speer. Plea in Behalf of the Immigrants from China   271

5.4.   A Reply to the Charges Against the Chinese   293

5.5.   Joel Franks. Chinese Shoemaker Protest in 19th Century San Francisco   305

Introduction

Volume I of Asian Americans in the United States is designed to be used in Asian American Studies 33A and 33B, a sequence of courses that examines Asian Americans in the United States historical and political process, and explores the manner in which culture, institutions, and American society are affected by the Asian American presence. Both Volume I and Volume II are comprised of selected readings from both primary and secondary sources. Volume I covers Asian Americans in the United States through the latter part of the 19th century. Volume II spans the latter part of the 19th century to the present. Each volume is divided into five sections. Part I introduces some concepts that have been utilized in analyzing non-Euroamerican groups in the United States and addresses the diversity in this country. Part II contends with Asian immigration, specifically the structural factors fostering migration from Asia. Part III addresses Asian American participation in the labor force in the United States. Part IV examines structural and social discriminatory practices which have been used against Asian Americans. Part V presents examples of responses and resistance to anti-Asian sentiment.

Concepts, Theories

1

Part 1. Concepts, Theories

1.0   Carlos Sluzki. Migration and Family Conflict
1.2.   W.E.B. DuBois. Excerpt from "The Souls of Black Folk"
1.3.   Robert Ezra Park. Excerpt from "Our Racial Frontier on the Pacific"
1.4.   Milton M. Gordon. Excerpt from "Assimilation in American Life"
1.5.   Robert Blauner. Excerpt from "Colonized and Immigrant Minorities"
1.6.   Edna Bonacich. Excerpt from "A Theory of Ethnic Antagonism: The Split Labor Market"
1.7.   Benjamin B. Ringer. Excerpt from "We the People" and Others
1.8.   Multiple Consciousness

A conceptual framework is a set of ideas that are used together to create a larger understanding of phenomena in the world. A conceptual framework or theory is not necessarily accurate or correct; it is one of a myriad of ways to look at processes. Within the context of this course sequence, AAS33A and AAS33B, socio-historical, political and economic theories will be addressed. In this section of the reader seven conceptual frameworks will be addressed. These are by no means the only explanations possible; nor are these ideas mutually exclusively. The concepts introduced in this section of the reader were selected on the basis of applicability to the material we will be covering in class.

The first article by Carlos Sluzki, MD. presents the notion of migration (meaning a change in location as opposed to immigration which specifies intentionality) and the accompanying difficulties thereof. Although not all Americans are immigrants, migration is a major factor in the social history of America. Forced migration, displacement both within and outside the United States, as well as consensual migration can be examined vis-a-vis Sluzki's theory of migration and stree.

The second idea brought forth is that of double-consciousness by W.E.B. Dubois (turn of the century) which deals with the impact of social and cultural norms on individuals. Although this idea was used to described the African American condition, it is an idea that has been generalized to other groups of people who are viewed as racially, ethnically, and socially different from the majority group in the United States.

Robert E. Park's race relations cycle is introduced as another early notions in race relations (1920's) in the United States. He brings for the idea of the inevitability of assimilation. Park's ideas were, and still are very influential in the development of social theory in the United States.

Built upon Park's assertions of race relations, Gordon further articulated and refined the notion of assimilation in this book, *Assimilation into American Life.*

In contrast to the previous two notions, Blauner cast race relations in terms of economic power relations—that of the colonizer (of the dominant group) and the colonized (racial minorities) within the United States. In doing so, he put forth the notion of internal colonialism.

Bonacich's work on split labor market theory shares some similarity with Blauner's in that the economics is split along racial lines, and that EuroAmerican workers view minority workers as threatening their interest because of the willingness of workers of color to work for less.

Ringer's dual systems approach to race relations focuses on the dual legal-political system which divides the populace into "people" and "other people." This division is then the justification for unequal access to human rights and privileges considered basic for all Americans.

The final idea introduced in this section deals with the notion of multiple consciousness as an alternative perspective to a single perspective or consciousness and advocates understanding of the multiplicity of traditions and perspective from which people come. This notion can be seen as related to, but not the same as, the notion of cultural pluralism.

Historical events and trends can be interpreted through these theories, and by the end of the semester you should be able to see how these ideas can be applied. This should give you a sense of interpretive social, political and economic history, and provide you with the tools to your own understanding of the historical legacy in the United States.

1.1

Carlos Sluzki

Migration and Family Conflict

Topical Introduction

Migration, voluntary or involuntary, is part of the American experience
for most groups in the United States. The following article provides an
overview of the migration process and the impact of migration stress on
the family system. The framework is particularly useful because issues
from preparation to intergenerational conflicts that might rise over generations are addressed. By virtue of addressing migration and not immigration, this particular model can address both voluntary and involuntary migration. Sluzki's view of migration and family process is oriented
towards intervention at certain points of the process to reduce the effects of migration stress. Although the plan could be beneficial for many
families, it is problematic to locate the very families that could use the
intervention. In spite of that difficulty, Sluzki provides some valuable
tools with which to examine and understand the process of migration,
be it from one country to the next, or from a rural area to an urban area,
or from town to town.

---

*The stages of the process of migration are described, with the impli-
cations of each for family conflict and appropriate therapeutic intervention.*

Millions of people migrate each year. They do it alone or in organized
aggregates, by their own decision or forced by decisions of others or
by natural cataclysms, carrying with them truckloads of household
items or a bundle of essentials. They travel on a luxury ocean liner or
crammed in the *Bodega* of a *sampan,* are received with press conferences or sneak in under barbed wire borders by night. They look forward with hope or backward with fear. They belong to a culture in
which high geographic mobility is the rule and count on skills to deal

with the process of migration, or they have been raised in a highly sedentary culture in which uprooting means near-catastrophe. They are thoroughly familiar with, or completely ignorant of, their situation on arrival, the language and customs of the new place, the people, the dwelling situation, the work they are going to have. One way or another, countless numbers of people manage to break away from their basic support networks, sever ties with places and people, and transplant their home base, their nest, their life projects, their dreams, their ghosts.

There is a unique drama that characterizes migration in each case. In fact, this drama often becomes a part of the treasured heritage of each family. The concrete anecdote covers the widest spectrum. It may consist of the sheltered move from coast to coast of an executive's family for reasons of promotion in his work or the precarious move of the family of a political refugee who is given asylum in another country as an option to continued jail and torture. It may be the hopeful move of a family to a medical center where an offspring may receive continuous treatment for a chronic disease or the doomed move of a Puerto Rican from a low-paying job in San Juan to a low-paying job in the Bronx. It may be the move forced by racial and religious persecution in Nazi Germany or present-day Uganda or Southeast Asia, and so on, in an endless variety.

However, despite this array of anecdotes and scripts that derive from the culture and the circumstances of each family, the process of migration—both across cultures and across regions within cultures-presents outstanding regularities. In fact, if we focus our attention on patterns, rather than content (as we shall do in this discussion), we may develop a model of the migratory process that has a reasonable degree of cross-cultural validity, a model that is, so to speak, "culture free," regardless of how culture-specific the styles of coping and the prevalent themes may be.[1]

Stages of Migration Process

The continuum of the process of migration can be broken down into the following discrete steps: (I) *preparatory stage,* (II) *act of migration;* (III) *period of overcompensation;* (IV) *period of decompensation;* (V) *transgenerational phenomena.* Each step has distinctive characteristics, triggers different types of family coping mechanisms, and unchains different types of conflicts and symptoms. Each of these basis phases of the migratory process will be described in detail in this paper, with emphasis on specific types of urgencies, conflicts, and crises. This will be followed by some general guidelines for preventive and therapeutic interventions that are relevant when dealing with families presenting conflicts related to the migratory process.

An attempt to represent graphically the continuum of migration renders a shape well known to students in the field of biology and experimental psychology; the *curve of performance under stress*. It is reproduced in an adapted fashion in Figure 1, illustrating the cycle and the different points of preventive and therapeutic intervention.

I. Preparatory Stage

This prologue to migration begins when the first concrete moves are made by family members toward a commitment to migrate. These moves can be an exchange of letters, a request of an application for visas, or any other act that substantiates the intent to migrate. The time span of this stage obviously varies with the circumstances but in most cases is also contingent upon the family style (from an "explosive" decision to a lengthy rumination).

In the course of the preparatory stage, a first "up and down" curve will frequently appear, expressed as a short period of euphoria and an also short period of overload, dismay, and poor performance, that habitually does not acquire major proportions and tends to be explained away as the natural result of efforts, tensions, and emotions. In the course of those ups and downs, however, new family rules about roles and functions in relation to migration begin to be negotiated among members. These rules, explored during the preliminary stage, will be fully incorporated once migration takes place.

Migration is described by migrants as an act loaded either with negative motivations and connotations (such as "to escape political oppression") or with positive connotations (such as "to make a better living"). It is important to realize that the choice of one given connotation over the other is sometimes reasonable, but on other occasions quite arbitrary, although not random. So, "to make a better living" (positive) may imply "to escape from a bad living situation" (negative). [The choice of one given emphasis as reason for migration—with the value judgment attached to it—may provide us with valuable clues about the family's coping styles, including rules about which roles are to be played by each member.]

In spite of the fact that it is usually the result of a collective decision, some people tend to be labeled as "responsible" or motivator of the migration. Did they move because it was beneficial for the job situation or the career of one member of the family—more frequently the husband—while the other one—more frequently the wife—was dragged behind? Did they move because one of the kids was chronically ill, and they needed to locate near an adequate medical facility? If so, who insisted on the move, and was it useful in terms of the care of the illness? Was somebody rescued by the move? Who experienced the greatest loss in the move? The anecdotes that consolidate rules of heroes and villains, victims and oppressors, remain frequently as family myths and appear repeatedly as themes of family feuds or as the unmentioned "skeletons in the closet."

Another important issue in this regard stems from the frequent assumption that if the move had a positive motivation or even far exceeded the family's expectations in terms of advantages, there is no reason to mourn what has been left behind; any sadness or mourning is immediately labeled as pathological or an act of ill will. In fact, those family members "in charge" of mourning have the greatest chance of being scapegoated by the rest (thus isolating those members in charge of the painful task of coming to terms with the past).

The opposite situation can also be found. Families who have escaped from extreme situations such as total annihilation may remain anchored to their past, in a state of permanent collective remembrance, mourning, and involvement with those dreaded circumstances from which they—and not others—escaped. In these cases, the member of the family who breaks away first from the collective family mourning is frequently scapegoated as a traitor (to the family, to those who stayed behind, etc.). The confrontation notwithstanding, this role accomplishes a collective need: that of testing the new reality (done by the "traitor") while appeasing the guilt (done by the "accusers").

II. The Act of Migration

Migration is a transition with little or no prescribed rituals. In most cultures and circumstances, migrants are left to deal with the painful act of migration with only their private rituals.[2] The most noticeable exception takes place in Israel, where the Ulpan—an initial residential program and intensive teaching of Hebrew to new immigrants—entails a whole complex ritual of initiation. There are also minor exceptions in other cultures, such as the "welcome wagon" ritual performed by neighbors to newly moved families in middle-class America.

It must be kept in mind that, although the very act of migration may constitute a brief transition (a three-hour leap by plane), in many other cases the act proper may take a considerable time. Such is frequently the case with people displaced by wars and with people who migrated with intermediary stays in countries of transition or in internment camps. This protracted process may lead to the establishment of strong allegiances among people exposed to the same vicissitudes, to the point of becoming a primary net as strong as the one left in the country of origin. Such has been the case, for instance, with European Jews escaping the Holocaust who shared long pilgrimages on board ships before reaching a country that would accept them (leading to surrogate-family names such as *schiffbrudern* and *schiffschwestern*— ship-brothers and ship-sisters). The same occurs at present with the "boat people" from Viet Nam.

The mode or *style of the migratory act* varies considerably. Some families "burn bridges," and the act of migration has the character of something final and unchangeable. Contrariwise, others affirm that they migrate "only for a while," regardless of the unlikelihood of a return. Some families decide a priori that the country they have chosen will be it, whereas other families explicitly include trial periods in their plans in order to decide among countries. Some families migrate in block and blindly, without any previous exploration of the field. Others organize the move cautiously, sending some members as "scouts" to prepare the terrain, secure jobs and dwelling, etc. Some families migrate legally and can have access to institutions of the country of adoption, whereas others migrate illegally, thus enhancing their (adaptive) mistrust and alienation from main-stream institutions. Finally, some families choose to migrate and some are forced to do so.

III. Period of Overcompensation

Migratory stress does not take its heaviest tool in the weeks or even months immediately following migration. On the contrary, the participants are frequently unaware of the stressful nature of the experience and of its cumulative impact. In fact, it is a period in which a heightened task-oriented efficiency can be noted aided by a strong increase in the split between "instrumental" and "affective" roles within the family, in the service of the basic need for survival and adaptation in an environment and a culture that is, to a greater or lesser extent, alien.

Ethnicity can be defined in terms of the orientation it provides to individuals by delineating norms, values, interactional modalities, rituals, meanings, and collective goals. That orientation—that *weltanschauung*—does not operate in a vacuum but is dialectically supported by regularities of the environment that generate the experience of *consonance*. A person walking in the street with a baguette under his arm is consonant—for a perceptual set tuned up for Paris, not Boston.[3] To be surrounded mainly by blond people in consonant—for Stockholm, not San Juan. For men to go arm in arm is consonant—for Rome, not Omaha. A 1:00 to 4:00 siesta break is consonant—for New Orleans in the summer or for Jamaica, not Brooklyn. In fact, each individual subscribes to a certain organization of reality and, hence, makes constant predictions about how things are going to be and how people are going to act and react. Each unpredicted variation on any of those features shatters that person's premises about reality and calls for a complex calibration of either the perceptions ("are my senses reliable?") or the prediction ("are my values, or is my common sense, reliable?"). These calibrating adaptive mechanisms are mobilized by the *dissonance* resulting from any mismatch between expectations and environment.[4]

In the period immediately following migration, the first priority of the family is sheer survival, that is, the satisfaction of its basic needs. Given those priorities, the process of cancellation of dissonance or the denial of its subjective impact is maximal precisely at the period in which the bombardment by dissonant experiences is also maximal. As a result of this mechanism, it is not infrequent to observe that recent immigrants show a clear focus of attention—of consciousness—while the overall field of consciousness is blurred or clouded (similar to certain patients with concussion who appear overall stunned and confused but maintain a narrow focus of clear consciousness).

A concurrence of extreme circumstances and lack of coping skills can trigger massive crises in this period, with family disorganization or multiple symptoms. But that is not the rule. In fact, the majority of migrating families manage to establish and maintain for months a relative moratorium on the process of acculturation and accommodation. During this period immediately following migration, therefore, conflicts and symptoms tend to remain dormant. The only observable feature is that previous family rules and styles tend to appear slightly exaggerated. For instance, if the members were mutually close, physically or emotionally, they will seem even closer, if they were mutually distant, they will increase their autonomy further, in spite of the fact that the lack of an extended social network may force them to spend more time together.

A moratorium technique developed occasionally is the collective myth that "they will return to the country of origin after some time." Families cling to the old country's norms and refuse to engage with the new environment. Needless to say, that coping strategy can last for only so long, and eventually the fantasy will collapse under the pressure of the new reality, triggering a major crisis.

One way or another, the period of apparent calm and overcompensation gives way, some six months after it started, to an era of major crisis, one in which the long-range responses to migration take place.

IV. Period of Decompensation or Crisis

This is a stormy period, plagued with conflicts, symptoms, and difficulties. In fact, the majority of the migrated families that are brought to the attention of family therapists can be placed at one point or another of this phase of decompensation. In it, the main task of the recently migrated family takes place: that of reshaping its new reality, maximizing both the family's continuity in terms of identity and its compatibility with the environment. These two facets of the task sometimes compete and require a reasonable compromise for their accomplishment. It is indeed a frequent and necessary adaptation to retain certain family habits, even though they differ from those of the new context, while getting rid of other traits because they go too much against the grain of the culture of adoption or because they would require an extended family no longer available. The balance is delicate and difficult to reach. The whole collective task is complex, painful, and unavoidable. Frequently (the crisis creeps into the family through the offspring children tend to catch up with the new culture and the new language (verbal and nonverbal) much more rapidly than their parents do, unleashing a clash of values and styles that strikes at the core of the family).

Many family rules and values that were effective in the country of origin may prove to be less adaptive in the culture and circumstances of the country of adoption. But for a family to change its styles and rules (some of which may have been pivotal ones) requires that the group activate delicate and complex *rules about changes of rules.* In many cases, families have not previously established these rules about rules and embark on the still more difficult task of developing them *de novo.*[5] For instance, how may parents reach an agreement on ways of discussing contraception with their adolescent daughters raised in the United States when the norms of their culture—and therefore their present rules—preclude the explicit discussion of issues about sexuality in general even within the parental couple?

The effect of the strengths and weaknesses of the family coping mechanisms in the context of the new culture is cumulative and will express itself in the course of the months, sometimes years, after the migration. Many family functioning rules will prove to be adaptive in both cultures and will now show any change. Many others will have undergone changes affecting the distribution of roles and norms that may involve every member of the family. Finally, many other patterns will be retained at the expense of a certain degree of alienation from the extrafamilial world. Some of these patterns are maintained because they become central to the family identity, as a sort of cohesive ritual. Others are kept simply because the family has not been able to develop ways to cope with the changes in role entailed by the change of rules.

As mentioned above, in order to cope with the immediacy of migration, families frequently develop a split between instrumental and affective roles: one member—usually the male—deals with (present and future-oriented) instrumental activities that entail a connection with the current environment, and the other—usually the female—centers on present and past-oriented affective activities that entail a sustained connection with the previous environment (including maintenance tasks such as letters, phone calls, etc., and mourning of what has been left behind.)[6] This rule about distribution of roles, that may be adaptive during the first few months, has the potential of a catastrophic runaway in the system if rigidly maintained. The outward-oriented member will develop autonomous adaptive traits and establish a new satisfactory network of his (her) own, and the inward-oriented one will maintain a relative isolation that becomes more marked by comparison. The autonomous member will experience the other one, relatively ignorant of the norms and customs of the new environment and with fewer new acquaintances and friends, as interfering with the instrumental need and reacts to that experience with still more autonomy. This further fences off and enhances the experience of solitude of the already isolated, past-oriented member, who will respond either by clinging more to the past or by clinging more to the other member, who, in turn, will feel dragged down by that situation and increase his (her) disengagement. The whole process escalates progressively into a major crisis of the relationship.[7]

It is interesting to notice the power of this rule about polarization of roles. In those families in which this split of roles escalates into a divorce, it can be seen that the past-oriented member frees herself (himself) from the fixed role *only after the separation;* forced at first by the need to cope, she (he) soon "discovers" her (his) previously untapped abilities to deal with the present environment and to plan the future.

An inverse case, not infrequent in migrant families of rural origin, is that the woman will find an unskilled job in the city more easily than the man, thus challenging drastically their previous family structure and roles. In these circumstances, even though on occasion a switch of roles may take place uneventfully, much more frequently the man will become symptomatic (depressive, alcoholic, or with somatic complaints), or a major crisis of family disorganization will ensue.

Some families manage to mourn what has been left behind and integrate it constructively into a blend of old and new rules, models, and habits that constitute their new reality. For them, the positive side of the experience outweighs the disruptive nature of the stress, and they emerge from the process—some three years after migration—with new individual and collective strengths. In other families, whatever has been left behind in the country of origin, may become increasingly idealized (making adaptation more difficult) or denigrated (making mourning and working through of the loss more difficult) (see Figure 2). High levels of intrafamilial confrontations may cause the family to consult a therapist, with some members representing the values of the country of origin. and some, those of the new society.

The factionalization will appear as tension and overt conflict between spouses, with the additional tug-of-war of offspring factions—or across generations, with the tightening of intragenerational coalitions. These tendencies build into a major interpersonal crisis or crystalize into a medical or psychiatric complaint. In fact, in order to deal with, or express, accumulated stress, tension, pain, and conflict, family members will frequently activate the socially acceptable and interactionally powerful pattern of the "somatic complaint" or the "psychiatric problem," and occasionally the socially less acceptable patterns of "social deviant" (e.g., as a juvenile delinquent).

V. Transgenerational Impact

Families, in their function as main socializing agents, convey not only the norms and mores of their culture at large, but also the specific styles, modes, values, and myths that constitute an ad hoc, family-specific view of the world and of their own history. It comes as no surprise then to discover that any long-term delay in the family's adaptive process will tend to become apparent when a second generation is missed in the country of adoption. Whatever has been avoided by a first generation will appear in the second one, generally expressed as a *clash between generations*.

This clash is maximally apparent in families belonging to cultural groups that have been ghettoized by choice or by force in their country of adoption. A neighborhood that mimics the country of origin constitutes an environment that buffers the cross-cultural exposure and slows any adaptive change. If the second generation becomes socialized in that same secluded environment, the process will repeat itself with no apparent consequences. However, if the process of socialization takes place in a milieu that reflects the norms and values of the new country, what has been delayed by the first generation will take the form of an intergenerational conflict of values.

Such is the case, for instance, with families of Chinese origin living in American Chinatowns. Offspring of immigrant parents, who are raised in the United States and who interacted actively with the larger society through schools, mass media, and informal and formal contacts of various sources, tend to clash dramatically with their parents in terms of values, norms, and mores. In a more or less subtle way, this intergenerational clash takes place in almost any immigrant family with an intensity that shows an inverse correlation with its previous capacity to thoroughly work through the complex process of migration.

In many cases, however, the clash is intercultural rather than intergenerational. The conflict between the child's dominant style of coping—congruent with the family culture—and the differently defined rules and boundaries within large sectors of the extrafamilial world results in a label of "delinquency" for the child's behavior and its consequences (see Minuchin et al., [6. pp. 351–352]).

To close this paper, it should be acknowledged that the general model underlying this presentation, rather than specific to the migratory process, can be applied to many other systemic and environmental changes to which families are exposed in the course of their life cycles. In its descriptive and pragmatic versatility lies, precisely, the power of this paradigm.

References

1. Cherry, Colin. *On Human Communication*. Cambridge and London. The MIT Press (Second Edition), 1966.
2. Falicov, Celia and Betty M. Karrer, "Acculturation and Family Development in Mexican-Americans," Conferences presented at the San Francisco Family Forum, November 11, 1976.
3. Flugelman, Ronaldo Juan and Susan H., "Foreign Student Families at the University of California at Berkeley: A Group at Risk," Working paper prepared for the Community Mental Health Program of the School of Public Health, University of California at Berkeley, 1977.
4. Hoffman, Lynn, "Deviation-Amplifying Processes in Natural Groups," in J. Haley, ed.: *Changing Families*. New York, Grune & Stratton, 1971.
5. Maruyama, Magoroh, "The Second Cybernetics: Deviation-Amplifying Mutual Causal Processes," *American Scientist*, 51: 164–79, 1963. Reprinted in Buckley W., Ed.: *Modern Systems Research for the Behavioral Scientist*. Chicago, Aldine, 1968.
6. Minuchin, S.; Montalvo, B.; Guerney, B. G.; Rosman, B. L.; and Schumer, F. *Families of the Slums,* New York. Basic Books, 1967.
7. Sluzki, Carlos E., "Acculturation and Family Conflict in the Latino Family." Conference presented at the San Francisco Family Forum, November 11, 1976.

Reprint requests should be addressed to Carlos Sluzki, M.D., Family Practice Residency Program, San Francisco General Hospital, San Francisco, California 94110.

1.2
W.E.B. Dubois
Excerpt from "The Souls of Black Folk"

Topical Introduction

Born in 1868, W.E.B. Dubois was an Afro-American scholar and political activist, who helped form the NAACP (National Association for the Advancement of Color People) and left an enduring legacy of commitment to the struggle against racism in the United States. Among his many fine pieces of writing is *The Souls of Black Folk.* In this book can be found Dubois's depiction of African American Double-Consciousness. While Dubois argues that double-consciousness shapes Black identity and Black culture, perhaps the following can also be applied to other excluded social groups in American life.

It is a peculiar sensation, this double-consciousness, this sense of always looking at one's self through the eyes of others, of measuring one's soul by the tape of a world that looks on in amused contempt and pity. One ever feels his twoness,—an American, a Negro; two souls, two thoughts, two unreconciled strivings; two warring ideals in one dark body, whose dogged strength alone keeps it from being torn asunder.

1.3
Robert Ezra Park
Excerpt from "Our Racial Frontier on the Pacific"

Topical Introduction

Robert E. Park was one of the foremost sociologists or race relations in the United States. Moreover, he spent considerable studying the experiences of Asian-Pacific peoples in the United States. A pioneering contributions to the literature of race relations theory is Park's Race Relations Cycle. While some theorists criticize Park's concept as naive and unappreciative of the power of conflict and institutional racism, it is useful to point out that Park originally wrote the following in the 1920s; a time when many Americans believed that people of color, as well as working class European immigrants were by nature inferior and incapable of being useful citizens of the United States. From Robert Ezra Park, "Our Racial Frontier on the Pacific," in *Race and Culture: Essays in the Sociology of Contemporary Man,"* (New York: The Free Press, 1964), 150–151.

The race relations cycle which takes the form, to state it abstractly, of contacts, competition, accommodation and eventual assimilation, is apparently progressive and irreversible. Customs regulations, immigration restrictions and racial barriers may slacken the tempo of the movement; may perhaps halt it altogether for a time; but cannot change its direction; cannot at any rate, reverse it.

It does not follow that because the tendencies to the assimilation and eventual amalgamation of races exist, they should not be resisted and, if possible, altogether inhibited. On the other hand, it is vain to underestimate the character and force of the tendencies that are drawing the races and peoples about the Pacific into the ever narrowing circle of a common life. Rising tides of color and oriental exclusion laws are merely incidental evidences of these diminishing distances.

1.4

Milton M. Gordon

Excerpt from "Assimilation in American Life"

Topical Introduction

Milton Gordon was among a number of social theorists who elaborated upon the ideas of Robert E. Park. Gordon developed an assimilation model which did not include Parks's emphasis upon a structural approach in the context of a world political economy. Milton Gordon, in *Assimilation in American Life,* succinctly delineated assimilation in terms of a process involving the incorporation of groups to a society. From his analysis of the American historical experience, Gordon identified three models of immigrant adjustment in American society. These are Anglo-conformity, melting pot, and cultural pluralism.

Over the course of the American experience, "philosophies," or goal-systems of assimilation, have grouped themselves around three main axes. These three central ideological tendencies may be referred to as "Anglo-conformity" (the phrase is the Coles's[1]), "the melting pot," and "cultural pluralism."[2] In preliminary fashion, we may say that the "Anglo-conformity" theory demanded the complete renunciation of the immigrant's ancestral culture in favor of the behavior and values of the Anglo-Saxon core group; the "melting pot" idea envisaged a biological merger of the Anglo-Saxon peoples with other immigrant groups and a blending of their respective cultures into a new indigenous American type; and "cultural pluralism" postulated the preservation of the communal life and significant portions of the culture of the later immigrant groups within the context of American citizenship and political and economic integration into American society. Various individual changes were rung on these three central themes by particular

Milton M. Gordon, *Assimilation in American Life: The Role of Race, Religion, and National Origins,* Oxford University Press, New York, 1964, pp. 85–86.

proponents of assimilation goals, as we shall see, but the central tendencies remain.

"Cultural pluralism" as an articulated goal-system of assimilation is a relative late-comer on the American scene, being predominantly a development of the experiences and reflections of the twentieth century. Whatever the unconscious or unexpressed cultural goals of non-Anglo-Saxon immigrant groups may have been, and regardless of the factual existence of some degree of cultural pluralism in the colonial and nineteenth century experiences, these eras of American life are characterized by implicit or explicit adherence to theories which postulate either the Anglicization of the non-English portions of the population, or the forging of a new American cultural type out of the diverse heritages of Europe.

1.5

Robert Blauner

Excerpt from "Colonized and Immigrant Minorities"

Topical Introduction

Robert Blauner conceptualized the relationships between racial minorities and American society in terms of colonization as a process of the subjugation of racial minorities. The internal colonial model takes up the issues raised by Robert E. Park in accounting for exploitation and oppression, which are secondary considerations for the assimilation perspective.

Blauner's conceptualization of colonization as a process, rests upon five elements: contact between dominant and subordinate groups is initially through the forced, involuntary entry of the racial minority; the culture of the racial minority is controlled by the dominant group such that some aspects of the culture is changed, destroyed, or kept static; a bureaucracy has control over the lives of the racial minority; a racial labor principle operates to assign minorities jobs in undesirable sectors of the economy, often labor intensive, low wage, non-industrial, offering little or no upward mobility; and racism as an ideology which defines racial minorities as inferior and promotes and justifies their differential treatment, socially, psychologically, and economically in the larger society.

People of color have never been an integral part of the Anglo-American political community and culture because they did not enter the dominant society in the same way as did the European ethnics. The third world notion points to a basic distinction between immigration and colonization as the two major processes through which new population groups are incorporated into a nation. Immigrant groups enter a new territory or society voluntarily, though they may be pushed out of their old country by dire economic or political oppression.

Robert Blauner, "Colonized and Immigrant Minorities," in Norman R. Yetman and C. Hoy Steele, *Majority and Minority: The Dynamics of Racial and Ethnic Relations,* Allyn and Bacon, Inc., Boston, 1975, pp. 338–339.

Colonized groups become part of a new society through force or violence; they are conquered, enslaved, or pressured into movement. Thus, the third world formulation is a bold attack on the myth that America is the land of the free, or, more specifically, a nation whose population has been built up through successive waves of immigration. The third world perspective returns us to the origins of the American experience, reminding us that this nation owes its very existence to colonialism, and that along with settlers and immigrants there have always been conquered Indians and black slaves, and later defeated Mexicans—that is, colonial subjects—on the national soil.

The first condition, already touched upon, is that of a forced entry into the larger society or metropolitan domain. The second is subjection to various forms of unfree labor that greatly restrict the physical and social mobility of the group and its participation in the political arena. The third is a cultural policy of the colonizer that constrains, transforms, or destroys original values, orientations, and ways of life.

1.6
Edna Bonacich
Excerpt from "A Theory of Ethnic Antagonism: The Split Labor Market"

Topical Introduction

Sociologist, Edna Bonacich, has done considerable work studying economic influences on racial and ethnic relations in the United States. During the early 1970s, she argued that perhaps "economic processes are more fundamental" than racial and cultural differences in explaining racism or, as she put it, "ethnic antagonism."

Due to labor markets split along ethnic lines, Bonacich maintained, white working class antagonism toward workers of color was and remains not irrational, but a rational, although unfortunate, response to what Euroamerican workers perceive as a menace to their interests. That is, they see that the availability of workers of color will lower their wages and threaten job stability. The following is taken from Edna Bonacich, "A Theory of Ethnic Antagonism: The Split Labor Market," in Ronald Takaki, (ed), *From Different Shores: Perspectives on Race and Ethnicity in America,* (New York: Oxford University Press, 1987), 140.

The Split Labor Market

The central hypothesis is that ethnic antagonism first germinates in a labor market split along ethnic lines. To be split, a labor market must contain at least two groups of workers whose price of labor differs for the same work, or would differ if they did the same work. The concept "price of labor" refers to labor's total cost to the employer, including not only wages, but the cost of recruitment, transportation, room and board, education, health care (if the employer must bear these), and the costs of labor unrest. The degree of worker "freedom" does not interfere with this calculus; the cost of a slave can be estimated in the same monetary units as that of a wage earner, from his purchase price, living expenses, policing requirements, and so on.

1.7
Benjamin B. Ringer
Excerpt from "We the People" and Others

Topical Introduction

Benjamin B. Ringer is a sociologist who believes that the study of American history and political institutions will provide insight into the relationship between power and race in the United States. He argues that it is important to look at how in America a dual legal-political system has developed since colonial days. This dual legal-political system has divided the "people" from the "other people." In so doing, Ringer argues, it has justified unequal access to the fruits of democracy and freedom in a land that declares itself a model of equality, democracy, and freedom. More than that, it has supported too often a cruel, even murderous, disregard for the humanity of the "others." The following is taken from Benjamin B. Ringer, *"We the People" and Others: Duality and America's Treatment of its Racial Minorities*, (London: Tavistock Publications, 1983), 7–8.

As colonists, the English created a society whose institutions were molded in their racial, religious, and national image. They took particular pride in the structure of self-governance they built, first in Virginia and later in the other colonies. In each instance the people of the colonist society had certain basic rights and immunities, but only the white colonist could be part of the people. This colonist heritage found expression in the Declaration of Independence and the Constitution as the thirteen colonies were transformed into a federated nation-state. Through this heritage, the sovereignty of the people were reaffirmed in both the political state and in the national community.

In each, "We the People" were to share various rights and immunities and were to be defined as citizens. Within the Domain of the People, universalistic, egalitarian, achievement-oriented, and democratic norms and values were to be the ideals. Membership in this People's Domain, though, was confined, as in the colonist society, to whites.

1.8
Multiple Consciousness

Although the notion of cultural pluralism and multi-culturalism is bantered about quite loosely, the social trend seems to be the increasing division and differentiation along lines of class, race/ethnicity and gender. One example of that is the destruction following the Rodney King Verdict. There has been an unease following the 1992 aftermath of the Rodney King verdict in Los Angeles, and although interethnic solidarity would be preferable, group process has always been difficult. It is not surprising for groups to become exclusive in order to heal, to lick to wounds that are still festering and bleeding. This is not to say that there are no interethnic alliances; however, these connections have occurred more on individual, interpersonal levels than on the level of social organizations.

The aftermath of the Rodney King verdict, the violence and destruction is evidence of the levels of frustration and hopelessness that people are feeling. Indeed, "many other groups now share with black folks a sense of deep alienation, despair, uncertainty, loss of a sense of grounding even if it is not informed by shared circumstance" (hooks, p. 17). It is the pervasiveness of this discontent and the abject hopelessness that breeds a hunger for renewal and new social order.

"Yearning is the word that best describes a common psychological state shared by many of use, cutting across boundaries of race, class, gender, and sexual practice" (hooks, 1990, p. 27).

The question that arises is what is the yearning for? As previously stated, there is much ado about multi-culturalism. But what is multi-culturalism? How can it be operationalized? Multi-culturalism cannot develop without multiple consciousness. Multiple consciousness is about affiliation and loyalty to groups, specifically two or more affiliations of a person's choice or circumstances. There are innumerable combinations that can exist. Multiple consciousness is a by-product of the growing diversity of our population and definitions that of various groups, sub-groups and affiliations that one person can have.

Multiple consciousness defies the traditional Western paradigm of dualism and opposition—of majority versus minority, thesis versus anti-thesis, of structure versus antistructure, of white versus black, of power versus powerlessness, of good versus bad. Multiple consciousness is the acceptance and incorporation of multiple perspectives within a whole. Put simply, if we were to chart dualism, it would be two points at the opposite ends of a continuum. By virtue of the positioning, not only does dualism obliterate all the other points which can exist on the continuum, it also obviates other points which might exist outside the realm of the continuum.

According to Anzaldua, multiple consciousness entails ''. . . a tolerance for contradictions, a tolerance for ambiguity. . . . She [/he] has a plural personality, she [/he] operates in a pluralistic mode—nothing is thrust out, the good the bad and the ugly, nothing rejected, nothing abandoned (Anzaldua, 1987, p. 79). Because the future depends on the breaking down of paradigms, it depends on the straddling of two or more cultures'' (Anzaldua, 1987, p. 80).

References

Hooks, Bell. *Yearning: race, gender, and cultural politics*. Boston: South End Press, 1990.

Anzaldua, Gloria. *Borderlands*. San Francisco: spinsters/*aunt lute*, 1987.

International Relations between Asia and the United States:
Immigration

Part 2. International Relations Between Asian and the United States: Immigration

2.1.   The First Naturalization Act of 1790

2.2.   Oscar Handlin. The Uprooted

2.3.   Eric C. Wolf. International Capitalism and Labor on the Move

2.4.   Herbert Gutman. Immigrant Culture and Social Change in Industrializing America

2.5.   Denett Tyler. "The American Share in the Opium Trade"

2.6.   John Quincy Adams. Lecture on the War with China

2.7.   Aaron H. Palmer. Memoir: Geographical, Political, and Commercial

2.8.   Harley Farnsworth MacNair. "The Chinese Alien: The Contract Laborer"

2.9.   Alexander Yamato. Labor in California

2.10.   Ping Chiu. Changing Economic Structure and Chinese Immigration, 1865–1880

2.11.   Chinese Railroad Workers

2.12.   John R. Commons et al. Chinese Laborers in Post-Civil War Massachusetts and the South

2.13.   Fraudulent Importation of Chinese, 1886

2.14.   Yuji Ichioka. The Origins of Japanese Immigration to the United States Mainland

2.15.   Immigration to Hawaii

Attitudes toward Chinese Americans and Asian Americans reflected an ethnocentric attitude of Western and American superiority. The following documents provide us with insight into America's attitudes towards Asia and China in particular. It is important to note that America viewed China as an important source of trade and labor.

The Naturalization Act of 1790 provides the foundation for immigration of non-Euroamerican groups to the United States.

John Quincy Adams in commenting on the Opium War reveals his assumptions about Chinese society and the Chinese people. Adams questions the right of China to determine the nature of commerce and trade with the West.

The arrival of Europeans and Americans to the Hawaiian Islands fundamentally altered its history and life. American and European merchants were attracted to the Hawaiian Islands because of the whaling industry and the China trade. They were able to obtain much needed supplies for their long voyages. American merchants also traded for sandalwood which was highly sought after in China and sold for many times its cost.

However, with contact, the Hawaiian people died in large numbers. European and American sailors brought venereal diseases. The arrival of American missionaries also undermined the native subsistence economy by advising the King to convert land into public and private property.

American merchants and missionaries sought to advance their economic interests by developing a plantation agriculture, particularly sugar cane. Native Hawaiians and Polynesians were used as field laborers. However, the demand for laborers was so great that the planters sought to recruit laborers from all across the world. With the proximity to Asia, planters recruited laborers from China, Japan, and the Philippines.

The Chinese diaspora must be placed in the context of the need of European empires for labor in the 19th century. The control of labor was institutionalized through the contract labor system. Chinese were kidnapped, coerced, or deceived into working in prolonged servitude.

Aaron Palmer writing in 1848 wanted to encourage the use of Chinese farming labor in California and envisioned San Francisco to be the gateway of the Pacific Rim. He further saw the need for a transcontinental railroad to connect the Ohio valley with San Francisco and Asia. The selection on the "coolie trade" documents the fact that Americans engaged in shipping Chinese people against their will to work as laborers.

The selection by Harley Farnsworth MacNair elaborates upon the status of Chinese as contract laborers in the United States, and the manner in which this status affected migration to the United States. Chiu also examines the impact of the changing economic structure on Chinese immigration. George elaborates on the problem of the Chinese on the West Coast in an article from the New York Tribune on May 1, 1869.

The selection on Chinese Railroad Workers further supports Palmer's position on the need for Chinese labor in the United States.

Not only were Chinese laborers used in the West and in the building of the transcontinental railroad, they were also utilized in the post-Civil War period in Massachusetts and the South.

Euroamerican responses to the use of Chinese labor was not always favorable. Oliver Morton expressed his views of the impact of Chinese immigration to the United States. The next selection also addresses issues of importation of Chinese laborers under fraudulent guises.

During the latter part of the 19th century the Japanese started to migrate to the United States mainland and Hawaii. Exaggerated accounts of what Japanese immigrants might find in the United States started this new wave of migration.

2.1

The First Naturalization Act of 1790

Topical Introduction

The Naturalization Act of 1790, the United States' first naturalization act, discloses further the racial contradictions that early U.S. political leaders sought to embed in American life. On the one hand, the Act asserts a relatively liberal attitude toward residency period before an alien can become a citizen. On the other hand, it racially restricts those people who can become naturalized citizens.

This piece of legislation, signed by President George Washington, possessed damaging consequences for Blacks, American Indians, and Asians. If immigrants of color can't become citizens, then how much political power do they possess? From U.S. Congress, *Debates and Proceedings,* 1790, vol. 1, 109

"that all free white persons,* who have, or shall migrate into the United States, and shall give satisfactory proof, before a magistrate, by oath, that they intend to reside therein, and shall take an oath of allegiance, *and shall have resided in the United States for one whole year* shall be entitled to all rights of citizenship, except being capable of holding an office under the State or General Government, which capacity they are to acquire after a residence of two years or more." (US Congress, Debates and Proceedings 1790:1109)

2.2
Oscar Handlin
The Uprooted

Topical Introduction

In *The Uprooted,* Oscar Handlin perceptively wrote, "Once I thought to write a history of immigrants in America. Then I discovered that the immigrants were American history." *The Uprooted* is a classic historical statement on immigration to the United States. As classical statements often seem to be, it ignores people of non-European origins. Nevertheless, its focus on immigration as an uprooting, alienating experience has influenced a great deal of scholars and teachers on the subject in general of immigration to the United States. The following, then, is an excerpt from Oscar Handlin, *The Uprooted: The Epic Story of the Great Migrations that Made the American People,* (New York: Grosset & Dunlap, 1951), 4, 5.

My theme is emigration as the central experience of a great many human beings. I shall touch upon broken homes, interruptions of a familiar life, separation from known surroundings, the becoming a foreigner and ceasing to belong. These are the aspects of alienation; and seen from the perspective of the individual received rather than of the receiving society, the history of immigration is a history of alienation and its consequences.

Migration took these people out of traditional, accustomed environments and replanted them in strange ground, among strangers, where stranger manners prevailed. The customary modes of behavior were no longer adequate, for the problems of life were new and different. With old ties snapped, men faced the enormous compulsion of working out new relationships, new meanings to their lives, often under harsh and hostile circumstances.

2.3
Eric C. Wolf
International Capitalism and Labor on the Move

Topical Introduction

Anthropologist Eric Wolf argues against typical explanations of migration from one society to another. In the first place, it has been a dynamic international process; far more complex than some peasant deciding that he would like to breathe the free air of America, while wearing Levis and watching MTV. Moreover, Wolf contends, migration has been related to the changing, world requirements of capitalism; requirements that often include the attainment of an inexpensive, reliable, and relatively powerless labor force.

We often think about immigration as a product of push and pull factors; that is those factors which push people out of a society and those factors which pull people to a society. America is often, then, portrayed as a magnet passively drawing to its shores the impoverished and discontented. Wolf, however, states that there is really little that is passive about the forces moving labor from one place to another. From Eric R. Wolf, *Europe and the People Without History,* (Berkeley and Los Angeles: University of California Press, 1982), 361

To meet the increasing demand for labor power, labor began to flow from regions where people were underemployed, or displaced from agriculture or cottage industries, toward regions of heightened industrial or agricultural activity. The subsequent growth and expansion of capitalism evoked massive relocations of human populations as people carried their labor and resources from areas where they were redundant or obsolete to new key areas of accumulation. This is not to say that population movements always occur in response to upswings and downturns of demand. Labor is often held fast by constraints, and governments are not always willing to allow their subjects to emigrate. Sometimes population movements precede rather than follow an upswing in economic activity, the increased supply of laborers pushing down wages and favoring investment. Nevertheless, capitalism has generally found laborers when and where it needed them, and migratory movements have carried labor power to market all across the globe.

2.4

Herbert Gutman

Immigrant Culture and Social Change in Industrializing America

Topical Introduction

Like Oscar Handlin, historian Herbert Gutman was determined to retrieve the historical experiences of ordinary men and women dealing with complex social change. Unlike Handlin, Gutman argued that immigrants to industrializing America from peasant or any kind of nonindustrial backgrounds possessed greater cultural and community resources to handle creatively industrializing, urbanizing America in the 1800s and early 1900s. Their responses might vary to their new social settings, but immigrants were not quite the dumbfounded folk depicted in *The Uprooted*.

The passage below comes from Gutman's influential essay, "Work, Culture, and Society in Industrializing America." Note that what he says doesn't just apply to immigrants, but migrants from rural areas to the city; such as the Black migration from the South to the North in the 20th century. Moreover, note as well, that Gutman was saying that the constant infusion of premodern, precapitalist people into the changing American working class brought significant social conflict. These people judged America through the perspectives of the world views, values, and ideologies they brought with them and frequently they felt compelled to indict America or, at least, particular Americans. From Herbert Gutman, *Work, Culture, and Society in Industrializing America: Essays in American Working-Class and Social History,* (New York: Knopf, 1976), 14–15.

The fact that the American working class was continually altered in its composition by infusions, from within and without the nation, of peasants, farmers, skilled artisans, and casual day laborers who brought into industrial society ways of work and other habits and values not associated with industrial necessities and the industrial ethos. Some shed these older ways to conform to new imperatives. Others fell victim to fled, moving from place to place. Some sought to extend and adapt older patterns of work and life to a new society. Others challenged the social system through varieties of collective

35

associations. But for all—at different historical moments—the transition to industrial society, as E. P. Thompson has written, "entailed a severe restructuring of working habits—new disciplines, new incentives, and a new human nature upon which these incentives could bite effectively."[12]

2.5

Denett Tyler

"The American Share in the Opium Trade"

Topical Introduction

A little known piece of history is the fact that American ships were actively involved in bringing opium to China from Turkey and India as early as 1805. In fact, opium was shipped to American ports where the opium was then sent to China. The Chinese associated Turkish opium with Americans. American ships carried opium on consignment for the British as well. Although the American navy was sent to China to see that no Americans were engaged in the opium trade, widespread smuggling by Americans was uncovered.

———————

The Americans were far more deeply involved in the opium trade at that time than appears from any statistics. The existence of the trade itself conferred on them a direct commercial benefit, for it reduced the necessity for the importation of specie by the substitution of bills on London. Opium was sold in ever increasing quantities, and the Americans, as well as the English and other foreigners, used the bills thus obtained in place of specie to purchase their return cargoes. As the supply of furs began to diminish, after 1820, and while the American cotton trade was in its infancy, the increased importation of opium from whatever country and by whomever transported, was a very important consideration. The system was vicious and short-sighted economically, as the merchants afterwards came to see. The consumption of opium demoralized the producing and consuming powers of China, led to greatly increased importation of specie, and the ill-will of the people, but when the capital of the American merchants was still relatively small, and the supply of acceptable specie limited, the opium trade, like slaves and distilleries, entered into the foundation of many American fortunes.

Dennett, Tyler, *Americans in Eastern Asia,* New York, Macmillan Co., 1922.

2.6
John Quincy Adams
Lecture on the War with China

Art. III. *Lecture on the War with China, delivered before the Massachusetts Historical Society, December,* 1841. By the hon. John Quincy Adams of Mass., U.S.A. Extracted from an American paper.

The existing state of the relations between the kingdom of Great Britain and Ireland, and the empire of China, opens for discussion questions of deep interest to the whole human race; and of pre-eminent interest to the people of the North American union. Great Britain and China are at war. The questions which immediately rise for consideration, in this conflict between two of the mightiest nations of the globe, are—

1. Which of the two parties to the contest has the righteous cause?
2. What are the prospects of its progress and termination?
3. How are the interests of other nations, and particularly of the United States, already, or likely to be hereafter, affected by it?
4. What are the duties of the government and people of the United States resulting from it?

For the solution of the first of these questions, we must resort to a statement of the facts in which the controversy originated, and for a candid application to those facts, of the laws of nature and of nations.

How far this reproach of a French writer upon the freedom of the seas, (Rayneval) is justified by the facts which he alleges in its support, is not now my purpose, nor have we time to inquire. It behooves us however to remember that the English language is now the mother tongue, not of one, but of many nations, and that whatever portion of them believe that the fountain of all human legislation is the omnipotence of the British parliament, we as one of those nations acknowledge no such supremacy. We think, with the great jurist of our mother country, that the omnipotence of the British parliament is a figure of speech rather too bold, and the first declaration of the act of our existence as a separate nation, was, self-evident, inalienable rights of all men by the laws of nature and of nature's God. This is the only omnipotence to which we bow the knee, as the only source, direct or indirect of all human legislation, and that thus the laws of nations are identical with the rights of men associated in independent communities.

The practical organization of our social system is not altogether consistent with our theory of the law of nature and of nature's God, which has given to all men the inalienable right to liberty. The existence of slavery is incompatible with that law of nature.

But we speak the English language, and what the men of other tongues call the right of nations, we call the law of nations. What then are the laws of nature by the rules of which the right and wrong of the present contest between Great Britain and China are to be ascertained? And here we are to remember, that by the laws of nations are to be understood not one code of laws, binding alike upon all the nations of the earth, but a system of rules, varying according to the character and condition of the parties concerned. The general law of nations is derived from four distinct sources, denominated by Vattel the necessary, voluntary, conventional, and customary, laws of nations. The necessary law is the application of the law of nature to the intercourse between independent communities, and this itself can be enforced only between nations who recognize the principle that the state of nature is a state of peace. It is a religious principle of the Mohammedan nations, that it is their duty to propagate their religion by the sword. Time was, when their cruel, absurd, and unnatural principle was inscribed on the holy banners of the meek and lowly Jesus. The vision of Constantine himself who seated Christianity upon the throne of the Cæsars—the vision by which he pretended to have been converted to the faith of the blessed Gospel, falsified all its commands, and perverted its nature. The cross of Christ was exhibited before his eyes, and the words inscribed upon it were, ''By this conquer''—conquer, persecute, enslave, destroy, kindle the fires of the holy fraternities, burn the heretic at the stake, toar his nerves to atoms by the rack, hunt him with blood-hounds, pluck out his vitals and slap them in his face—all for the salvation of his soul—by this conquer!

The empire of China is said to extend over three hundred millions of human beings. It is said to cover a space of seven millions of square miles; about four times larger than the surface of these United States. The people are not Christians. Nor can a Christian nation appeal to the principles of a common faith to settle the question of right and wrong between them. The moral obligation of commercial intercourse between nations if founded entirely, exclusively, upon the Christian precept to love your neighbor as yourself. With this principle you cannot refuse commercial intercourse with your neighbor, because commerce, consisting of a voluntary exchange of property mutually beneficial to both parties, excites in both the selfish and the social propensities, and enables each of the parties to promote the happiness of his neighbors by the same act whereby he provides for his own. But China, not being a Christian nation, its inhabitants do not consider themselves bound by the Christian precept, to love their neighbors as themselves. The right of commercial intercourse with them reverts not to the execrable principle of Hobbes that the state of nature is a state of war, where every one has a right to buy, but no one is obliged to sell. Commerce becomes altogether a matter of convention. The right of each party is only to propose—that of the other is to accept or refuse, and to his result he may be guided exclusively by the consideration of his own interest, without regard to the interests, the wishes, or the other wants of his neighbor.

This is a churlish and unsocial system;—and I take occasion here to say that whoever examines the Christian system of morals, with a philosophical spirit, setting aside all the external and historical evidences of its truth, will find all its precepts tending to exalt the nature of the animal man; all its purpose of peace on earth and goodwill towards men. Ask the atheist—the deist—the Chinese, and they will tell you that the foundation, of their system of morals is selfish enjoyment. Ask the philosophers of the Grecian schools—Epicurus, Socrates, Zeno, Plato, Lucretius, Cicero, Seneca, and you will find them discoursing upon the Supreme Good. They will tell you it is pleasure, ease, temperance, prudence, fortitude, justice, not one of them will whisper the name of love; unless in its gross and physical sense; as an instrument of pleasure, not one of them will tell you that the source of all moral relation between you and the rest of mankind is to love your neighbor as yourself—to do unto him as you would that he should do unto you.

The Chinese recognize no such law. Their internal government is a hereditary patriarchal despotism, and their own exclusive interest is the measure of all their relations with the rest of mankind. Their own government is founded upon the principle, that as a nation they are superior to the rest of mankind. They believe themselves and their country especially privileged over all others—that their dominion is the celestial empire, and their territory the flowery land. At a period of their history so remote that they have no authentic records of the times,* to make their separation from the rest of the world more effectual, they built a wall 1500 miles long between themselves and their next neighbors, the Tartars, which however has not saved them from being more than once conquered. The last time that this happened was in the year 1644, and the second century is about closing upon the dominion of the Mantchou Tartars. That conquest however

*The Great Wall was built about B.C. 240, by the emperor Chí Hwángtí of the Tsin dynasty. He was contemporary with Hannibal. The Chinese records of this event are among the most authentic they have, for this emperor stands preeminent for his power and his conquests.—Ed. Chi. Rep.

produced no other revolution of government than the transfer of the imperial sceptre from one family to another. It is a remark of Hume that if the conquest of France by Henry V. had been maintained by his successors, the result would have been to convert England into a French province; such in the natural course of events must be the result of the conquest of a larger by a smaller adjoining people. And this is precisely what has happened with China and Tartary. The principle of the Chinese government is, that the whole nation is one great family, of which the emperor is the father. His authority is unlimited, and he can, not only appoint such of his sons as he pleases to succeed him, but may even transfer the succession to another family. Idol worship, polygamy, infanticide, are the natural consequences† of such a system within the realm, and the assumption of a pretension to superiority over all other nations regulates their intercourse with foreigners.

To the Greeks and Romans of antiquity, the very existence of the Chinese nation was unknown. The first notice of them received by the Europeans of the middle ages, was from the Venetian Marco Palo in the 13th century. When the Portuguese two hundred years later found the way round the cape of Good Hope to India, they soon pushed forward their navigation and their enterprize along the whole coast of China. They were allowed to trade for several years at various ports; but abusing this privilege and their navigating power, they were excluded from all access to the empire. A few years later the coast was infested by pirates. One of these named Ching Chílung obtained possession of the island of Macao; others held the whole coast in a state of blockade, and besieged Canton, itself destitute of all naval power. The officers of the celestial empire were obliged to have recourse to those very Portuguese to defend and deliver their country from the depredation of a single bold and desperate pirate. They sent from Sancian, where they had a trading establishment, an expedition which raised the siege of Canton, and drove Ching Chílung back to Macao, where to escape from the fate which awaited him, had he fallen into the hands of his pursuers, he died by his own hands. In reward for this service, the emperor of China gave to the Portuguese the island of Macao, which they hold to this day, and from which station they,

---

†In our humble opinion, these consequences can hardly be said to follow, because the emperor's authority is unlimited, nor do we exactly see how they grow out of it at all: the power of the emperor of Russia is probably as unlimited as that of his imperial brother at Peking, but these evils are surely not general in his dominions.—*Ed. Chi. Rep.*

and the other navigating nations of Christendom, have carried on their commercial intercourse with the interior of China.*

This grant, in full sovereignty of an island at the very entrance of the China seas, to a foreign and Christian power, would seem to be a wide departure from the fundamental system of excluding all foreigners from admission within the empire, but it was in truth a necessary consequence of that system. The seclusion of the empire from all other nations was a necessary renunciation of all maritime enterprise, and all naval armament. The coast was thus left defenseless against the assaults of single desperate adventurers. The traffic which the Portuguese solicited, was altogether advantageous to the Chinese. The Portuguese brought gold, silver, and precious stones. They took away silks, nankeens, porcelain, varnish, medicinal plants and tea, the produce of the soil and manufacturing industry of the country. A small island upon the coast as a permanent abode for the Portuguese traders, given to them as a possession, was a compromise for their claim of admission to the territory necessary for carrying on that importation of the precious metals, and that exportation of Chinese industry, the benefits of which could not but be felt, and could not be overlooked.

Other navigating Christian nations followed in the wake of the Portuguese. The Spaniards, the Dutch, the English, the French, and the Danes,—successively came as rival competitors for the lucrative commerce. It was chiefly, though not always confined to the port of Canton, but no European was ever admitted within the walls of that city. The several trading nations were allowed to establish small factories, as counting-houses, on the banks of the river without the city; but they were never suffered to enter within the gates, they were not permitted to introduce even a woman into their factory. All their intercourse with the subordinate government of the province was carried on through the medium of a dozen Chinese traders denominated the hong-merchants. All their remonstrances against wrong, or claims of right, must be transmitted not directly to the government, but through the hong, in the form of humble supplication called by the Chinese a *pin*—and all must be content to receive the answers of the viceroys in the form of edicts in which they, their sovereigns, and their nations, were invariably styled ''outside barbarians;''—and the highest compliment to their kings was to declare them reverently submissive to

*For notices of the travelers who visited China before Marco Polo, and the intercourse carried on with this people, see Chi. Rep., vol. III., page 107. There is, also, in this paragraph some confusion regarding the doings of the pirates, one or two of whom are confounded. Ching Chílung died in Peking. But see Chi. Rep. vol. III., page 64, and Ljungstedt's Macao, page 12, for an account of this and other pirates, and the tenure by which the Portuguese obtained and still hold Macao. Nor is it from this port alone that the other navigating nations of Christendom have carried on their commercial intercourse with China.—*Ed. Chi. Rep.*

his imperial majesty, monarch of the Celestial empire,—and father of the Flowery land. It is humiliating to think that not only the proudest monarch of Europe, but the most spirited and enlightened and valorous nations of Christendom have submitted to this tone, and these principles of intercourse, so long as to have given them, if prescription could give them, a claim of right, and a color of conformity to the law of nature.

There are three principles of the law of nature applied to nations, laid down in the preliminary chapter to Vattel's treatise, a close attention to which is indispensably necessary to the adjustment of the question of right and wrong in the issue of fact between the British and Chinese governments:

"The first general law, which the very end of the society of nations discovers, is that each nation ought to contribute all in its power to the happiness and perfection of others."—"But the duty towards ourselves having incontestibly the advantage over our duty with respect to others, a nation ought in the first place, preferably to all other considerations, to do whatever it can to promote its own happiness and perfection." Here is a fallacy. The first and vital principle of Christian morality is to love your neighbor as yourself—to do unto others as you would that they should do unto you. It does not permit you to promote your own happiness and perfection in preference to all other considerations. It makes your neighbor's happiness, so far as your action is concerned, a part of your own. It does not permit you to sacrifice his happiness to yours, any more than yours to his. The importance of this distinction will be seen—by referring to the second and third preliminaries laid down by the same author, and by deducing the consequences inferable from them all.

"Nations being free and independent of each other, in the same manner as men are free and independent,—the second general law of their society is, that each nation ought to be left in the peaceable enjoyment of that liberty it has derived from nature. From this liberty and independence, it follows that every nation is to judge of what its conscience demands, of what it can or cannot do, of what is proper or improper to be done; and consequently to organize and determine, whether it can perform any office for another without being wanting in what it owes to itself."

Now for the third general law. "Since men are naturally equal, and their rights and obligations are the same, as equally proceeding from nature, nations composed of men, considered as so many free persons living together in a state of nature, are naturally equal, and receive from nature the same obligations and rights." Hence, "If it [a nation] makes an ill use of its liberty, it offends; but others ought to suffer it to do so, having to right to command it to do otherwise. The nation that has acted wrong, has offended against its conscience, but as it may do whatever it has a right to perform it cannot be accused of violating the laws of society.''

Let us separate the question of right and wrong, from that of the right of either party to compel by force the performance of right by the other, and how stand these three corner stones of Vattel's laws of nations towards each other? If it be true that each nation ought to contribute all in its power to the happiness and perfection of others, how can it be true that a nation ought in the first place, and preferable to all other considerations, to do whatever it can to promote its own happiness and perfection, and to be the exclusive judge of what that is? If the vital principle of all human society be that each is bound to contribute to the happiness of all, it surely follows that each cannot regulate his conduct by the exclusive or even by the paramount consideration of his own interest. In applying his own principles to the cultivation of commerce, Vattel begins by laying it down as a moral obligation. He says expressly, that nations are obliged to cultivate the home-trade—because it promotes the welfare of the community—and, ''From the same reason, drawn from the welfare of the state, and to procure for the citizens everything they want, a nation is obliged to promote and carry on a foreign trade.'' And yet, because every one has a right to buy, and every one an equal right to refuse to sell, therefore every nation, having exclusively, or in preference to all other considerations, regard to its own interest, has a right to interdict all commerce with other nations. Here is a manifest inconsistency between the two principles. The vital principle of commerce is reciprocity; and although in all cases of traffic, each party acts for himself and for the promotion of his own interest, the duty of each is to hold commercial intercourse with the other—not from exclusive or paramount consideration of his own interest, but from a joint and equal moral consideration of the interests of both. If the object of any particular traffic is advantageous to one party, and injurious to the other, then the party suffering has an unquestionable right to interdict the trade, not from exclusive or paramount consideration of his own interest, but because the traffic no longer fulfills the condition which makes commercial intercourse a duty.

The fundamental principle of the Chinese empire is anti-commercial. It is founded entirely upon the second and third of Vattel's general principles, to the total exclusion of the first. It admits no obligation to hold commercial intercourse with others. It utterly denies the equality of other nations with itself, and even their independence. It holds itself to be the centre of the terraqueous globe, equal to the heavenly host, and all other nations with whom it has any relations, political or commercial, as outside tributary barbarians reverently submissive to the will of its despotic chief. It is upon this principle, openly avowed and inflexibly maintained, that the principal maritime nations of

Europe for several centuries, and the United States of America from the time of their acknowledged independence, have been content to hold commercial intercourse with the empire of China.

It is time that this enormous outrage upon the rights of human nature, and upon the first principle of the rights of nations, should cease. These principles of the Chinese empire, too long connived at and truckled to by the mightiest Christian nations of the civilized world, have at length been brought into conflict with the principles and the power of the British empire; and I cannot forbear to express the hope that Britain, after taking the lead in the abolition of the African slave trade and of slavery, and of the still more degrading tribute to the Barbary African Mohammedans, will extend her liberating arm to the farthest bound of Asia, and at the close of the present contest insist upon concluding the peace on terms of perfect equality with the Chinese empire, and that the future commerce shall be carried on upon terms of equality and reciprocity between the two communities, parties to the trade, for the benefit of both, each retaining the right of prohibition and of regulation, to interdict any article or branch of trade injurious to itself, as, for example, the article of opium; and to secure itself against the practices of fraudulent traders and smugglers.

This is the truth, and I apprehend the only question at issue between the governments and nations of Great Britain and China. It is a general, but I believe altogether mistaken opinion, that the quarrel is merely for certain chests of opium imported by British merchants into China, and seized by the Chinese government for having been imported contrary to law. This is a mere incident to the dispute; but no more the cause of the war, than the throwing overboard of the tea in Boston harbor was the cause of the North American revolution.

The cause of the war is the pretension on the part of the Chinese, that in all their intercourse with other nations, political or commercial, their superiority must be implicitly acknowledged, and manifested in humiliating forms. It is not creditable to the great, powerful and enlightened nations of Europe, that for several centuries they have, for the sake of profitable trade, submitted to these insolent and insulting pretensions, equally contrary to the first principles of the law of nature and of revealed religion—the natural equality of mankind—

Among the expedients to which the British government had resorted to hide their faces from the shame of submission to their principle of commercial intercourse with China, was that of granting the monopoly of trade to a company of merchants. The charter of the East India Company was the instrument of this monopoly; and as the Company possessed none of the attributes of sovereignty, whatever compliances their thirst for gain might reconcile with their self-esteem as men or their pride as Britons, was supposed to involve no sacrifice of the national honor and dignity. They submitted, therefore, to accept the permission to trade with the people of China, as a boon granted to their humble supplication, called a *pin*. But their trade was to be confined to the single port of Canton, in an empire of seven millions of square miles, with a population of 360,000,000 of souls. Even into that city of Canton no British subject was ever to be suffered to get his foot. They were permitted to erect, on the banks of the river below the city, the buildings necessary for a counting-house, over which they might display the degraded standard of their nation, but from which their wives and families were to be for ever excluded.— For the superintendence of this trade, certain officers were appointed by the East India Company—and it was to be exclusively carried on with ten or twelve Chinese merchants of the city, called hong-merchants, through whom alone, the outside barbarians had access by the *pin* [i.e. petition] to the government of the city.

It has been seen how the British government and nation had accommodated themselves to this self-arrogating system of the Chinese. It was by establishing a monopoly on their part adapted to the monopoly of the Chinese system. The exclusive right of trading with China was granted to the East India Company, and all the commerce of British subjects with the celestial empire was transacted by means of commissioned supercargoes, appointed by those merchant princes, without diplomatic character, and without direct intercourse with any officer of the Chinese government.

But on the expiration and removal of the East India Company's charter in 1833, the exclusive right of trading with China was discontinued, and thenceforth the quasi-political intercourse between the two nations, transacted by mere commercial agents of the East India Company ceased, and in the third and fourth year of the reign of William IV., an act of parliament was made and passed, 'to regulate the trade to China and India.' In pursuance of the powers conferred upon the crown by this act, the sailor-king issued three orders in council. 1.— Constituting and appointing William John, lord Napier, W. Henry Chicheley Plowden, and John Francis Davis, 'superintendents of the trade of British subjects in China,' with an order for the government of British subjects within the Chinese dominions. 2.—Creating a court of justice for the purposes therein mentioned. 3.—Imposing duties on the ships and goods of British subjects trading to China, for the purposes therein mentioned, that is, of defraying the expenses of the establishment. The order for the imposition of duties was afterwards rescinded, and the order for the constitution of a court of justice was suspended for further consideration. The chief superintendent lord Napier was *instructed* to announce his arrival at Canton, by letter to the viceroy. The superintendents were instructed to take up their residence at the port of Canton, and to discharge the duties of their commission within the river or port of Canton, or at any other place within that river or port, or at any other place thereafter to be designated by an order in council, and *not elsewhere*.

One of the most remarkable circumstances attending all these transactions is, that in giving these instructions to the superintendents to take up their residence at Canton, and to the chief superintendent to announce his arrival by letter to the viceroy, they appear not to have been aware of the possibility of any objection to this course of proceeding on the part of the Chinese. Accordingly, on his arrival in China, after organizing the board of superintendents at Macao, lord Napier with his colleagues and the secretary of the commission proceeded immediately to Canton. For the scenes which ensued of dramatic interest, partaking at once of tragedy and farce, recourse may be had to the official dispatch of the chief superintendent to his Britannic majesty's secretary of state. 'In obedience to his majesty's commands (says lord Napier in his letter of 9th August 1834, to lord Palmerston) conveyed to me by your lordship, of the date of the 23d of January last, desiring me to announce my arrival at Canton by letter to the viceroy, which being rendered into Chinese by the Rev. Dr. Morrison, the Chinese secretary and interpreter, was carried to the city gates by Mr. Astell, (the secretary to the commission) accompanied by a deputation of gentlemen from the establishment.'

[*For lord Napier's account of this transaction, see pages 26 and 27 of this vol.*]

You have now, in this portion of the narrative of the first dispatch from lord Napier to lord Palmerston, the primitive and efficient cause of the present war between Great Britain and China. It was in the attempt to execute two points of the instructions to the superintendent. That the chief superintendent should announce his arrival at Canton, by letter to the viceroy, and the other, that the superintendents should take up their residence at Canton. Lord Napier, with the open-hearted and inconsiderate boldness of a British sailor, attempted to execute these points of his instructions to the letter, without for an instant conceiving that each of them was in direct conflict with the vital and fundamental laws of the celestial empire. This ignorance was very natural and very excusable in a captain of the British navy, but how it came to be shared by the council and the secretary of state of the British empire, is more unaccountable. The instructions were explicit and positive. Had there been the remotest suspicion at the time when they were prepared, that their execution would meet with resistance by the Chinese authorities, it could not have failed to be noticed in them, with directions how the superintendents were to proceed in such an event. Until then the official protector of British commercial interests in China, had been a supercargo of the East India Company, denominated by the Chinese a *táipán,* whose representations or remonstrances in behalf of British subjects to the governor of the two provinces, Kwángtung and Kwángsí, were always presented in the form of petitions, and always communicated through the medium of the hong-merchants, without obtaining or claiming direct access to the Chinese dignitary himself. That this mode of communication was to cease from the time of the expiration of the exclusive privileges of the East India Company, was equally well known to the British and Chinese governments, and in the controversy which immediately followed this first collision between lord Napier and the governor of Canton, the latter once and again asserts that ample warning had been given to the British merchants that when, by the expiration of the privileges of the East India Company, the functions of the *táipán* would be superseded, some suitable messenger must be substituted to settle with the hong-merchants those trifling and insignificant concerns of commerce which it was far beneath the dignity of the government of the celestial empire to provide for or to notice.

But I am already trespassing upon your patience—a brief and summary notice of the sequel, is all that your time will at present allow. The proud and generous British noble mariner persisted in his determination to hold direct communication with the governor of the two provinces, Lú, and to continue his residence at Canton, till he was obliged to call for an armed force from the British frigate in which he had performed his passage, and for the frigate and another to force the passage of the river for the protection of his person from assault by the armed force of the governor, who on his part issued edict after edict against the barbarian eye, the laboriously vile Napier, who had come by sea more than ten thousand miles to the flowery land of the celestial empire, for what purpose, the chief of the two-eyed peacock feather could not tell, but against all reason, and ignorant of all dignities, pretending to correspond with the viceroy of the provinces of Kwángtung and Kwángsí, upon matters of trade, by letter, instead of by petition, and to assume the functions, which for a century and some tens of years had always been performed in all humility by a táipán, petitioning through the medium of the hong-merchants. Three of the principal hong-merchants attempted for several days to negotiate a compromise between the governor and the noble lord superintendent, without success, till at length an edict was issued by the governor which suspended the British trade. The British commerce in China was prostrated at a blow, and the only alternative left to lord Napier was to retire under numerous insults and indignities to Macao, where on the 13th day of October, 1834, he died of chagrin and a broken heart.

And here we might pause:—do I hear you inquire, what is all this to the opium question, or the taking of Canton? These I answer are but incidents in that movement of mind on this globe of earth, of which the war between Great Britain and China, is now the leading

star. Of the four questions which I have proposed this evening to discuss, we have not even reached the conclusion of the first.

The justice of the cause between the two parties:—which has the
righteous cause? You have perhaps been surprised to hear me answer
Britain—Britain has the righteous cause. But to prove it, I have been
obliged to show that the opium question is not the cause of the war,
my demonstration is not yet complete. The cause of the war is the
kotow!—the arrogant and insupportable pretensions of China, that she
will hold commercial intercourse with the rest of mankind, not upon
terms of equal reciprocity, but upon the insulting and degrading forms
of the relation between lord and vassal. The melancholy catastrophe
with which I am obliged to close, the death of the gallant Napier, was
the first bitter fruit of the struggle against that insulting and senseless
pretension of China. Might I, in the flight of time, be permitted again
to address you, I should pursue the course of the inquiry, through the
four questions with which I have begun. But the solution of them all
is involved in the germinating element of the first, the justice of the
cause. This I have sought in the natural rights of man. Whether it may
ever be my good fortune to address you again, is in the disposal of a
higher Power; but with reference to the last of my four questions,
What are the duties of the government and the people of the United
States, resulting from the existing war between Great Britain and
China? I leave to your meditations the last event of that war, which
the winds have brought to our ears—the ransom of Canton. When we
remember the scornful refusal from the gates of Canton in July, 1834,
of Mr. Astell, bearing the letter of peace and friendship from lord
Napier to the governor of the two provinces, and the contemptuous
refusal to receive the letter itself, and compare it with the ransom of
that same city in June, 1841, we trace the whole line of connection
between cause and effect—may we not draw from it a monitory lesson, written with a beam of phosphoric light—of preparation for war,
and preservation of peace?

Note. One of the strongest inducements to place this lecture of Mr.
Adams upon the pages of the Repository has been in this manner to
exhibit the principal arguments that can be stated in behalf of this
view of the merits of the present struggle between China and England. These remarks are the views of a man of extensive experience
in public life, and as such are worthy of attention and deference; and
they also show in a lucid manner one of the strongest reasons why the
Chinese government has not the right to shut themselves out from the
rest of mankind, founded on deductions drawn from the rights of men
as members of one great social system. While, however, we differ
from the lecturer with regard to the influence the opium trade has had
upon the war, for it has been without doubt the great proximate cause,
we mainly agree with him as to the effect that other remoter causes

springing from Chinese assumption, conceit, and ignorance have also had upon it. In its progress, these features have been more and more prominently brought forward, and on the part of this government, the war is probably at present regarded as one of supremacy or vassalism, according as the Chinese win or lose. We do not see how the war could have arisen, had not the opium trade been a smuggling trade,— we think it would never have gone on as it has were the Chinese better acquainted with their own and others' rights. But whatever be its course, it must we think, be the hearty desire of every well-wisher of his race, that the almighty Governor of the nations would in his own chosen way educe lasting good to both parties, and cause that these two mighty nations may in their future intercourse be a mutual benefit.—*Ed. Chi. Rep.*

2.7
Aaron H. Palmer
Memoir: Geographical, Political, and Commercial

Topical Introduction

Memoir: Geographical, political, and commercial, on the present state, productive resources and capabilities for commerce, of Siberia, Manchuria and the Asiatic islands of the Northern Pacific ocean; and on the importance of opening commercial intercourse with those countries, &c. Addressed to His Excellency James K. Polk, President of the United States. By Aaron H. Palmer, Counsellor of the Supreme Court of the United States, Corresponding Member of the National Institute, Washington, &c.

NEW YORK, *January* 10, 1848.

SIR: I have the honor of transmitting you, herewith, a brief memoir on the present state, productive resources, and capabilities for commerce, of several of the comparatively unknown countries of the East, which are daily becoming of importance to us in a political as well as commercial point of view, and where a new world may be opened to the trading enterprise of our countrymen.

The territories of Oregon and California, now in rapid progress of settlement by enterprising citizens of the United States, together with the great and increasing value of American navigation employed in commerce and the whale fishery in the northern Pacific, are eminently entitled to the fostering care of our government, and require the early adoption of a comprehensive system of policy, both for their protection and development, and to secure the permanency of our commercial and maritime supremacy on that ocean. Early measures should be taken for the reconnaissance and survey of the most feasible route for a ship canal to unite the Atlantic and Pacific, and also for a railroad from a point on the Mississippi to San Francisco or San Diego, in

California, to accelerate intercommunication between the different sections of our magnificent and mighty republic on both oceans.

It appears from official data that the American whaling vessels alone in the Pacific exceed in number 700, making an aggregate of about 240,000 tons, and give employment to upwards of 20,000 officers and men; that the capital invested therein amounts in value to upwards of $40,000,000, the annual product of the fishery being estimated at $10,000,000; and that during the year ending the 31st December, 1847, the whole number of our merchant vessels which cleared for ports in the Pacific and to ports in the East Indies amounted to 181.

I would also take leave to suggest the importance of an early revision of our commercial convention with Russia of the 17th April, 1824, for the admission of our flag into the ports of Siberia, Kamtschatka, the Kurile and Aleutian islands, in the northern Pacific ocean, as well as those of the Russian colonies on the northwestern coast of America; by which a new and profitable commerce may be opened, mutually beneficial to both nations.

I consider it equally important that our government should insist on the right of navigating the great Manchurian river Amúr and its affluents, and of trading with the colonial dependencies of China, upon the same footing as the Russians; and that we claim the further privilege of commercial intercourse at Tinghae, in the Chusan Archipelago. The favorable position of that port, with its safe anchorages, accessible to the largest ships at all seasons, lying near the embouchure of the great Yangtsckang river, and within two days' sail of Japan and Corca, give it superior advantages over every other port in China for trade, and as a depot and halting station for the American trans-Pacific line of steamers, which it is contemplated to establish between Panama and China, in connexion with the line now in progress from Panama to Oregon.

The memoir is extracted from my forthcoming work, entitled "The Unknown Countries of the East," and is arranged under the following heads, viz:

1. *Siberia, its valuable products and rich gold mines.*
2. *Russian overland trade with China at Kiakta, &c.*
3. *Manchuria and the river Amúr, &c.*
4. *Island of Tarakay, or Saghalien.*
5. *Russian and Japanese Kurile islands, &c.*
6. *Steam communication with China: superior commercial advantages of Chusan, &c.*
7. *Special mission to the East: steam navigation on the Indus and Brahmaputra, &c. Extensive caravan trade with Northwestern and Central Asia, &c.*

8. *Policy of encouraging immigration of Chinese agricultural laborers to California: railroad from the Mississippi to the bay of San Francisco.*

9. *Skip canal from the Atlantic to the Pacific;* to which are appended an outline chart of the coast of Northern Asia and the adjacent islands in the Northern Pacific, and a map of the isthmus of Nicaragua; together with a prospectus of the new work above mentioned, for which your patronage and the aid of Congress is most respectfully solicited, to enable me to complete it under the auspices of our government according to the plan therein indicated.

I have the honor to be, with the highest respect, sir, your Excellency's most obedient servant.

AARON H. PALMER

His Excellency James K. Polk
President of the U.S., Washington.

8. Policy of encouraging immigration of Chinese agricultural laborers to California.—Railroad from the Mississippi to the Bay of San Francisco.

With the view of bringing the fertile lands in California under early cultivation, I would suggest the policy of encouraging immigration of agricultural laborers from China to that territory. No people in all the East are so well adapted for clearing wild lands and raising every species of agricultural product, especially rice, cotton, tobacco, sugar, and silk, as the Chinese. They are the principal cultivators, agricultural laborers, mechanics, and ship-carpenters, throughout the various islands of the Indian Archipelago, Java, Borneo, Penang, Singapore, Malacca, Siam, Cochin China, the Philippine islands, &c., where they are estimated to exceed 2,000,000, nearly one-fourth of whom are established in Siam: the culture of sugar, the principal export of that country, is almost exclusively in their hands. A large amount of the traffic, and a greater proportion of the carrying trade of those countries, is conducted by them. The better class of the settlers are described as enterprising, keen, laborious, and persevering; and those in traffic, expert, speculative, and judicious.

The establishment of a colony of Chinese cultivators at some eligible location on the coast of California, would, as a natural consequence, attract thither their trading junks, and lead to the opening of a direct commercial intercourse from thence with China, and all the eastern countries with which the Chinese carry on their junk trade. The superabundance of the population of that immense empire, annually compels vast numbers to emigrate. A channel for emigration once opened, great multitudes from that over peopled country would wend their way to California. Some of their junks are of 1,500 to 2,000 tons burden, and frequently arrive at Singapore, and other places in the Indian Archipelago, with 1,200 emigrants on board, seeking employment. The junks are divided into seven or more different compartments, water-tight, usually belonging to different persons on board for the voyage. They are now beginning to build fast-sailing ships after our models. The greater proportion of emigrants are from Amoy, in the province of Fokien.

Emigration, instead of being prohibited as formerly, under severe penalties, is now encouraged by the Mandarins. A considerable number of Chinese coolies have been engaged to work for a term of years, at low wages, on the coffee and sugar plantations of the French island of Bourbon. Arrangements are in progress, under the sanction of the colonial authorities of Australia, to introduce the culture of sugar, cotton, and rice, on an extensive scale, in tropical Australia, and to supply the planters with predial laborers from China. Several ship loads of natives of the New Hebrides and Solomon's group have likewise been imported into the same colony, to serve as shepherds and agricultural laborers.

The commodious port of *San Francisco* is destined to become the great emporium of our commerce on the Pacific; and so soon as it is connected by a railroad with the Atlantic States, will become the most eligible point of departure for steamers to Oregon, China, the Indian Archipelago, &c. Coal of an intermediate species between bituminous and anthracite, burning more easily than the latter, but a little harder, and giving out less smoke than the former, has been recently found in large strata in its vicinity.

It is stated, on reliable authority, that the country along the valley of San Joaquin, between the bay of San Francisco and the Mississippi, is comparatively level, presenting less difficulties in execution, and more advantages in a commercial point of view, than any other projected route for a railroad between the Atlantic and Pacific, within the territorial limits and occupancy of the United States.

By this route it is proposed "that the railroad should start from the Mississippi, near the mouth of the Ohio, or at such a point that the navigation will never be interrupted by ice; thence to the vicinity of Arkansas; thence along the prairie ridge, which separates the waters which flow into Arkansas from those which flow into the Mississippi and Missouri, to the point where the road passes from Missouri to New Mexico, and by San Miguel, to Santa Fe, thence up the valley to Rio del Norte, to the mouth of Abeca creek; thence through a pine forest of low sandy hills, ninety miles, to the Rio de la Plata, which is a tributary of the San Juan, and this is a tributary of the Colorado. It should cross the last named river to the northwest side, and proceed along the trail from Santa Fe to California to a point between the Mahawee river and the San Bernadine mountains; thence through about ten miles of low hills to the great valley of the San Joaquin; thence down that fertile valley about five hundred miles on a level, to the tide water of the bay of San Francisco. By this route the road will pass over a dead level of about eight hundred miles at the eastern, and about five hundred miles at the western end; will have no mountains to cross; will be really free from snow in all parts; and will afford an outlet from New Mexico to both oceans, to terminate at the best port on the western coast of America.''

2.8
Harley Farnsworth MacNair
"The Chinese Alien: The Contract Laborer"

Topical Introduction

The Chinese diaspora must be placed in the context of the need of European empires for labor in the 19th century. The control of labor was institutionalized through the contract labor system. Chinese were kidnapped, coerced, or deceived into working in prolonged servitude.

I

The effect of steam traffic upon the emigration of the Chinese was almost revolutionary: by the use of steamships instead of sailing junks not only did greater numbers leave China than ever before, but they spread to many new parts of the world. In California and Australia discoveries of gold drew free Chinese workers, but the same quarter of a century that saw these changes heralded another change which affected materially the emigration of Chinese. This was the abolition of slavery in the British Empire, and the attempt to discourage it throughout the world.

Unfortunately, the abolition of slavery without the removal of its causes could not at once be an unqualified success. The sugar and cotton plantations of the New World needed cheap and forced labor. Indian slavery of the Spanish era had been followed by African slavery; just prior to 1850 this latter gave way to Chinese slavery in the shape of contract labor: "The time had now come for yellow to take the place of black at the behest of anti-slavery sentiment, not

Harley Farnsworth MacNair, *The Chinese Abroad: Their Position and Protection, a Study in International Law and Relations,* The Commercial Press, Limited, Shanghai, China, 1933, pp. 209–227.

more intelligent than that of a Chinese prince, who, pitying an ox, ordered a sheep to be sacrificed instead.''

During the period 1847–1874, it has been estimated that between a quarter and a half million laborers were shipped from Amoy, Canton, Hongkong, and Macao—especially from the two places last named—to Cuba, Peru, Chile, and the Sandwich Islands. In 1864, for example, from Macao there were shipped to Cuba 4,479 and to Peru 6,243; in 1865, 5,207 to Cuba, and 8,417 to Peru. During the same years 2,716 laborers were shipped from Canton by Cuban agents acting under the French flag.

The sufferings of these laborers caused by the methods used by European, American, and Chinese agents in getting them to leave China; the terrible conditions under which they were shipped abroad, as bad as those on the old African slave ships; and their exploitation on the plantations of the New World combine to form one of the darkest stains on the record of the relations of China and the West, a record, it may be added, for which the blame must be pretty equally divided between Chinese and Westerners.

The need for cheap labor in the West and the overflowing population of China built up a lucrative business for conscienceless traders of East and West. The supply came chiefly from three sources, says a contemporary account; ''prisoners taken in the clan fights . . . of the province of Kwangtung, and who are sold by their captors to Chinese of Portuguese man-buyers upon the interior waters; villagers or fishermen forcibly kidnaped along the coast; . . . and thirdly, individuals who are tempted by prowling agents to gamble [in Macao] . . . and who on losing . . . surrender their persons in payment according to the peculiar Chinese notions of liability in this respect.''

The ''crimps,'' as the collecting agents were called, received from seven to ten dollars a man delivered to the coolie depots, or barracoons, in Macao; here the coolie ''signed'' a ''contract'' for eight years of service; on reaching Cuba the surviving coolies were put up at auction with their contracts and sold for an average of seventy-eight pounds. The legal right of the coolie to appeal to the Spanish courts for enforcement of his rights in case of illtreatment or lack of payment was assured him but ''no instance is on record of such a proceeding.''

Had it been possible from the first to regulate this traffic the Chinese government would not have done so, for to regulate it would have been to recognize the right of Chinese to expatriate themselves, and this was not done until 1860.

The Hongkong government in 1853 attempted to ameliorate conditions by prescribing ships' regulations for space and food. No other coolie ships were bound by such regulations, however, and, with the exception of those British official agencies which were engaged in shipping coolies to Demerara and Trinidad, these ships left largely from non-treaty ports. In the same year, properly regulated emigration of laborers to Cuiana began; and in the next year a shipload of emigrants reached Kingston, Jamaica. On September 1, 1854, a prohibition was placed on the emigration of coolies to the Chincha Islands, Peru, on account of the conditions of the trade, but upon improvement of these conditions the ban was lifted on February 3, 1855; in the same year, however, the whole traffic was stopped by the enactment of the Chinese Passengers Act. In March, 1857, closed coolie barracoons were discovered in Hongkong and immediately broken up. During the years 1867–1869 the emigration regulations became more and more strict; in 1870 contract emigration from Hongkong to non-British colonies became illegal. Finally, in April, 1873, the chief justice of the colony announced from the bench that any one in Hongkong participating in the traffic, either directly or indirectly, would be liable to punishment for felony under the Imperial Act for the suppression of slavery.

From 1858–1861 the administration of the city of Canton was in the hands of an Anglo-French commission; aided by the commissioners and the various consuls, the viceroy of Kwangtung in 1860 established a system to regulate emigration by means of licensed receiving depots at Canton and Swatow which were to be inspected by Chinese officers; emigrant ships were to be inspected by customs officers.

In October, 1864, following the English and French precedents, Spain concluded a treaty with China. In this, the right of Chinese subjects to take service under Spanish subjects in the colonies, after the making of necessary regulations for the protection of the laborers by the Chinese local authorities and the Spanish representatives, was recognized.

During the winter of 1865–1866, the British and the French ministers in Peking conferred with Prince Kung, head of the Ministry of Foreign Affairs, who was as opposed to the malpractices of the coolie traffic as were the foreign envoys themselves. On March 5, 1866, a convention to regulate the engagement of Chinese emigrants by British and French subjects was signed by Sir Rutherford Alcock, Henry de Bellonet, and Prince Kung. Elaborate and specific regulations for the protection of the emigrant, whether free or contract, were laid down; in the case of the latter type the specifications of the contract were prescribed, including among others the hours of work, the number of working days a year, the length of the contract, provisions for illness, and for return of the laborer to China.

Prince Kung made three declarations: "1st, that the Chinese government throws no obstacle in the way of free emigration, . . . but that all attempts to bring Chinese under an engagement to emigrate, otherwise than as the present regulations provide, are formally forbidden, and will be prosecuted with the extreme rigor of the law. 2d, that a law of the empire punishes by death those who, by fraud or by force, may kidnap Chinese subjects for the purpose of sending them aborad against their will''; and thirdly, that emigration of collie labor abroad was authorized at ports only where it could be supervised jointly by the consuls and the Chinese authorities.

The envoys of the United States, Russia, and Prussia approved the convention but did not participate in its formation. The French government did not approve of certain provisions in the convention, although both the English and French governments approved it as a whole. Eighteen months were spent in discussing the matter and in making minor changes; the result was that the agreement was never ratified. But ''the Chinese government has consistently declared that contract emigration, when carried on, could be permitted only under the conditions prescribed in this convention.''

To evade even the slight restrictions placed on the emigration of coolies from Canton, and those of the customs officers in the open ports, the emigrant dealers fell back largely on Macao where they were protected by the Portuguese. From here the evil trade went on until March, 1875, when the Portuguese home government, at the instigation of England, supported by France and Germany, put a stop to it.

The conditions under which the contract laborers worked in the New World were almost incredibly bad; for the most part they were considered and treated as slaves without the protection of any government. An unprejudiced observer wrote: ''I believe the coolie slave trade to be as bad as that of the negroes. During the passage, which is always horrible, the latter perhaps suffered rather more; but, once arrived at their destination, the slaves found in the very interest of their proprietor a guarantee of comparative well-being. The coolies have not even this advantage; and they tell me that their fate is the more lamentable because they belong to a race which is more civilized and more intelligent than the negroes.''

The Spanish desired a new emigration convention in 1873; the question of the coolie emigration caused strained relations between the Tsungli Yamen and the Spanish legation in Peking, for reports of the hardships and cruelties undergone by the contract laborers in Cuba and Peru were reaching the Chinese court. The imperial government decided to send a commission to Cuba in 1874. This commission reported to the Tsungli Yamen on October 20, and in it occurred the following statements: ''The depositions and petitions show that eight tenths of the entire number declared that they had been kidnaped or decoyed. . . . On arrival at Havana they were sold into slavery. . . . During the past years a large number have been killed by blows, have died from the effects of wounds, and have hanged themselves, cut their throats, poisoned themselves with opium, and thrown themselves into wells and sugar caldrons. . . . On the termination of the contracts the employers, in most cases, insist on a renewal of engagements, which may extend to even more then ten years. . . . Almost every Chinese met by us was, or had been, undergoing suffering, and suffering was the purport of almost every word we heard.''

The Spanish were unable to obtain a new convention until November, 1877, almost three years after the Macao trade had been stopped. The new agreement abrogated the previous contract arrangement; enforced emigration was denounced and the Spanish government agreed that the Chinese in Cuba should be treated as subjects of the same standing as those of the most-favored nation. China recognized the right of free emigration to Cuba: emigrants were to be supplied with printed passports by the customhouse taotais, which, after being viséed by the Spanish consul, were to be forwarded into the Chinese consuls whom Spain now agreed should be established in Cuba by China. Chinese subjects in Cuba were to be registered at the consulates of their country. The Spanish government, ''anxious to prove its friendship and good wishes to His Majesty the Emperor of China,'' agreed to repatriate at its own expense, ''persons who formerly had a literary occupation in China, as also those who had official standing, and the members of such families. . . . Old men who, on account of age, are unable to work, and who petition to return to China, as well as Chinese orphan girls who desire to return to their country, will be repatriated in like manner.'' Workmen whose contracts had not expired were to fulfill them, but to enjoy the advantages of newcomers; workers whose contracts had expired might leave Cuba or remain at their pleasure.

Coincident with the signing of the treaty between China and Peru on June 26, 1874, a special agreement respecting the Chinese immigrants in the latter country was signed. In recognition of the fact that some Chinese subjects were suffering ''grievances'' in Peru the government of that country agreed that China should send a commission to ''institute a thorough investigation into the condition of Chinese immigrants in all parts of Peru,'' which commission was to receive the assistance of all local or provincial authorities. Where cases should be found of illtreatment of immigrants whose contracts had not expired, the commission was to report to the local authorities; if employers of Chinese denied the charges of illtreatment, the complaints were to be forwarded by the local authorities to the tribunals for ''judicial inquiry and decision,'' and cases might even be carried to the higher courts of justice for further investigation, the immigrants being placed on an equality in matters of legal procedure with subjects of the most-favored nation.

In the case of immigrants whose contracts had expired, and in which there had been a stipulation that the employer should send them back to China, the Peruvian government agreed to compel the employers to carry out the contract; in similar cases, where there had been no return stipulation, and where the immigrant was indigent, the government promised to "cause them to be repatriated gratuitously in the ships which leave Peru for China."

With the exchange of ratifications of the treaty to which this Special Agreement was appended, on August 7, 1875, and of those to the Spanish convention on December 6, 1878, the worst abuses of the unrestricted and unregulated contract labor of the old régime came to an end.

II

The story of contract labor in the Sandwich Islands, or Hawaii, is a less gloomy one than the above. While some of the laborers for Hawaii were "captured" in the manner previously described, their lot in the Pacific islands was quite different from that of their brothers in Cuba and Peru at the same time.

The legal basis for the introduction of contract labor into Hawaii was the incorporation in the Master and Servants Act of that kingdom in 1850 of a section recognizing that "all engagements of service contracted in a foreign country to be executed in this" were valid except that "engagements made for a longer period than ten years be reduced to that limit."

In 1852, Captain Cass, in two trips of the bark *Thetis,* took in two hundred eighty Chinese laborers who were on contract to "serve for a term of five years at three dollars per month in addition to passage prepaid and food, clothing, and shelter provided by the planter who had engaged their services." Such labor cost slightly less than nine dollars a month in as much as it was reckoned that transportation cost fifty dollars a man and his maintenance about five dollars a month.

The secretary of the Royal Hawaiian Agricultural Society in his annual report of 1852, referred to the Chinese as "quiet, able, and willing men." An account in the *Chinese Mail* contrasted the conditions of the Chinese laborers in Hawaii with those in South America. Captain Cass was referred to as "a man of much humanity and good sense," who had "entered into engagement with the planters of the Sandwich Islands to import Chinese laborers for the sugar plantations,—the planters binding themselves to pay the laborers four dollars a month from the time of their arrival; while cooks, house servants, and gardeners have been engaged at salaries as high as sixteen dollars,—and as the wages are not promised merely, but paid, and the coolies are well treated, they are not only contented but have urged their friends at home to join them."

Special precautions were taken by the passage of various laws between 1872 and 1892 for the protection of all contract laborers, Chinese and others, in the kingdom of Hawaii. In 1872 a law was passed requiring a contract to be acknowledged before an authorized government officer by both master and servant stating that the contract was clearly understood and a voluntary one. By a law of 1876, the length of a working day, if not already specified in the contract, was declared to be nine hours, with additional pay for extra time. A sanitary standard for plantation camps was fixed by a law of 1880; this prescribed the type and repairing of houses, the amount of air space for adults and children, drainage, and sewage. In 1882, it was provided that there should be no extension of the term of labor as a punishment for desertion. This was punished by fine and imprisonment only. Those who received ill usage by their masters might apply to the courts where, if the complaint was sustained, the employee was freed from his contract and the master fined. In 1884, a law declared that "every laborer serving under written contract shall be entitled to his full pay under the contract, according to the time he has worked, and no master shall deduct from the wages of any such laborer for lost time, more than the amount of money representing such lost time." Transfers of Chinese contracted employees from one employer to another was allowed after 1892, only with the consent of the both laborer and employer.

The Board of Immigration report of 1888–1890 estimated the plantation wages of Chinese contract laborers to be $17.61 a month, while those of free Chinese laborers was estimated at $17.47.

Opposition to the importation of Chinese laborers began in 1875 and culminated with the restriction and exclusion acts of 1885–1895. By 1888, there were 5,728 Chinese plantation laborers out of a total of 15,578 of all nationalities. A modification of the exclusion laws occurred in 1895 to permit employers to import Chinese laborers provided they would at the same time "introduce European or American agricultural laborers equal in number to one tenth of the Chinese permitted" them within a year after the date of the permit. by 1897, Chinese to the number of 7,364 had been brought in under this arrangement.

The conclusions of a careful student of contract labor in the Hawaiian Islands are of value in themselves and as a basis for comparison of the same in other lands: "Much misunderstanding has arisen concerning this method of meeting the labor demand of the sugar planters. The evil reputation of the coolie trade—a reputation well earned in Cuba and in the Chincha Islands—has attached itself to every attempt to transfer the superabundant population of Asia to the lands where their labor is in demand. It must be acknowledged that the penal enforcement of a labor contract is inconsistent with the trend of modern labor legislation. It suggests slavery. But how otherwise could the laborer, guiltless of property and in debt for his passage money, secure his master against breach of contract? The labor contract, moreover, was the only practical method of securing labor in a country so remote from the sources of supply. Laborers could be induced to immigrate only by the offer of passage prepaid and a guarantee of employment at a living wage. Planters could not be expected to meet these terms unless they were guaranteed against loss by a legal claim on the laborer for a definite term. Finally social security would have been threatened by the importation of alien laborers in numbers far exceeding the native population, but for the fact that these men were held upon the plantations by the labor obligation. . . .

"Contract labor as practiced in the Hawaiian Islands was fully justified by the peculiar social and industrial conditions there prevailing. As administered by the Board of Immigration, the system was calculated to advance the interests of the laborers quite as much as those of the planters. That it has done so is evident from the property statistics of the twelfth census. The value of the farm lands in which Chinese are interested as owners, part owners, managers, cash tenants, or share tenants is $2,700,335. . . . The Chinese residents in the Hawaiian Islands pay taxes on $3,287,802 of personal property. . . . It would not be difficult to prove that for the Oriental laborer the labor contract has been the highroad to fortune." These observations and conclusions are of especial value in reference to contract labor in British and Dutch Malaysia and in South Africa.

2.9

Alexander Yamato
Labor in California

It is exceedingly important to examine the historical experience of Asian Americans in California and especially San Francisco. Not only was it a major port of entry for those from Asia, San Francisco was also the major site of the anti-Oriental movement to exclude Chinese and Japanese from immigrating to the United States. San Francisco had a reputation as being a city largely consisting of immigrants. For instance, in the late 1860s, four foreign born ethnic groups constituted one-third of all immigrants (Cherny and Issel, 1979:10). These immigrants came from Ireland, China, Germany, and Italy. Thus, by 1900, 75% of San Franciscans had parents who were foreign born (Cherny and Issel, 1979:29). The Irish and the Chinese both immigrated in large numbers in the period from the 1860s to the 1880s (Cinel, 1982:18). German immigrants arrived in the city between 1880 and 1900 (Cinel, 1982:18). The German immigrants were a diverse population, being equal to the number of Irish immigrants in the 1880s, but heterogeneous, some being Protestant, others Catholic, and still others Jewish (Cherny and Issel, 1979:29). Peak immigration for Italians to San Francisco was between 1900 and 1924. Jewish immigrants were among the early pioneers in San Francisco, and unlike the experiences of Jews on the East Coast, did not encounter the degree of resistance or opposition (Decker, 1978:117–188; Rosenbaum, 1980:17). Blacks migrated from the South and other parts of the United States from about the 1850s but never arrived in large numbers until the beginning of World War II.

White ethnics such as the Irish and Italian, although they encountered initial discrimination in the late 19th Century, were woven into a society based upon cultural pluralism whereby these immigrants were able to establish ethnic social institutions, such as ethnic churches, language schools, cultural societies, and other organizations renewing their ties and maintaining a continuity with the traditions of their previous country. San Francisco, during this period, expanded greatly both as a developing industrial, manufacturing port of trade to a cosmopolitan city with a multi-cultural, multi-lingual population but with the Anglo cultural norms predominating (Burchell, 1980:180). Through the late 19th Century, San Francisco's population was characterized by extremely high mobility rates. For example, only 10% of the population of 1880 were residents of the city in 1860. Seventy-five percent of the native born and 67% of the foreign born living in the city in 1880 had arrived only in the 1870s (Decker, 1978:171).

67

Similarly, among the English, French, and Irish, there were high rates
of out-migration. Only the Irish were able to maintain their proportion
of the population through the period of Irish immigration. The numbers of Eastern and Southern European immigrants, including Italians,
increased, as well as the Chinese population which constituted 9% of
the city's population (Decker, 1978:171). However, racial groups,
were definitely not considered or treated equally. According to
Burchell, a historian of the Irish in San Francisco, the presence of the
Chinese reduced perceived differences between the American born
population and Irish immigrants and defined the limits of accept-
ability. A definition which Burchell cites as being a common understanding of "American" was articulated by Frank Soule, a Whig
political leader in 1853:

> Under the term 'Americans' are included the natives of Great Britain
> and Ireland, who are less easily distinguishable from native Americans
> than are other foreigners. Many, however, of the British-born, are
> American by adoption and naturalization. Since the common language
> of the Americans and British is English, and their customs and habits
> of thought are generally the same, there seems no impropriety in call-
> ing them all in California simply Americans (Burchell, 1980:181–182).

The European ethnics were able to establish a form of cultural
pluralism where each group established ethnic institutions according to their dialect, locale, and religious orientations. One writer,
di Leonardo, believed that the presence of the Chinese and the Japanese displaced the prejudice that would have been directed towards
new immigrants (di Leonardo, 1984:56). One Italian American told of
a story of young Italians in the early 1900s, "tying the long hair of
Chinese people in a knot and then running like hell!" (di Leonardo,
1984:56). Although the Chinese population had drastically been reduced due to exclusionary immigration laws, the Chinese were still
objects of causes which created solidarity among white workers and
solidified union support (Knight, 1960:41–42). In fact a sustained opposition to Catholics, such as one led by the Know-Nothing movement in other parts of the country, never materialized and instead the
Chinese were singled out (di Leonardo, 1984:56).

In the 1850s there was a well established way of treating racial
minorities, carried on with succeeding racial groups. Unlike other
groups, such as European immigrants, which merchants assisted to
obtain entry into merchant occupations, through employment in entry
level positions such as clerks or accountants, or through establishing
aid associations or societies, Blacks were relegated to service labor as
cooks and waiters (Decker, 1978:118, 120). While certain immigrant
groups and migrating groups found opportunities in San Francisco,
they "viewed all Latins and Chinese with contempt" (Decker,

1978:120). The 1880s marked the decline of opportunities for those attempting to improve their occupational standing from workers to small merchants, as manufacturers and department stores displaced the role of small merchants, wholesalers, and small shops (Decker, 1978:195). Only one-third of the merchants in business in 1880 were still in the city ten years later (Decker, 1978:193). Changing economic conditions and access to capital determined those who survived. Those qualifying for credit had to satisfy an ethnocentric determination of their character: "ethnic, religious, and racial background, personal dedication to the Protestant work ethnic, moral and ethical behavior" (Decker, 1978:258).

Various lessons can be learned from comparing the labor experience of racial minorities with that of European ethnic groups. First, as Lieberson had found in his study comparing Southern and Eastern European immigrant occupational patterns with those for Blacks, there is a queuing effect such that the presence of a racial group acts to place them lowest in the hierarchy for jobs and other needs, and also allows the new European immigrant groups access to more desirable jobs than are available to Blacks (Lieberson, 1980:378–379). It is clear that the various ethnic groups carved out economic niches, according to prior background and skills or because of a traditional role for those of a certain ethnic group even though those skills were not brought with them. Thus, Italian immigrants who were fisherman or farmers in Italy continued their vocations in San Francisco. However, there were those Italian or Irish working as domestic workers who learned the work in the United States, and later immigrants fell into the occupation.

It is intriguing to examine San Francisco labor history and to compare and contrast the experience of racial minorities with that of European immigrant groups. What is interesting is the fact that Chinese labor was the only racial minority employed in large numbers in the manufacturing industries of San Francisco. Chinese labor rather than Black labor was actively recruited to work particularly on the construction of the railroads and mines in the 1850s and 1860s and later these workers settled in San Francisco, a fledgling manufacturing city at the time and were employed in light industry. The effect of the migration and immigration of immigrant groups was to increase the labor pools and a restructuring of employment of various ethnic groups. Thus, Chinese and Black labor were displaced in the skilled trades. Of the European immigrant groups on the other hand, while there was a great deal of turnover and migration, a labor movement did develop organizing workers of different nationalities, religions, and cultures, as well as a parallel organization of capital in employer's associations (McWilliams, 1979:129–130).

In accounting for the division between Chinese and non-Chinese, Saxton believes that it was clearly the case of white workers of diverse backgrounds becoming melded into a united political group in opposition to capital but striking out at the Chinese, considered to be the agent of capital (Saxton, 1975:258–259). Similarly, Edna Bonacich accounts for discriminatory acts such as exclusionary movements as an articulation of perceived or real feelings of unfair competition between "higher priced" labor and "cheap" labor (Bonacich, 1973:591). However, the labor history of San Francisco reveals that the Chinese were already established as labor, and that unionized labor, rather than attempting to organize Chinese and Black workers, sought with capital to displace minority workers from favored positions. Also, later immigrant groups such as the Italian, although experiencing a degree of discrimination, were not excluded as an immigrant group as was the Chinese. Although the peak of Italian immigration was about thirty years later than the Chinese, the Italian were able to establish themselves in agriculture and fishing, whereas the Chinese faced restrictive legislation, regulating their economic participation. The Italian were contemporaneous with the Japanese, but the Japanese found themselves treated and viewed in the same way as the Chinese before them.

The following selection is taken from Ping Chiu, *Chinese Labor in California, 1850–1880: An Economic Study,* State Historical Society of Wisconsin, 1967. Ping Chiu's book is important in understanding the historical experience of Chinese Americans and Asian Americans because he places the immigration and labor struggles of Chinese Americans in the broader context of the political economy of California in relation to the United States economy. Chiu examines the "myth" of the Chinese as "cheap labor."

References

Bonacich, Edna. 1973. "A Theory of Middlemen Minorities," *American Sociological Review,* Vol. 38 (October): 583–594.

Burchell, R. A. 1980. *The San Francisco Irish, 1848–1880,* Berkeley: University of California Press.

Cherny, Robert W., and William Issel. 1981. *San Francisco: Presidio, Port, and Pacific Metropolis,* San Francisco: Boyd & Fraser Publishing Company.

Cinel, Dino. 1982. *From Italy to San Francisco,* Stanford University Press.

Decker, Peter R. 1978. *Fortunes and Failures, White-Collar Mobility in Nineteenth-Century San Francisco,* Cambridge: Harvard University Press.

di Leonardo, Micaela. 1984. *The Varieties of Ethnic Experience, Kinship, Class, and Gender Among California Italian Americans,* Ithaca: Cornell University Press.

Lieberson, Stanley. 1980. *A Piece of the Pie, Blacks and White Immigrants Since 1880,* Berkeley: University of California Press.

McWilliams, Carey. 1979. *California: The Great Exception,* Santa Barbara: Peregrine Smith, Inc.

Rosenbaum, Fred. 1980. *Architects of Reform, Congregational and Community Leadership Emanu-El of San Francisco, 1849–1980,* Berkeley: The Judah L. Magnes Memorial Museum.

Saxton, Alexander. 1975. *The Indispensible Enemy: Labor and the Anti-Chinese Movement in California,* Berkeley: University of California Press.

2.10
Ping Chiu
Changing Economic Structure and Chinese Immigration, 1865–1880

Chapter IV

Before plunging into a detailed discussion of the Chinese as industrial and agricultural workers, it may prove worthwhile to offer a cursory review of general economic conditions in California. Mining had dominated early California's economy insofar as it was the main field for investment and employment, while other sectors of the economy were oriented toward the needs of mining and of the miners. Because of this California constituted a distinct economic region in spite of its close trade relations with the rest of the world. The economic welfare of the state depended primarily on the production of gold. Wages rose and fell with the income and employment opportunities of individual pioneer miners. Local "manufacturing" was supplementary to, instead of in competition with, imported goods. California had its own price and wage levels, and the impact of Eastern business conditions had neither been immediate nor direct.

The dominance of gold, however, waned after the mid–1850's as a result of a reduction of gold yield, the rapid growth of especially wheat production, and the rise of manufacturing in the 1870's. This changing economic structure was a sign of maturation and coincided with the emergence of a national market. Thereafter, an increasing segment of California's economy was in direct competition with that of the East. Prices, wages, and levels of business activity began to conform with the national norm. With this development California's economy entered into a new era. The adjustments entailed by this change induced many new problems, and among them was that of Chinese labor in manufacturing industries.

The decline of the dominant position of mining in the state can be illustrated by the merchandise-treasure export ratio, and the merchandise export-import ratio (or balance of trade).

Table 15
California's External Trade Ratio, 1848–1871

Year	Merchandise-Treasure Export Ratio	Merchandise Export-Import Ratio
1848–54	1: 29	—*
1855–58	1: 13	1: 2.1
1859–60	1: 6.4	1: 1.4
1860–65	1: 4	1: 0.86
1866–68	1: 2	1: 0.89
1868–71	1: 1.5	1: 1.37

*Reliable data on imports not available

Again, the rapid development of agriculture together with the concurrent growth of wheat exports was primarily responsible for the changes in California's external trade. With the development of agricultural exports, the treasure outflow was reduced vastly. This, in conjunction with the reduction of gold production, the triumph of company mining, the advancement in banking, and the maturing local economy, brought about a reduction of interest charges. Last, but not least, the decline of individual mining terminated the most important outlet for self-employment in early California. Thus the major deterrents to the development of industry, scarcity of capital and labor, were diminished. Therefore, the rise of manufacturing in California came after the Civil War, after the Chinese left the mines en masse, and after the labor force of the Central Pacific Railroad had reached its maximum point in 1867.

The postwar depression touched the state only slightly. In contrast with the East, the year 1866 was one of the most prosperous in California. In spite of financial stringency in England and New York, money in San Francisco was easy, with the exception of the mid-year period.

In the next year, however, there was considerable unemployment in San Francisco. As a result, there was a flurry of anti-Chinese agitation and a full round of debate as to the consequences and desirability of the employment of Chinese labor. A cursory glance at those present at the Anti-Coolie Labor Meeting, March 6, 1867, will betray the fact that with the exception of the cigar makers, none of the trades were in direct competition with the Chinese. There were wine merchants, ship carpenters, plumbers, masons, boilermakers, tinners, stevadores, warehouse assistants, carriage makers, shoemakers (Chinese labor entered this field after 1867) and lumbermen. In other words, the urban anti-Chinese movement from its very beginning was dominated by skilled labor and non-factory, or sweatshop workers, who were in no way competing with the Chinese labor.

The leadership and their followers in the 1867 anti-Chinese movement essentially constituted noncompetitors for the Chinese. They had no specific legislation or remedies except immigration restriction, much as the anti-Chinese agitations in the 1870's. The passage of laws discriminating against the Chinese in certain other areas of activities in no way affected job opportunities for the majority of the participants in the movement. The expulsion of the Chinese from a certain locality (as the miners did in the 1850's) would be similarly ineffective.

As in the case of 1852 there were clear divisions of interests and opinions within the state. Through persistent lobbying and agitation, the anti-Chinese forces had succeeded in persuading the Democratic party to take up Chinese exclusion as a campaign issue. The movement failed to gain momentum. This can be explained in part by the fact that the number of workers who competed directly with the Chinese was relatively small. The budding sweatshop industries in San Francisco were still in their infancy. Furthermore, the recession was spotty. Shipping was reported as "uniformly active at remunerative rates; importers and jobbers enjoyed full average employment; farmers had reaped unprecedented harvests; mining was rated as fair. In other words, depression was pretty much limited to certain segments in San Francisco.

The great debate of 1867 was in essence a repeat performance of the 1852 drama but with a different cast. The anti-Chinese elements, this time predominantly wage laborers instead of independent miners, argued that the Chinese depressed wages, deprived white workers of their employment, and that their customs, laws, language, religion and civilization in general were incompatible with the American way of life. The governor, the Republican party, the employers, and a large number of important newspapers took the position that Chinese labor was essential, if not indispensable for the economic well-being of the state. They argued that white labor had not been displaced but on the contrary the utilization of Chinese labor resulted in a vast expansion of job opportunities for all.

In 1869 California suffered a mild recession, and the divergence between levels of trade, profit, and employment heightened in 1870. A mild business downswing coincided with substantial unemployment in San Francisco. Again, the nonmanufacturing workers were at the forefront of the anti-Chinese crusade.

Agricultural prosperity in California greatly mitigated the severity of the depression of 1873. Farm prosperity made up a portion of the increase in exports and absorbed a large amount of imports. General business downturn commenced in 1874.

During the 1870's, California's annual merchandise export fell far short of its import, with the exception of 1875, 1878 and 1879. Initially the unfavorable balance of trade was not profound because the gold price was steady in the years 1871 to 1873 and a modest upward trend in commodity price appeared during the same period. The advance of import in 1876, however, was coincidental with a strong national downward trend in commodity prices, and a major reduction of westbound railroad freight charges. For the first time in the history of California, there was an "industrial" depression.

As California kept gold as its medium of exchange throughout the Greenback era, the consequences of the general price decline was particularly grave from October 1875 to October 1876, when commodity prices fell and gold price went up and from October 1877, to July 1879, when commodity prices declined at a faster rate than the price of gold. In short, the deflationary trend was even stronger in California than in the country as a whole.

The impact of declining prices on California's manufacturing can also be illustrated by the beginning of recessions (upper turning points) in the major industries in regard to the size of labor force, total value of product and the value of product per worker. The following table was compiled from the *San Francisco Municipal Reports* and the data were collected on a fiscal year basis (that is, 1874 means from July 1, 1874, to June 30, 1875).

The woolen industry in California, organized on a factory production basis from the start and in competition on the national market, was the first to be affected. Boot and shoe manufacturing—partly factory, partly sweatshop in operation—felt the recession a short time later. Other industries did not feel the impact of recession until 1876 or after the major price drop of October 1875 to October 1876.

In slipper and shirt manufacturing, during the 1876–1877 season, values of product per worker declined. There the total labor force and product value remained steady or actually rose. Indeed sweatshops often sought to combat price drops by increasing output. Therefore, in the fiscal years of 1876 and 1877 profit diminished as a result of stable or rising output and declining prices. As the depression deepened in 1877 and 1878, sweatshops began to cut production: the shirt industry in 1877, and the slipper industry in 1878.

In the case of slipper making, prices and profits declined first. Production cuts followed at an interval of two years, though labor still remained in the industry for another three years. In contrast, the reductions of output and labor force were concurrent in the shirt manufacturing industry. This disparity of labor mobility can be explained in part by the lack of similarities between slipper and shoe making, as the former were not made of leather.

Table 16
Upper Turning Points of Selected Industries

Industry	Size of Labor Force	Value of Product	Value of Product Per Worker
Woolen textile	1875	1874	1874
Boots and shoes	1878	1877	1874
Slippers	After 1880	1878	1876
Cigars	1879	1876*	1876**
Clothing	After 1880	After 1880	1876
Shirts	1877	1877	1876

*Total product instead of value of product
**Units of product per worker

The clothing industries included, however, various sub-branches. Hence, the trend was not as clear as in slipper or shirt manufacturing. Increase there in total product value and labor force after 1876 was due in part to an influx of shirt makers and the entry of female workers during a depression. In woolen mills, however, price drop and production cut were simultaneous and soon a sizable labor force had been laid off.

The effects of the 1875–1876 price drop were profoundly felt in California. A number of new industries had developed in the intervening years since the milder shock of 1870, and were in competition with Eastern producers on the local market. Many of the economic dislocations in California during the late 1870's were caused by Eastern competition, by the conflict between the emergence of a national market and a maturing regional economy. Had California remained predominantly a mining community in the 1870's, price drops in manufactured goods would have been most beneficial.

Moreover, the 1870's were a transitional period in numerous industries from sweatshops to factory modes of production. High requirements for capital and managerial skills of factory production prevented the majority of sweatshop owners from entering the field. Mass-produced, low-priced products encroached on local markets which had been hitherto served by local sweatshops. California manufacturers were faced with the danger of elimination in the late 1870's. Unable to fight these economic forces, small manufacturers and laborers in California chose to wage their battle against the Chinese.

Aside from these external or inter-regional factors, California's manufacturers had serious regional problems to cope with. The effects of high interest rates and high wages have been discussed previously. It suffices to state here that if these were of great importance in the

1850's and the 1860's, they were more so in the 1870's when Eastern competition was not latent but intense, not intermittent but constant.

The scarcity of women laborers posed a serious problem for the development of various light industries in California. The preponderant male population in a mining frontier is a fact too well known to require lengthy documentation here. As late as 1880, for every female worker in manufacturing, there were eleven male workers in California.

In addition to the unequal distribution of the sex ratio in its population, high per capita income in early California also kept white women and children out of the labor market. Many industries were compelled to start with Chinese labor. In the mid-1870's for the first time in the history of California, a substantial number of females and minors were seeking employment. Many complained that the Chinese barred them from employment.

Large scale substitution of females for Chinese labor in jobs usually held by women in other states was not entirely feasible in California in the late 1870's. There simply were not enough of them. The fact that they sought employment in a glutted labor market caused their number to be greatly exaggerated by casual observers. Secondly, they were entirely inexperienced. According to John S. Hittell, a certain shop giving work to all skilled female applicants could obtain only twenty female sewing-machine operators. Moreover, it took them entirely too long to acquire a new skill. For instance, in shirt making, the females needed one to two years to finish their apprenticeship in contrast with six to eight months for the Chinese. According to the same source, even when the girls were paid at a higher rate on piece work they failed to make anything near the same wage as the Chinese.

Moreover, boys and girls (in California any member of the fair sex was a girl) were subjected to discipline with great difficulty. As one employer related his experience:

> I never could rely upon them performing their work satisfactorily. If I would leave the factory and go up the street, when I came back I would find them throwing matches all over the factory, the floor covered with them, and they would be burnt up; and sometimes I would find them on the top of the two story building chasing each other all over the roof. By such things they destroyed a great deal of property, and I found I could not control them at all.
>
> The next change I made was to try girls in the packing of matches and putting them up, and I found more difficulty with them than I did with the boys, and I could not do anything with them.
>
> It was utterly impossible to set them to work and give them instructions that they would abide by. They would make little changes today, little changes tomorrow, and in a week you would find them doing entirely different work from the instructions you gave them.

As for the Chinese he stated:

> You take a Chinaman, a green China boy, into your factory and
> show him just how to do a thing, and if you leave him and come back,
> if it is a year afterward, you find him doing the work precisely as you
> instructed him.

He attributed the disciplinary problems to high income of the California worker.

> I think it is more the force of habit, their custom of living, the parents not having to depend on the labor of children to contribute to the
> family support. I think, probably it would be a proper instruction to
> place upon it to say that the laboring class here, as a general thing,
> depended upon the labor of the head of the family for the family support, and that they do not depend upon the labor of their children. I
> think that is the cause.

From the late 1860's, as gold yield declined and manufacturing developed, cost-price spread became the primary concern. California's wage structure, therefore, is another key issue. As we have mentioned before, the general wage level in California rose and fell with the income and employment possibilities of independent miners, but the degree of Eastern contact or competition, direct and indirect, exercised a strong influence in determining the wage level of specific trades.

Seamen's pay is a case in point. The income level of the miners set the minimum below which the crew members refused to work, and price differentials between East and West, or freight charges or profitability, determined the maximum level that the shipper would be willing to pay. It would not be difficult to recruit seamen in the East at $15 a month, but as soon as the ship docked at San Francisco, their pay had to be raised to $80, $100, $150 or even $250 to avoid desertion, or to recruit new members. As general price levels began to decline in California during the mid-1850's price differences between Eastern states and the Pacific coast were reduced. Seamen's pay on clipper ships was the first to approach the national average of $20 per month in San Francisco.

The year 1853 had been the first year in which anything resembling a standard wage rate in California came into existence. The following is a table of remunerations on various trades before and after a series of strikes in July and August, 1853.

The differences in pay between the bricklayers and carpenters, on the one hand, and shoemakers and tailors on the other, were astounding indeed. There seems to be no evidence of a dire shortage of the former, or a glut of the latter. Among the predominantly male population of a mining frontier, tailoring was not likely to be done at home. Furthermore, after the strike most trades were able to obtain substantial

Table 17
Wage Rates in 1853

Trades	Wage Rate Before Strike (Per Day)	Wage Rate After Strike (Per Day)
Bricklayers	$8–10	$10
stone cutters, plasterers*	8	10
Carpenters, joiners	7	10
Printers	7	10
Tinners	4–8	7
Shoemakers,** tailors	4	4
Common laborers	4	4

*Plasters got only $9 per day.
**Or $100 per month without board.

wage increases; tailors and shoemakers were notable exceptions. The strength of "unions" appears irrelevant in this case. What really depressed the wage of the latter group was the volume and the price of imports. Commodity prices set the upper limit of wage level. For those trades whose services could not be performed in the East and then transported to the Pacific coast, the remuneration for labor was on the whole high. Conversely, heavy imports coincided with low wage rates.

If this had been the case in 1850's, it was all the more true in the 1870's. Degree of Eastern competition in great part explains employment and wage patterns in the shoe, cigar and clothing industries. Chinese labor in these trades was the consequence of low price and low wage. It was not the cause, hence their expulsion would have been a very ineffective means to raise wages, or even employment.

The low pay of the common, unskilled laborers in the late 1860's and afterwards was a major cause of labor unrest. In the short run, workers were embittered for having been denied what they considered as a living wage. In the long run, labor mobility was hampered. Wage differentials between the skilled and unskilled kept workers in their own trade even when opportunities in other fields seemed better. This is not to infer that there would be perfect labor mobility otherwise, but to point up a person's reluctance to leave a $3.50 or $4.50 job for a $1.00 or $1.50 while learning a new skill.

As long as common laborers were primarily employed in odd jobs, and their wages constituted only a fraction of the total costs, pay was relatively high. But the labor intensive industries, such as construction work and numerous sweatshop industries, could not operate at that wage level. Thus, large scale levees were seldom contemplated in early California through many towns and much farmland were repeatedly flooded. Again, costly as it might be to ship machinery to the mines, road building was a rather late development. Scarcity of capital and labor was an important factor. It was no hindrance, however, to the construction of mining canals. Anticipated returns on investments were the real deterrents. In the fabulous era of the mines, cost or wage was no concern, but that day was soon over. It was not until the displaced Chinese miners joined the ranks of the pick and shovel brigade that the construction boom in irrigation, reclamation levees, railroads, and harbor improvements actually started. Not until the Chinese were available in great numbers were various manufacturing industries established and orchards extensively cultivated.

The presence and the availability of a large Chinese labor force had, in a few instances, "prevented" strikes on the part of white workers from being successful. However, the overall effect on wage levels was probably negligible. Low wage rates had been established, in most cases, before the entry of the Chinese. Moreover, many of the strikes were for an increase in wages; such demands rarely were successful except during a period of expansion.

It is next to impossible to discover and to interpret the effects of Chinese labor on the employment of white workers in construction and related fields. With only scattered information on the financial condition of such projects, it would be imprudent to venture an opinion as to the employer's ability or willingness to pay the wage differentials between the Chinese and white laborers—$30 to $32.50 for the former, and $30 to $35 with board for the latter. Some credibility must be given to the employer's claim that had it not been for the Chinese, many projects would not have been started.

Remuneration of labor on a racial basis had been the custom in Southern California; such differential discrimination was only latent in the North until the 1860's when an increasing number of Chinese left the mines in search of other employment. By the mid-1860's, a standard rate of $1 per day had been established except for those with special skills. Because of this uniform pay, there was a greater mobility among the Chinese workers. A transfer of jobs entailed little or no reduction in pay.

As might have been suspected, the flow of immigrants from China reflected job opportunities for the Chinese in California. To a point, the employers' assertion that the demand for labor regulated the volume of immigration contains a certain element of truth.

In general, Chinese immigration until 1880 can be divided into four periods. These in turn reflect the circumstances in California. From 1850 to 1863 mining afforded the Chinese fair opportunity. In spite of riots and persecutions, these years saw the first wave of heavy immigration. From 1864 to 1867, as the placer mines were giving out, more Chinese left California than immigrated there. From 1868 to 1876 the agricultural, manufacturing and construction boom touched off another wave of immigration. From 1877 to 1880, as the depression deepened, departures nearly counterbalanced new arrivals.

From 1852 to 1863 the fluctuations of annual Chinese immigration corresponded closely to the opportunities in mining, and the intensities of anti-Chinese sentiments. Until 1852, Chinese immigration was insignificant, and most of the immigrants stayed in the cities. In the golden years of surface mining, 1852 and 1854, net immigration figures reached the all time peak of 18,258 and 13,754 respectively. Reactions on the part of white miners were both immediate and violent, and in the following years, 1853 and 1855, departures exceeded arrivals. Population flow across the Pacific resumed immediately, though at more moderate rates, as the yield of surface mines declined. According to the San Francisco Custom House, figures for the eight years, 1856–1863, there was a net gain of 28,357 Chinese immigrants in California, which was less than 90 per cent of the two-year total for 1852 and 1854. Judging from the receipts of the Foreign Miner's Tax, the low point of Chinese in mining came at some time just before 1860, when not more than 70 per cent of the Chinese were engaged in mines. At the peak year, 1863, the figure rose to 80 per cent or 85 per cent.

For the years 1864–1867 departures surpassed arrivals from China in spite of employment opportunities in railroad and manufacturing. These were the twilight years of individual mining. During this period, about 10,000 Chinese left the mines. Nevertheless, at the end of 1867, 45 per cent to 50 per cent of the Chinese were still miners. About 8,000 or 21 per cent were employed by the railroad, and about 1,200 to 1,400 in the cigar, shoe and woolen manufacturing industries. It was also during this period that an increasing number of Chinese found employment as domestic servants and launderers. Unfortunately precise information is not available. A few Chinese had left for the mountain states in search of gold. However, the trend toward wage labor was unmistakable.

From 1868 to 1876 Chinese immigration reached a new peak. During this period, it was the building manufacturing industries in San Francisco, hop and fruit raising in Santa Clara County, truck gardening in and around San Francisco, Sacramento and lesser cities, levee, irrigation and reclamation projects, and later fruit raising and harvesting in the San Joaquin Valley, that attracted and absorbed the new immigrants from China. By 1876, manufacturing industries employed most of the Chinese—about 14,000 in San Francisco and more than 15,000 in the state as a whole. The Chinese mining population continued to decline during this period. By 1876 less than 12,500 remained. Construction and agricultural laborers, including those employed by

Table 18
Major Occupations of Chinese in 1880

Occupation	Number	Percentage of the State Total
Agricultural and harvest laborers	3,380	14.2
Gardeners and garden laborers	2,146	48
Farmers and tenants	1,590	–
Domestic servants	7,918	34
Hotel, restaurant keepers and helpers	630	10
Common laborers	11,710	20
Launderers	5,435	79.6
Peddlers	1,287	–
Boot and shoe makers	2,359	52
Brick makers	316	44
Cigar makers	2,717	84.4
Woolen mill operators	254	32.7
Clothing factory laborers	644	
Tailors and sewing machine operators	855	–
Miners	10,024	27
Fishermen	1,193	39

the railroads, were no less numerous than the miners. Seven thousand were employed as servants, and five thousand in laundries.

As the recession set in, an anti-Chinese movement spread and immigration waned. At the same time Chinese were leaving California in increasing numbers for other states and territories, especially Washington, Nevada, Arizona, Wyoming, Oregon, New York, Colorado and Louisiana. In 1870, there were only 13,972 Chinese in the United States residing outside of California; a decade later this figure reached 30,333.

In spite of anti-Chinese agitation and under-employment in the late 1870's, Chinese in the manufacturing industries still remained in their respective trades. The trend toward service industries remained at an initial stage. Table 18 shows the major occupations of Chinese in 1880.

2.11
Chinese Railroad Workers

Topical Introduction

Charles Crocker, who was Superintendent of the construction of the Central Pacific Railroad, possessed a relatively favorable attitude toward the work of Chinese immigrants. During the mid-1870s, a congressional committee travelled to California to investigate Chinese immigration. Among the people testifying was Crocker, who was among the minority of those who had anything positive to say about Chinese immigrants. Note, however, how he and his company encouraged ethnic rivalry in the construction of the Central Pacific Railroad in the late 1860s. From U.S. Senate, *Report of the Joint Committee to Investigate Chinese Immigration,* 44th Congress, 2nd Session, Report no. 689, (Washington: Government Printing Office, 1887), 667.

By the Chairman:

Q. What are their powers of endurance?—A. They are equal to the best white men. We tested that in the Summit tunnel, which is in the very hardest granite. We had a shaft down in the center. We were cutting both ways from the bottom of that shaft. The company were in a very great hurry for that tunnel, as it was the key to the position across the mountains, and they urged me to get the very best Cornish miners and put them into the tunnel so as to hurry it, and we did so. We went to Virginia City and got some Cornish miners out of those mines and paid them extra wages. We put them into one side of the shaft, the heading leading from one side, and we had Chinamen on the other side. We measured the work every Sunday morning; and the Chinamen without fail always outmeasured the Cornish miners; that is to say, they would cut more rock in a week than the Cornish miners did, and there it was hard work, steady pounding on the rock, bone-labor. The Chinese were skilled in using the hammer and the drill; and they proved themselves equal to the very best Cornish miners in that work. They are very trusty, they are very intelligent, and they live up to their contracts.

2.12

John R. Commons et al

Chinese Laborers in Post-Civil War Massachusetts and the South

Topical Introduction

Typically, when people think about Chinese workers in 19th century they think about Chinese railroad workers in the Far West. These documents below suggest, however, a greater diversity of Chinese working class experiences in post-Civil War United States. In the South, after the Civil War, the white elite was rightly concerned that Blacks freed from slavery were reluctant to provide the kind of cheap, reliable, and controllable labor its members felt was necessary to bring the Southern economy back to life. In the Northeast, manufacturers hoped that the use of Chinese workers would spell the end of white trade unionism. Of course, Euroamerican workers saw the introduction of Chinese workers in a very different, less optimistic light. The following documents were excerpted from John R. Commons, et. al., (eds.), *A Documentary History of American Industrial Society*, Vol. IX (Cleveland, OH: The Arthur H. Clark, Company, 1910), 80–88.

(b) The Chinese

(x) To supplement the Negro.

Memphis *Daily Avalanche*, July 16, 1869. On July 13 to 15, 1869, a convention, arranged by southern capitalists and planters, was held at Memphis, Tennessee, on the subject of labor immigration. The committee on finance, General Pillow, chairman, recommended the organization of a stock company to supply planters with laborers. The committee on transportation reported the figures made by the Union Pacific Railroad "for the transportation of Chinese from California to Memphis, forty-four dollars and seventy cents in lots of five hundred and upward."—Philadelphia *Inquirer*, July 21, 1869. The committee on Chinese Labor submitted the following report.

The committee assumes it is the sense of this Convention, that even if the present labor element among us could be utilized and profitably employed, it would still be utterly inadequate to the wants of the Southern and South-western States, and that we not only have ample room and superior inducements to offer the European immigration, but that it is also desirable and necessary to look to the teeming population of Asia for assistance in the cultivation of our soil and the development of our industrial interests; and that China, especially, is capable of supplying us with a class of laborers peculiarly adapted to our circumstances and the necessities of our situation. . . . The idea, then, that there is any danger of too great an accession to our population, provided it be of the kind we desire, is simply the madness of the moon. And if God in His providence, has opened up the door for the introduction of the Mongolian race to our fields of labor, instead of repelling this class of population as heathens and idolaters, whose touch is contaminating, would we not exhibit more of the spirit of Christians by falling in with the apparent leadings of Providence, and whilst we avail ourselves of the physical assistance these pagans are capable of affording us, endeavor at the same time to bring to bear upon them the elevating and saving influence of our holy religion, so that when those coming among us shall return to their own country, they may carry back with them and disseminate the good seed which is here sown, and the New World shall thus in a double sense become the regenerator of the Old.

The question specially referred to the consideration of your Committee is as to the best means of introducing this Asiatic labor, and this is the question of paramount importance to our people. Your committee has conversed fully and freely with Mr. Koopmanschaap, the agent of California Chinese Immigration, who has a large experience in that field of enterprise; and also with Mr. Tye Kim Orr, a native Chinaman of intelligence and cultivation, who has travelled a great deal, and is perfectly familiar with our language and habits.

The information derived from the gentlemen has satisfied your committee of the very great difference between different classes of Chinamen, and the great care and caution that will be necessary in procuring supplies that may be ordered by our people, since those following mechanical pursuits or lounging about the towns and cities of China are wholly unfit for agricultural pursuits and very frequently are of a malicious and unreliable character, while those of the rural districts of China are industrious, docile and competent agricultural laborers and exhibit as much fidelity in the performance of their duties and obligations as any people in the world.

Mr. Koopmanschaap did not come prepared to make engagements for the delivery of laborers here now, but the chief object of his visit was to acquaint himself with the wants of our people, and the extent of the demand, which he finds to be much greater than he anticipated; and his purpose is to return to California without delay, and make a special visit to China with a view to make some definite arrangements commensurate with the demand, information of which will be communicated to the public here at the earliest period practicable. His present estimates of the expenses incident to employing Chinese labor are to a great extent conjectural. He thinks that laborers can be transported from some Chinese port to Memphis via San Francisco and the Pacific Railroad in some six weeks, or two months at the outside, and delivered here at an expense not exceeding one hundred dollars per head. He supposes the companies he represents will be willing to deliver them here at that rate, guaranteeing the laborers to be of the description ordered or represented, the transportation money to be secured and paid on delivery of the laborer at Memphis.

As to the rate of wages, and reimbursement of the transportation money, those are matters of contract, which must be ultimately controlled, as all such questions are, by the law of demand and supply. The wages these laborers receive in China are merely nominal, but in California, the urgency of the demand in the mines and upon the railroads, has fixed the wages of labor at a figure that we would be unwilling to meet. The first importation made by us will doubtless be the most expensive, and the monthly wages, exclusive of rations, will, perhaps, be from eight to twelve dollars. These estimates are, however, as already remarked, merely conjectural; and in a great enterprise like this, so inseparably connected with our progress and prosperity, individually, and as a people, we must practice the virtues of patience and perseverance, submit to temporary sacrifice, and be hopeful of the future. Two facts are patent—China has the labor that we need, and it can be procured to an unlimited extent. When the supply of this labor becomes a business, competition will of course spring up, and the expense of procuring it will be reduced to a minimum which must fall far below the expenses incident to our present labor system, whilst its great advantage over that system, and the impetus it will impart to all of our industrial interest, will, it is confidently believed, very soon silence all objections, and remove all the prejudices now existing in the minds of our people. Respectfully submitted,

J. W. Clapp, Tennessee, Chairman; Wirt Adams, Mississippi; G. W. Gift, Tennessee; L. C. Garrett, Arkansas; J. C. Goodloe, Alabama; W. H. Sutton, Louisiana; J. Patton Anderson, Tennessee;—Dupree, Louisiana; E. Richardson, Louisiana.

On motion of Judge Sutton, the report was adopted.

(2) To counteract the Knights of St. Crispin. The Springfield *Republican*, June 17, 1870, p. 8, col. 2.

The van of the invading army of Celestials, seen in a vision by Wendell Phillips, greatly feared by all democrats, and not particularly welcomed by anybody, except in dire necessity, have arrived at North Adams, in the persons of seventy-five Chinamen engaged by C. T. Sampson to man his shoe factories, and free him from the cramping tyranny of that worst of American trades-unions, the "Knights of St. Crispin." These men were engaged in San Francisco through a Chinese business firm, by Mr. Chase of North Adams, who went out for that purpose. They are to be paid twenty-three dollars a month the first year, twenty-six dollars a month for the second and third years, and sixty dollars a month a Ah Sing, their foreman, who speaks and writes English fluently. Their passage is paid to Adams, their quarters and fuel furnished, but they of course board and clothe themselves. If any man be worthless, the San Francisco house forfeits twenty-five dollars and sends another in his place. The most sacred part of the Chinaman's religion, his body's burial with his ancestors, is also nominated in the bond, Sampson pledging to box up each corpse and send it to Kwong Chong Wing Company in Frisco, who will take charge of the rest of it. . . .

The Boston *Commonwealth*, June 25, 1870, p. 2, col. 2.

They are with us! the "Celestials"—with almond eyes, pigtails, rare industry, quick adaptation, high morality, and all—seventy-five of them—hard at work in the town of North Adams, making shoes. And their employer, and all the neighbors, say they are excellent in skill and deportment, ready learners, respectful and obedient, and almost as good as the same number of intelligent American workmen. These "Celestials" belong to no striking organizations—do not care to be out nights—don't worry about their pay—do not presume to dictate to their employer—and have situations guaranteed to them for three years. And the secret of it all is this: the Crispins of that town not only sought to establish their own pay and hours, but they demanded the discharge of their associates delinquent on the lodge-books of their organizations. Refusing to accede to this dictation, their employer, Mr. Sampson, saw the entire crowd of members in good standing with the lodge leave the shop, and himself, with unfilled contracts, on the brink of ruin. Being a man of energy he bethought him of the Chinese, of whom favorable reports had reached him as shoemakers in California. Thither he at once posted, and in a few weeks seventy-five of their countrymen entered the handsome village of North Adams, and in a day or two were at work in the deserted factory; while all Crispendom, near and remote, have since been watching the experiment, in mortal fear that their occupation is gone.

Now comes the question of the hour. Shall we give welcome to these Asiatic mechanics? It is a hard thing to supplant native workmen with them. But it is a harder thing to be dominated in our enterprise and industry by a secret, oath-bound labor organization, that listens to no reason, and whose practice is to rule or ruin. Mr. Sampson has solved for himself the problem. He is to be a free man—free to make his contracts, and conduct his business as he will, as well as nominally free under the guarantees of the law; and he has only done what every man of spirit and energy should do, if possible—triumphed over every obstacle that hindered the development of his prosperity, so long as he deprived no other man of his liberty to work, to accumulate, to rise in the social scale. That he is not a reckless and unprincipled man is shown that he has at once commenced the education of his new help, and some of them have ventured voluntarily into the Sunday-school connected with his church. We cannot question that American civilization can absorb this new element, moulding all races into one superior, predominant class. We have infinite trust in that Wisdom which made of one blood all nations to adapt this ancient people to the new world. Annoying as may be the perturbations of labor in the process, we believe that the nation, civilization, and humanity, will be benefited by this commingling of the races.

The Boston *Investigator,* July 6, 1870, p. 78, col. I.

The Voice of Free Labor. A large and enthusiastic meeting of the workingmen of this city was held in Tremont Temple last Wednesday afternoon and evening. Its object was to take some measures relative to the importation of coolie labor into Massachusetts. Many speeches were made, the substance of which is embodied in the following Resolutions passed by the meeting:

Whereas, efforts are now being made to introduce into the manufactories of this state coolie labor from China in order to cheapen, and, if possible, degrade the intelligent, educated loyal labor of Massachusetts, therefore be it

Resolved, that while we welcome voluntary laborers from every clime, and pledge them the protection of our laws, and the assurance of equal opportunities in every field of industry, still we cannot but deprecate all attempts to introduce into the manufactories of this State a servile class of laborers from China, or elsewhere, who come in fulfilment of contracts made on foreign soil, and with no intention to become American citizens or aid in the permanent development of American resources.

Resolved, that in the language of the Massachusetts Bill of Rights, Government is instituted for the common good, for the protection, safety, and happiness of the people, and not for the profit, honor, or private interest of any one man, family, or class of men. Therefore, the people alone have an incontrovertible, unalienable and indefeasible right to institute government, and to reform, alter, or totally change the same when their protection, safety, property, or happiness require it; and we, therefore, declare our fixed and unalterable purpose to use the power of the ballot to secure the protection, safety, property, and happiness of the working people of this commonwealth as against this new attempt of capital to cheapen labor and degrade the working classes by importing coolie slaves for that purpose.

Resolved, that we tender our thanks to the Hon. Henry Wilson for his earnest efforts to secure the passage of a law prohibiting the fulfilment on American soil of these infamous contracts for coolie labor, and we call upon our representatives in Congress to use all their influence to secure the passage of such a law as is due alike to the best interests of the country, as well as a measure of justice to the coolie, who, ignorant of the value of labor, accepts conditions degrading alike to him and to us.

Resolved, that the conduct of the Massachusetts Legislature, in twice refusing to take action calculated to check the introduction of the coolie system into this state, deserves the rebuke and condemnation of every working man in the State, as well as the condemnation of every man who believes the dignity of labor or the supremacy of liberty over tyranny.

Resolved, that we ignore all elements, whether in this meeting of out, which have for their tendency the strengthening of any man's chance for political honors who is not pledged to represent the greatest number of the people for the people's good, and who is not willing to be held accountable to the people for his political actions.

Resolved, that we have voted for protection to American industry at the suggestions of the rich manufacturers who owned the protected products, thinking to help ourselves, but we now find that, under the scheme of protection, capital is to get the protection and American labor is to be reduced to the Chinese standard of rice and rats, and we cut loose, now and forever, from the false and lying knaves who have beguiled us.

Resolved, that the rights of workingmen will gain no successful foothold in Massachusetts until the workingmen repudiate those time serving politicians who think to retain office at any price of double dealing.

Resolved, that we cordially endorse the course of Hon. Henry K. Oliver, Chief of the Bureau of Labor Statistics, and his assistants, for the able report on the condition of labor in this State, and pledge ourselves all the aid in our power by collecting and placing before the people the true condition and needs of the working classes.

2.13
Fraudulent Importation of Chinese, 1886

Letter from The Secretary of the Treasury

In response to Senate resolution of March 9, reports of Special Agent Spaulding relative to the charge of fraudulent importation of Chinese. MARCH 17, 1886.—Referred to the Committee on Commerce and ordered to be printed.

Treasury Department,
Office of the Secretary,
Washington, D.C., March 16, 1886.

SIR: I have the honor to acknowledge the receipt of a copy of a resolution of the Senate, dated the 9th instant, in which I am directed to transmit certified copies of two reports made to this Department in November last by Special Agent O. L. Spaulding, in relation to the charge of fraudulent importation of Chinese into the United States, and in reply to transmit herewith certified copies of reports of Agent Spaulding, dated respectively the 2d and 5th of November last. I also transmit copies of the three inclosures which accompanied the report of November 2.

Respectfully yours,

D. Manning,
Secretary.

Hon. John Sherman,
President pro tempore United States Senate.

———————

Office of Special Agent Treasury Department,
San Francisco, Cal., November 2, 1885.

Hon. Daniel Manning,
Secretary of the Treasury:

Sir: In obedience to your instructions I have investigated the charges made of the violation of the Chinese restriction act at this port, and beg to submit the following report:

By the terms of the act which was approved May 6, 1882, the coming of Chinese laborers to the United States was suspended after ninety days from its passage for ten years, except such as were the United States November 17, 1880, or should have come into the same before expiration of the said ninety days.

The law was amended July 5, 1881, but for the purpose of this report the amendments are not material.

It devolved on the Secretary of the Treasury and his subordinate customs officers to devise regulations and facilities for giving the law practical effect. It is not strange that the best methods were not adopted at first.

It must be admitted that grave mistakes of administration were made, but it is probable those now most forward in criticism would not have formulated a perfect system at once.

At the outset it was found that a liberal compliance with section 4 was impracticable. It was manifest that the clerical work of registration and filling out certificates could not be done on shipboard. It is the work of a week to pass six or seven hundred Chinese passengers, a number not unusual for a departing steamer to carry, and it could not be undertaken on board till after the landing of all incoming passengers. As this is often not completed until near the time of the vessel's departure, the delay and inconvenience to the public and to business interests incident to a literal compliance with the law would be such as to practically nullify it. It would involve the transfer to the ship of the records and seal of the custom-house, and demand the constant presence on board of a deputy collector; while the danger of escapes would fully equal the danger of fraud under the present practice. Substantially the following plan has been adopted with the approval of the Treasury Department, and I believe it has been recognized by the courts as within the spirit of the law: A room has been set apart at the custom-house, known as the registration office, where Chinese intending to depart from the United States may apply for registration and for certificates entitling them to return. Three clerks and an interpreter are assigned to duty in the office. Applicants are admitted singly, and each gives to the interpreter his name, age, occupation, &c. These particulars the latter repeats to the clerks, who simultaneously write them out, one upon white paper already signed by a deputy collector, which has come to be known as the "white tag," the second in the office register, and the third in the certificate furnished by the Department in books of 100 certificates each, which from the color is called the "red" certificate.

The applicant is then measured, and his height, physical marks, and peculiarities are entered both in the register and in the certificate. He then receives the white tag, which entitles him to the red certificate of corresponding number at the ship on her departure. The certificates, checked by the clerk in charge, are then signed and sealed by a deputy collector. Formerly the certificates were returned to the clerk, who retained them till the day of the ship's sailing, when he attended on board, and exchanged them for the white tags. It was his duty to cancel and return to the custom-house certificates not called for.

At first the surveyor was charged with the delivery of the certificates, but from early in 1883 to July last a single clerk was entrusted both with the custody and the delivery.

He accounted to himself for the entire number by the return to himself of an equal number of white tags and unclaimed certificates. It was known only to himself whether these returns equaled the number of certificates signed and whether all the outstanding certificates were delivered to Chinese who had actually departed. It will be seen there was no check upon his exchange of certificates for white tags elsewhere than on board the ship, and thus putting afloat certificates to be sent to China for fraudulent use. Whether he was a party to such transactions is not now considered. Attention for the present is simply called to the loose practice. It gave opportunity to a dishonest official, and a possible temptation to an honest one, to engage in an unlawful business requiring no capital and promising profitable returns.

The landing of returning Chinese has always been in charge of the surveyor, and to July last was practically in the hands of one and the same inspector. This officer, aided by an interpreter, examined each passenger, compared his physical peculiarities with those noted in his certificate, and if found to agree put a chalk mark on him, which was recognized by the inspector at the gang-plank as evidence of his right to go ashore. The surrendered certificates were for the present retained by the inspector, who subsequently made returns, subject, however, to no supervision. Opportunity was here given him to land unauthorized persons, and even to reissue certificates for use again. That the temptation to do this was frequent appears from statements of other officers that they were offered considerable sums of money to aid in landing improper persons, especially Chinese women, who were rated in Chinatown as high as $2,500 for purposes of prostitution. Besides laborers returning with certificates, there were Chinese merchants, laborers claiming residence prior to the passage of the law, and other excepted persons.

Generally merchants could be distinguished, but difficulty was experienced in determining the rights of laborers claiming prior residence. In such cases a special showing was required. If this was held insufficient by the collector or the surveyor the passenger was refused landing. Some were also refused landing as their descriptions did not correspond to those contained in the certificates presented by them.

The United States courts were then appealed to in the passengers' behalf and the writ of habeas corpus was invoked.

A new and presumably profitable kind of litigation sprang up, and the calendars of the courts were burdened with Chinese cases. Seventy-five writs were issued in August last. The recognized attorney's fees in each case is $100, to which must be added clerk's, district attorney's, and marshal's fees and the charge ($5) of the interpreter. The writ was sometimes employed in the aid of transit passengers who held through tickets for Victoria, but who sought to land here.

The petitioner, on being brought into court, was admitted to bail pending the hearing. As his case was strengthened by exhibiting at the hearing a knowledge of the city, the principal streets and public buildings, it is obvious he had gained substantial advantages by his temporary landing. This will avail him less in the future, as under the present practice of the United States district court his statement is at once taken by the district attorney.

The action of the courts is the subject of some public criticism, a matter, however, not within the province of this investigation. The number of Chinese arrivals at San Francisco from foreign ports since the passage of the act to August 1, 1885, embraced:

Laborers	12,654
Other than laborers—males	2,121
Females	625
Total	15,400

Landed as follows:

Laborers:

On certificates	11,452
On special showing	758
On writs of habeas corpus	390
On Chinese certificates	1
Escaped	53

Other than laborers:

On certificates	108
On special showing	857
On writs of habeas corpus	504
On Chinese certificates	621
Escaped	31

Females

On certificates	189
On special showing	80
On writs of habeas corpus	193
On Chinese certificates	163
Total landed	15,400

Of those landed on writs, 1,000 were discharged; the remainder were either remanded, departed the country before a hearing, or are held awaiting decision of the courts. Early in the present year it began to be rumored that Chinese laborers were being landed on certificates purchased of brokers in Hong-Kong, who procured them of customs officers in San Francisco.

A little later it was publicly charged and generally believed that the chief clerk in the registration office was the guilty official. It was said that Chinese men and women in the employ of these brokers obtained white tags of the registration office which they surrendered to their employers, who in turn exchanged them with the clerk for the corresponding certificates. His extravagance and irregular habits indicated an income much beyond his salary and lent color to the charge. An investigation by the collector disclosed no positive evidence of his guilt and he was retained till July last, when, on being transferred to other duty, he resigned.

The figures I first obtained at the custom-house indicated that he had issued 225 more certificates than he had accounted for. He insists, however, that the excess was issued to the crews of various ships in exchange for old ones surrendered. From the manner in which the books were kept they do not disprove his statement, while it is equally true they were kept so as to be an admirable cover to just such frauds as are charged. The statements implicating him are hearsay and from Chinamen. It is noticeable that those who insist these statements should be accepted as true, on other occasions assert that a Chinaman cannot be believed even under oath. But as these hearsay statements come from widely different sources (in one instance from a white man of character) apparently without collusion, and indicate a general belief of the Chinamen that he has engaged in the sale of certificates, I cannot pronounce him innocent, though I have found no legal evidence of his guilt. I do not think his sales if made, reached the thousands sometimes asserted, but as certificates for men were rated about $80, and for women $300, in Hong-Kong, if he received a moiety of this on the few hundred named he realized a considerable sum. Since his retirement it is said certificates cannot be found in "Chinatown" and that the business has ended.

The whole matter is now the subject of investigation by the grand jury—a body that can compel the attendance and testimony of witnesses, and it may find evidence not at my command which will set the controversy at rest. It is conceded that Chinese laborers arrive with certificates purchased at Hong-Kong, but it is also claimed that they were obtained of their rightful owners who remain in China, or from the relations of lawful holders who have died at home.

The number of certificates which had been issued at all the Pacific ports up to August 1, 1885, aggregates 35,235, and of this number there has been returned but 14,726, leaving outstanding 20,509; with this number outstanding some will find their way back in the hands of wrong persons. Abundant material for frauds of this nature can be found without resort to purchase from Government officers. Occasionally a man entitled to land will be found possessed of another man's certificate through the carelessness of the officer who delivered it and from no fault of his own, as but few of these people can read their certificates. Corrupt practices were also charged upon the landing inspector and the interpreter associated with him last summer. If one is guilty the other is. The former possessed the confidence of the surveyor and was retained in service, though the latter was discharged on the surveyor's request. I believe, however, no specific charge was made against him. About the same time a second officer was assigned to duty with this inspector, but the impatience of the latter with his associate and his hostility to the new order of things led to his transfer to other duty, followed by his suspension, and later by his discharge on the late reduction of the force.

It comes from Chinamen that he received money for landing improper persons, but the statements are all second and third hand. Some of the charges are based on his frequent visits to Chinatown, which certainly opened him to suspicion, but the surveyor says he went there by his order. He certainly had the opportunity to make money by corrupt practices, and he is not credited by the public with the virtue that a refusal to do it implies. But his guilt is not established, and as he is out of the service I think it unnecessary for me to delay my report for further investigation, especially as the grand jury is considering the matter with better facilities than myself for getting at the facts. I am satisfied that the extent of the frauds has been exaggerated, and that if any have been committed by custom officers they have been confined to three or four persons at most, who are now out of service.

Both the collector and surveyor were aware of the complaints, but they believed them unfounded, and continued the suspected officers in their old positions when good administration would at least have demanded their transfer to other duties.

It is due, however, to the collector and surveyor to say that no suspicion of personal dishonesty attaches to either of them, and it should also be said of them that they have spared no personal effort to enforce the law.

The existing methods of business are largely due to them, and, though not perfect, they are in line of a decided reform in the Chinese business. The practice of the registration office remains unchanged, except that the applicant for a certificate signs his name in the register; but the certificates, when signed, are now registered by the deputy collector, and retained by him till the day of the ship's departure, when they are given to the surveyor for delivery.

Two inspectors deliver the certificates to the passengers as they go on board the vessel, and take up the corresponding white tags. All certificates not delivered are at once canceled by passing them over a bill-file, and are returned to the deputy collector, who verifies the return of white tags and canceled certificates by comparison with his register. "Not claimed" is stamped on the certificates and opposite the corresponding numbers in the several registers.

The landing of Chinese passengers continues in the charge of two inspectors and an interpreter. Surrendered certificates are immediately passed over a bill-file, and the holder, if found entitled to land, is given a landing ticket, which is surrendered to the inspector at the gang-plank.

The canceled certificates are compared with the landing tickets, verified by the passenger manifest, and then registered and filed at the custom-house. In an examination I found some of the certificates did not sufficiently describe the party named therein.

The physical peculiarity noted was vague and uncertain, as "flat nose," "large features," "small features," &c., a description not at all peculiar to the holders of the certificates.

In other cases peculiarities and marks were given that could be simulated by one purchasing the certificate, as, for example, "hole in right ear," "scar on forehead," "mark over right eye," &c.

The reason assigned for these faulty descriptions was the order of the Treasury Department that but one line of the record book should be used for the description, and this admitted the noting of but one peculiarity. Chinese laborers cannot be easily described. They look much alike. Individuals often have no marked peculiarities, and a sufficient description in such cases can only be had by taking several of such slight ones as can be found. More space should be given in the blank forms for entering physical peculiarities, or two lines should be used. The necessity of this will at once be obvious to one who undertakes to describe a Chinese laborer. It has been urged that the photograph of the departing Chinaman would furnish a sure means of identifying him on his return. Undoubtedly this would be an additional test of identity, but by no means an infallible one.

Chinese merchants now leave their photographs on departure, but in some cases there have been doubts of their identity on return. In one instance the photographer who took the picture was in doubt as to the identity of the man. If at least three physical marks or peculiarities appear in the certificate, identification can be had by them—sometimes by one—as certainly as by a photograph.

With honesty and intelligence at both ends of the line—at the registration office and the ship—such a description will guard against false personations, and without honesty and intelligence the photograph will fail. At first I was inclined to favor the photograph, but on further investigation I am of the opinion that it is unnecessary.

If other means of identification than those now employed are thought necessary, I suggest further experiments with the thumb marks, descriptions of which have been sent to the Department. This means of identification is said to have been employed in eastern countries for hundreds of years, and to be infallible. While I am not prepared to recommend its adoption, I believe it worthy of consideration before resorting to the doubtful and expensive expedient of the photograph.

It is charged, and by many believed, that a loose and corrupt administration of the law has tended to increase the Chinese population of the United States beyond that of 1882. In proof of this, attention is called to alleged smuggling of Chinese into the country and to their escape from ships, to the large excess of arrivals over departures in certain months, and to the apparent increase of Chinese population in San Francisco. It is true that a few men have escaped from vessels at the wharf and that some have been smuggled into the country. It is safe to assume the same thing will happen again, but this fact alone is evidence neither of dishonesty nor incompetency of the officers. Merchandise is smuggled, and will be, so long as we have tariff laws, and Chinamen who think and act for themselves can still more easily be smuggled or smuggle themselves into the country.

2.14

Yuji Ichioka

The Origins of Japanese Immigration to the United States Mainland

Topical Introduction

While Chinese immigrants encountered restrictive immigration measures in the 1880s (see part iv), Japanese immigrants to the United States grew in numbers. Still, by 1890, there were must 2,039 Japanese residents in the United States, according to Census figures. Significant social, economic, and political changes accompanying the Japanese government's attempt in the 1870s and 1880s to modernize Japanese society from above encouraged people to find opportunities to escape debt or military conscription. Among these opportunities was migration to Hawaii and mainland United States. However, exaggerated accounts of what Japanese immigrants might find in the United States helped pull them to American shores. Below is a quote from a guide written in the late 1880s. From *Kitare, Nihonjin* (Come, Japanese), this passage can be found in Yuji Ichioka, *The Issei: The World of the First Generation Japanese Immigrants: 1885–1924,* (New York: The Free Press, 1988), 11–12.

Come, merchants! America is a veritable human paradise, the number one mine in the world. Gold, silver, and gems are scattered on her streets. If you can figure out a way of picking them up, you'll become rich instantly to the tune of ten million and be able to enjoy ultimate human pleasures. Come, artisans! Sculptors, lacquerers, carpenters, painters—anyone skilled in the least in the Japanese arts—can earn a lot of money by making fans, ceramics, and lacquerware. Come, students! Working during the daytime, you'll have time to attend night school in the evening. And if you earn your school expenses by persevering for two to three years, it's not far-fetched to think of graduating from a college.[15]

In 1889 the *Ōsaka Mainichi* published *Beikoku Jijō* (American Conditions) which also contained descriptions of student life in San Francisco.

2.15

Immigration to Hawaii

Topical Introduction

By 1900, Hawaii was clearly established as a multi-cultural society, created significantly by way of immigration of Asian immigrants. The following is excerpted from an abstract of a report of the U.S. Immigration Commission. From the Reports of the Immigration Commission, *Abstracts of Reports of the Immigration Commission,* vol. 1 (Washington: Government Printing Office, 1911)

Immigration Conditions in Hawaii

Early Immigration

While the purpose of the following report is to describe immigration conditions in Hawaii since annexation, these conditions can not be understood without a cursory survey of the conditions that preceded them.

The native population of Hawaii has been constantly decreasing since the introduction of modern civilization. Contemporary with this decrease has been a large industrial development calling for a growing population of laborers. The main industry of Hawaii, sugar planting, has to compete with countries employing colored labor, and the rate of wages has not hitherto been high enough to attract a voluntary immigration of Americans or Europeans. An additional obstacle in the way of European immigration has been the cost and time of travel from Europe to Hawaii, and the only route by which immigrants have successfully been brought from Europe is around Cape Horn. One result of this remoteness has·been that few European emigrants to Hawaii ever returned to their native country, and consequently the advantages that the Territory possesses for emigrants have not been advertised in Europe by those returning from the islands in the same way as have the advantages of America.

Consequently Hawaii has had to choose between voluntary immigration from the Orient or assisted immigration from America and Europe; and for a long period even immigration from the Orient required the stimulus of prepaid passages and other inducements. Prior to annexation practically all the immigration to Hawaii from Japan and China was thus assisted.

The problem of importing laborers received consideration in Hawaii as early as 1852. At that time the main labor force was native, but there had been for some decades a small immigration of Chinese traders and farmers, as well as of white missionaries, merchants, and adventurers. The presence of the Chinese as voluntary immigrants suggested at an early date the importation of coolies of this nationality as agricultural laborers, but this movement acquired to volume until shortly after the American civil war. At that time the growing market on the coast, the decline of the whaling fleet business, and other conditions, partly local and partly general, greatly stimulated the sugar industry and caused an increasing demand for labor. This demand was accentuated by the reciprocity treaty of 1876, which opened the American market to the Hawaiian planters.

By the latter date the system of indentured service was well established in Hawaii. Introduced originally to secure regular work from the natives, and based upon the seaman's shipping contract laws of the United States, this institution was easily applied to Asiatic coolies, and continued the prevailing form of labor contract until the annexation of the islands by the United States of America.

There was little essential difference between the contract labor laws of Hawaii and those still in force in Sumatra and the Straits Settlements, and formerly in force in Queensland. Except in minor details the law did not differ materially from that under which many thousands of English, Scotch, Irish, and German laborers were brought to America in colonial days. The immigrants contracted to work for a specified number of years, which might vary from five to ten, at a stated wage. Failure to perform this contract might be punished by imprisonment, and, during the early years of the law, by an extension of the time of service. The passage of the immigrants was prepaid by the Government or by the planters.

This system resulted in making the population of Hawaii predominantly oriental. Until 1883 practically all the labor thus imported was Chinese; thereafter the Japanese began to come in, at first in small parties and later in increasing numbers, until by the time of annexation they were the most important single element in the population. During the eighties, partly in order to diversify the labor force and prevent any single nationality becoming predominant of the plantations, and partly to build up a domiciled citizen population. Portuguese and other European immigrants were brought to Hawaii in considerable numbers under the same contract that was employed in the case of orientals. From the first, however, partly in consideration of their higher standard of living and partly because these European immigrants brought families with them, while the orientals were mostly single men, the rate of pay and the quarters furnished Europeans were better than those furnished the Asiatics.

By the year of annexation, 1900, the result of this immigration policy had been to create a population composed as follows:

Work, Occupation, Community

3

Part 3. Work, Occupation, Community

3.1.   Joel Franks. The Chinese Laundry and the Chinese Restaurant
3.2.   California Trade Unions and the Anti-Chinese Movement
3.3.   Joel Franks. Ping Chiu's Chinese Labor in California 1850–1880
3.4.   James H. Okahata (Ed). Excerpt from *A History of Japanese in Hawaii*
3.5.   John A. Whitney. One Contemporary View of the Status of Chinese Labor in the United States
3.6.   Joel Franks. Chinese Shoemakers in Industrializing San Francisco

One of the key issues joining Asian Americans to the historical development of a culturally diverse United States has been the quest for inexpensive, reliable, and controllable labor. American Indians, African-Americans, Hispanics, European immigrants, women, and children have all been, willingly and unwillingly, drawn into this search, as well as Asians and Pacific Islanders. The early European conquerors of the Americas needed people to mine silver and gold, harvest sugar, rice, tobacco, and indigo, drain swamps, drive carriages, nurse babies, keep house, and even serve in the military. However, among Europeans in the Americas there were never enough willing hands to do these tasks. Others would have to be persuaded or compelled to meet the Americas' labor requirements. But some remained unpersuaded and some met force with counterforce.

Even after the Declaration of Independence proclaimed that "all men are equal," coerced labor remained a stark American reality. African-American slavery was the most notable reminder of the oppressive nature of America's need for labor. On the Pacific Coast, coerced Native Californians provided much of the labor enriching Spanish Missions and Mexican Ranches. Farther to the West, an American by the name of William Hooper attempted to fashion a cheap, reliable, and disciplined labor force out of Native Hawaiians during the 1830s. According to Gary Y. Okiriro:

> Despite Hooper's offer of 12 1/2 cents a day for workers and fees of 25 cents per man, paid to the chiefs each month, Hawaiians preferred kin-based production. During the 1840s, the Hawaiian legislature passed laws against idleness and vagrancy that carried penalties of eviction from neglected farms, repossession of those lands, or punishment at hard labor. (Okihiro: 1991, 15)

In other words, Hawaiians were going to recognize the value of free labor in an emerging capitalist economy even if forced to do so.

While some Native Hawaiians were transformed into agricultural labor for Hawaii's sugar plantations, others held on tightly to their subsistence, kin-based economies. In any event, Native Hawaiians were wrongly regarded as lazy, ill-disciplined, and incompetent. Moreover, the native population declined quickly and substantially due to disease. In part, this calamity was brought on by contact with Europeans, as well as the loss of their traditional means of Hawaiian livelihood due to the growing commercialization of Hawaii. Plantation owners, claiming an overwhelming need for labor, looked, consequently, to China for help.

These plantation owners did not just happen upon China as a source of labor by accident. By the time of Hooper's arrival in Hawaii, sandalwood was shipped from the islands to China, while Chinese sugar masters had established several mills on Maui and Hawaii. Hooper himself had taken note of these mills and the skill and industry of their Chinese work forces. In 1836, he stated that "(w)e may deem it at a future day, necessary to locate some halfdozen Chinese on the land, if the establishment grows it will require them. The superintendent cannot feed the mill, boil the juice, make sugar, etc., and to trust it to the natives is worse than nothing." (Takaki: 1989, 22)

It was not, however, until the 1850s that Hawaii began to seriously recruit workers from China; thus beginning a flow of Chinese, then Japanese, Korean, Filipino, and East Indian workers to the island sugar plantations by the 1900s. The work was long, arduous, and poorly paid.

The plantation owners insisted upon keeping their work forces ethnically divided in order to guarantee their controllability. And until the 1900s, they were relatively successful at keeping labor militancy at bay.

On the United States mainland, a more diversified economy embraced Chinese immigrant labor from the 1850s through the 1870s. The California Gold Rush initially beckoned Chinese immigrants, who, despite the impressions of Euroamericans, were not coolies. Indeed, an international coolie system did prosper in the mid-nineteenth century. Sucheng Chan writes:

> Where the indigenous population did not provide a large enough labor supply, the European colonizers shipped hands from other lands . . . (A)fter Great Britain stopped participating in the African slave trade in 1807 and especially after slavery was abolished in the British empire in 1833, (East) Indians and Chinese became the two main groups of nonwhite international migrant workers. Indians went to what were then and what became British colonies (in Southeast Asia, Africa, South America, the Caribbean, Indian Ocean, and Pacific Ocean). . . . Large number of Chinese were recruited to work in some of those places and in Peru and Cuba as well. (Chan: 1991, 4)

What should be added here is that many, if not most, of these workers were coerced into this system and pressured to remain. That is, their labor status was largely unfree; albeit there were substantial differences between them and African American slaves.

The Chinese who came to California left their homeland on a relatively voluntary basis. It is important to make this point, because to a great extent the anti-Chinese movement in California and elsewhere fervently associated Chinese coolies with Black slaves; as degraded labor that represented a threat to independent white labor and America's free institutions. Nevertheless, many Chinese immigrants to the United States mainland lacked complete freedom. In order to come to California, the Chinese poor often took advantage of the credit-ticket system. Ronald Takaki asserts that "(u)nder this arrangement, a broker would loan money to a migrant for the ticket for passage, and the latter in turn would pay off the loan plus interest out of his earnings in the new country." (Takaki: 1989, 35) Thus, Chinese immigrants on the U.S. mainland arrived seriously in debt to one of their fellow countrymen and clearly inclined to follow the demands of various labor contractors in order to attain and keep the work that would help them pay off what they owed.

Thanks, then, to the efforts of American society and their fellow countrymen, Chinese workers found it difficult, but not impossible, to overcome profound barriers to upward and lateral occupational mobility, as well as meaningful political expression. These barriers made Chinese workers attractive to those in pursuit of what they hoped would be a cheap, reliable, and controllable labor force to build railroads, serve food, make cigars and shoes, and cultivate the land. Edna Bonacich puts the matter clearly:

> Ultimately, the selection of Asia rather than . . . Europe as a source of labor for the West comes down to the fact that capital in California and Hawaii, varying backed by different levels of government, could impose harsher conditions on Asian immigrants than it could on the Europeans. (Bonacich: 1984, 161)

Asian immigrants in nineteenth century California could not become a citizen. The disenfranchisement of mainland Chinese and subsequently, Japanese immigrants, gave Asian workers a peculiar status. Bonacich notes "(t)he implications of this peculiar status are so staggering, in terms of the ability of capital to control them, that it alone can explain why Asians were cheap labor." (Bonacich: 1984, 162)

Without citizenship rights' an ethnic group lacks significant political voice. Among the serious consequences can be an inability to effectively fight expulsion from the country and exclusion from admission if business interests allying with labor find this ethnic group's presence in the United States undesirable. Even the threat of deportation could offset Asian immigrant labor militancy.

It should be stressed, moreover, that Asian immigrant workers possessed needs that somewhat corresponded with the requirements of Euroamerican capitalists; thus allowing the latter greater opportunity to impose their terms on Chinese, then Japanese, labor in the nineteenth century. For example, many Asian immigrants came to the United States as sojourners intending to remain only long enough to save sufficient money to aid their families in China or Japan. Sojourning was not peculiar to Asian immigrants. Still, in any event, it made sense for nineteenth century Asian immigrants, for, aside from the obvious problem of white racism, the cost of living was high in nineteenth century California and a family was not easily supported on the wages paid Asian workers. At the same time, Asian immigrants very likely viewed life in the United States as holding forth little in the way of guarantees that one would be taken care of during old age and illness. Thus retaining ties with village and kin in Asia, rather than asserting one's working class rights in the United States, was of greater concern to a nineteenth century Asian worker. As a result, American capital and Asian labor seemed to help each other out. But the trade-off was scarcely even. Asian communities and Asian immigrants themselves generally provided for the supply and support of Asian labor to the United States; not American capital. "The result," writes Bonacich, "was a kind of vicious circle, perpetuating a form of migrant labor or sojourning." Capitalist development in nineteenth century California, then, "made use of the persistence of a pre-capitalist sector in Asian countries. Needless to say, this pattern is found elsewhere in the world as well." (Bonacich: 1984, 166)

But to state that nineteenth century Asian labor was exploited in California, as well as Hawaii; to state that it was made substantially powerless tells only a part of the story. As Sucheng Chan points out, if Chinese workers were generally paid less than Euroamericans, this did not prove that they valued their labor any less; if Chinese workers failed to daily act as militantly opposed to Euroamerican capital as many white workers, this did not prove that they valued their dignity as human beings any less. Moreover, as these documents in this section point out, Asians took on a variety of occupations in order to survive the many obstacles placed in their paths in nineteenth century America. They weren't just miners, railroad workers, and "house boys." They harvested crops in places like Hawaii and the deep South. They labored in factories in New England and San Francisco. They established laundries and restaurants throughout the United States. They toiled as wage workers and entrepreneurs. They brought their skill, courage, and endurance to the forefront of those who helped build America. (Chan: 1986)

References

Bonacich, Edna. 1984. "Asian Labor in the Development of California and Hawaii," in *Labor Immigration Under Capitalism: Asian Workers in the United States Before World War II*. Berkeley and Los Angeles. University of California Press.

Chan, Sucheng. 1986. *This Bittersweet Soil: The Chinese in California Agriculture, 1860–1910*. Berkeley and Los Angeles: University of California Press.

1991 *Asian Americans: An Interpretive History*, Boston: Twayne Publishers.

Okihiro, Gary Y. 1991. *Cane Fires: The Anti-Japanese Movement in Hawaii, 1865–1945*. Philadelphia: Temple University Press.

Takaki, Ronald. 1989. *Strangers From a Different Shore: A History of Asian Americans*. Boston: Little Brown, 1989.

3.1

Joel Franks

The Chinese Laundry and the Chinese Restaurant

During the 1850s and 1860s, durable stereotypes emerged concerning Chinese work in laundries and restaurants. Chinese immigrants did not initially come to the United States in order to work in laundries or restaurants. Rather, they came to the United States by the thousands in the late 1840s and 1850s in order to mine the California gold fields. But Euroamerican hostility against Chinese miners was so powerful that significant numbers of these people decided to take up other occupations that would free them from white antagonism and yet provide them with something of an important economic niche in the United States.

Accordingly, they performed work that largely served white people; in particular, young Euroamerican males living in the American frontier hundreds of miles away from "the little woman."–mom, sister, or wife. In so doing, Chinese immigrants serviced the domestic needs of people who either couldn't or wouldn't clean or feed themselves on a regular basis. They also unwillingly serviced the racist notion that people of color, like women, belong in occupations in which they will happily do the bidding of white men. Thus, in the minds of many Euroamerican males, the fact that Chinese immigrants did laundry and restaurant work reinforced the viewpoint that the Chinese were, like Blacks and women, an ideally servile, dependent people unfit for full participation in American life.

As for the Chinese immigrants working in laundries and restaurants, they were not enthusiastic about the occupations they had undertaken. Yet they recognized that white males in places like Gold Rush California benefitted from their work. For example, a young 49er would have to send his pants to Hawaii by way of San Francisco if he wanted them cleaned. The emergence of Chinese laundries near the Gold fields cut down on the turn around time considerably. Moreover, as Sucheng Chan points out:

> men of any nationality willing to cook and feed others found it rela-
> tively easy to earn a living. A few observant Chinese quickly realized

that cooking would provide a more steady income than many other occupations. In time, thousands of Chinese worked as cooks—in private homes, on farms, in hotels and restaurants—all over the American West. (Chan: 1991, 34)

Chan also discloses that through laundry work and cooking, Chinese worker-entrepreneurs gained access to largely Euroamerican customers in towns and cities throughout the country. She writes that ''operating laundries and restaurants allowed (Chinese immigrants) to find an economic niche for themselves . . . (in) the Midwest and along the Atlantic seaboard.'' (Chan: 1991, 33) Nevertheless, a certain precedent was being established whereby Asian immigrants could gain a moderate amount of racial toleration while supporting a harmful stereotype of Asians as congenial, servile people.

Reference

Sucheng, Chan. 1991. *Asian Americans: An Interpretative History,* Boston: Twayne Publishers.

3.2
California Trade Unions and the Anti-Chinese Movement

Topical Introduction

While employers' scarcely regarded Chinese immigrants as social equals, trade unions were very central to the effectiveness of the anti-Chinese movement. The one thing that workers, regardless of other differences, could agree upon in San Francisco, was that the Chinese must go. At the same time, it should be stressed that while 19th century trade unions could pulsate with democratic aspirations, they often found a variety of reasons to bar people from membership. Women, African-Americans, and lesser skilled workers all witnessed trade unions turning their back on them. Thus, sadly, it is not surprising that Euroamerican trade unions disliked Chinese immigrants and welcomed their exclusion. Below are summaries of the concerns of several unions in California. Note particularly the issues facing the Boot and Shoemakers White Labor League and the Cigarmakers International Union, No. 228. Chinese workers had made the greatest inroads in the manufacturing of consumer goods such as boots and shoes and cigars. These were, then, highly competitive industries where cutting labor costs was a key way to remain profitable. But even where Chinese workers were not introduced in significant numbers, Euroamerican trade unions still faced severe problems. Perhaps, Henry George was right. From, *3rd Biennial Report of the Bureau of Labor Statistics of California,* (Sacramento: State Printing Office, 1888), 118–119.

Boot and Shoemakers White Labor League

There are about two hundred and fifty women who find employment in this city. There are no women in the union. There is no fixed scale of wages, but the by-laws make it impossible for a member to take the position of another, who has been discharged, for less wages than he got. There are many departments in the shoemaking trade, and few men, only, understand them all. The bottomers and lasters work by the piece, while the sole leather men and cutters by the day. Wages range downwards from $18 a week; the average is about $13. Most of the members prefer piece work. The Chinese competition is continuously forcing wages down. There are between three and four thousand Chinamen employed in this trade. The league only contains those white men who work in the factories, not those employed in the custom trade. It would take about two years to learn one branch of the trade. There is only one firm antagonistic to the league.

Bookbinders Union

The men work ten hours a day, and only in extraordinary cases does a dull month occur. The union has no fixed apprentice system, and the employers are trying to get as many of them as possible into their shops. The union relies mainly on the difficulty of the work to keep too many apprentices out. There are many girls working in the shops, but they mostly do the folding work, not the proper binding. The union pays sick benefits.

Journeymen Butchers Protective Benevolent Association of the Pacific Coast

Wages range from $7 to $22.50 a week. The average is about $15 a week. The work is steady all the year round. The working day is from 4 A.M. to 6 P.M. Sunday is not free. There is a city ordinance against keeping butcher shops open on Sunday, but doubts are entertained as to its validity. In some markets the men have to go to work on Saturday at 4 A.M., and do not leave off until 10 P.M., to resume work again on Sunday morning from 7 A.M. till 12 noon. This Sunday work is not paid extra. The union is agitating the questions of shorter hours and no Sunday work.

Cane and Willow Workers Union

It takes but a few weeks to learn something of the work, but unless the man is a quick worker he will not be able to make wages, and to become that will take about a year. Wages range from $1 to $2 a day. The union has been instrumental in driving the Chinese out of the trade, and also in raising the wages a little. There are three shops in this city employing respectively fifteen, eighteen, and twenty men. There is only one shop in which the union is properly organized. The union is opposed by certain men who work in one of the shops on fancy chair work, and who are paid at the rate of $18 a week. To be able to pay these high wages the employer keeps other wages down, and as the union wages are lower the men refuse to join the union. The trade is suffering from foreign importations of demijohns from Hamburg and Antwerp. There is a duty on such importations, which, however, seems to be evaded in some mysterious manner.

Cigarmakers International Union, No. 228

The union has a scale of wages. All work is done by the piece. A slow worker may make only $7 a week, while a fast one may reach $21 or $22. The average is about $10. The eight-hour day is introduced everywhere, and the work is steady all the year round. There is a good feeling between the men and the employers, who are thoroughly familiar with all the union rules. Each factory has its shop collector, who collects the dues, and in special cases, calls special meeting of the shop. The union pays sick benefits and strike benefits; also $50 burial money. There is also a traveling benefit of $20 paid, to allow a member to go to a place where he can find work. This amount must, however, be refunded to the union as soon as the beneficiary is able to do so. The union is directing its efforts principally against the Chinese competition. There are about four thousand five hundred Chinese cigarmakers in this city. There are about one hundred and sixty factories employing white labor, exclusively. The work is considered rather unhealthy on account of the dry dust flying about in the shop, which, when inhaled, seems to affect the lungs of a great many of the men.

Journeymen Bakers National Union, No. 24

This is a German-speaking union. Most of the men have learned their trade in Europe. It takes about three years to learn it. A day's work is eleven hours for the five days and sixteen hours for Saturday. No Sunday work. There is another union in this city in which many of the bosses are members. This union is mostly to be remembered for having got an ordinance passed against Sunday work in bakeries, only to see the same first violated and then declared invalid by the Courts, through the exertions of one of its own members, who had himself been one of the first to sign an agreement to keep the ordinance. This other union is now only a beneficiary association for bakers. The work is considered very unhealthy, on account of the exhaustive night work and the poor ventilation in the cellars where the men must work; also, because the work forces a man to run out often from the heated rooms into the chilly night air. There are about one hundred and twenty-four establishments giving employment to bakers in this city. The union is at present engaged in a fight with about twenty of them. Union No. 24 controls Oakland and Sacramento; in the former there are a few American shops. In Sacramento there are twenty members, forming a section of No. 24. They have absolute control of the bakeries in that town. There are some ten shops. The average wages there are $13, and $5 for board, and the day's work consists of ten hours, with twelve for Saturday. No. 24 pays no benefits of any kind. Initiation fee, $3, and monthly dues 50 cents.

American Bakers National Union, No. 51

The union has a fixed scale of wages, ranging from $12 to $20 per week, with board. There are men working for less than union wages, with the permission of the union, but should any of these lose their job, the union does not take up their case, further than to forbid any of its members to go in the places of such men at lower wages than these had received before. Should the men lose their job because they had demanded union wages, the union is ready to back them up. The union has just succeeded to introduce the ten-hour working day, with fourteen hours for Saturday. The American bakers complain that the importation of bakers from Germany, willing to work for reduced wages, some years ago lowered the standard of wages in this city very considerably. This has, however, been checked since the formation of the National Union.

3.3
Joel Franks
Ping Chiu's Chinese Labor in California 1850–1880

The remarkable historian of Asian American life, Sucheng Chan, has written that Ping Chiu's *Chinese Labor in California, 1850–1880* "is the only in-depth study of Chinese economic life in nineteenth century California." (Chan: 1986, 5) Indeed, Chiu's small book is a gem of a pioneering effort to uncover the laboring experiences of a people marginalized from American society and marginalized from practically all of American historical scholarship. Published in 1963, *Chinese Labor in California, 1850–1880* has received little attention aside from that given it by scholars like Sucheng Chan who are concerned with reconstructing the social and economic history of Asian Californians in the 19th and early 20th centuries. However, even though few know what has happened to Ping Chiu in the last several years, it is important to understand that while in the 1960s Euroamerican history students were talking about writing fully the multi-cultural history of working people in the United States, Ping Chiu, unknown to nearly all of them, had taken a small, but significant step, toward accomplishing the difficult task of making American history truly inclusive of all Americans.

Chiu explored the part played by Chinese labor in mining, railroad building, agriculture, and industries. However, this summary will focus upon his discussion of Chinese agricultural and industrial labor, as well as his interesting analysis of the "conflicting views on the effects of Chinese immigration on California's economy;" an analysis which remains quite relevant considering the on-going and frequently bitter debate on the impact of recent immigrants on American economy and society.

Agriculture

The need for farm labor in California was particularly urgent for fruit growers. The problem for these fruit growers was that wages were relatively high in the state. Thus, according to Chiu, they found that

117

"cheap Chinese labor was indispensable." Moreover, growers felt they could count upon a fixed labor cost when it came to Chinese labor no matter how much they might require workers. That is, growers believed that even when their demand for labor grew they would not have to pay Chinese labor any more.

Chiu writes that what attracted Chinese labor to agriculture was not, as many students of the subject have indicated, just the closing down of work on the Central Pacific Railroad in 1869. As important, if not more so, was the decreasing opportunities for Chinese workers in California mining during the 1860s.

For their part, California farmers found little attraction as a group to the anti-Chinese movement. However, he does explore a class difference between California farmers on the issue of Chinese exclusion and expulsion. Small farmers, moved by the anti-monopoly issued from urban anti-Chinese organizations, might have found groups like the Workingmen's Party of California attractive. Some large farmers, eager to expand the supply of Chinese labor, may have "calculated" that by supporting urban anti-Chinese activists they would take advantage of the growing number of Chinese workers unable to find jobs in California larger towns and cities. "Consciously trying to maintain a common front against the railroad," 1 Chiu writes, "or intimidated by the threat of violence, farm producers began to replace Chinese with white laborers in the mid-1870s." (Chiu: 1963, 87)

It should be added here, however, that the most thorough student of Chinese in California agriculture, Sucheng Chang, condemns Chiu's arguments regarding the anti-Chinese movement's relationship to white farm employers as unconvincing and needlessly speculative. Chan, for her part, shows that Chinese workers possessed a staying power in California rural areas that was underestimated by analysts such as Chiu.

Industry

Chinese labor was active in Californias woolen mills, as well as clothing, shoes, cigars, and other industries. Chiu points out Euroamerican industrialists were motivated by economic developments and white labor militancy to hire Chinese workers; not a commitment to racial and ethnic equality.

In regards to the woolen industry, Chiu agrees with John S. Hittell, who wrote extensively about the Pacific Coast economy in the late 1800s, "that the major impediments to its rapid growth were the scarcity of capital, low investment return, and uncertainty of labor, while labor was thought to be too high in price, too scarce in its supply, and too unreliable in its character." (Chiu: 1963, 90)

The woolen industry, therefore, pioneered the use of Chinese workers in the early 1860s. White workers rarely objected at this time, because there was sufficient opportunities for Euroamericans inside and outside of industry. A recession in 1867 initiated anti-Chinese sentiments among white laborers. But since this recession lasted only a short time anti-Chinese expressions faded only to pick up again with the next recession in the mid-1870s. Even then, according to Chiu, Euroamerican woolen mill owners generally resisted getting rid of all their Chinese workers.

The reason why Euroamerican woolen mill owners were so insistent upon hiring Chinese was that they were convinced "that the employment of Chinese labor assured a degree of continuity in production by checking strikes." (Chiu: 1963, 92) However, they feared an all Chinese work force would also prove difficult to control. Accordingly, they believed that "the best assurance against strikes was a mixed labor force" of Chinese, Euroamerican female workers, and a few Euroamerican male workers. (Chiu: 1963, 92)

The extremely competitive California clothing industry offered employment to Chinese workers for similar reasons as the woolen industry; the scarcity and cost of labor. On the East Coast, females provided a large percentage of the operatives in the clothing firms. Chiu argues that in San Francisco, for example, "adjustment to industrial discipline was a slow and painful process for women in San Francisco."

> Mastering the process of button-holing, hemming, or finishing meant acquiring an entirely new work pattern. In addition, the work was dictated by the rhythms of the machine and not by human individuality. The Chinese had a new but simple process to learn while women had a great deal to unlearn. Furthermore, a factory was not a sewing session where social functions dominated. Girls were prone to gossip and slowing down in one division held up the whole production or occasioned possible waste of material. These were luxuries the employers could ill afford. (Chiu: 1963, 96)

The clothing trade also witnessed a significant emergence of Chinese-operated firms. Euroamerican industrialists expressed concern over the turn-over in their Chinese workers; a turn-over they believed was facilitated by Chinese desiring self-employment. Apparently, a Chinese operative would work long enough to acquire the skills and capital to open his own shop or join a cooperative. Chiu writes that "(i)t was reported as soon·as a Chinese learned his trade, he would fall sick, and recommend another Chinese to take his place. When the latter became familiar with his work, sickness promptly overtook him, and so on and so on." (Chiu: 1963, 95) Fortunately for these Chinese entrepreneurs, according to Chiu, the capital needed to start a clothing firm was not exorbitant.

In shirt making, Chiu makes a major point of arguing how the competition of Eastern manufacturers made the employment of "cheaper" white female and Chinese workers mandatory for California firms.

> With cheaper Eastern shirts sold at $9.50 per dozen, those made by Chinese were priced at $15 and by whites at $21. The only plausible salvation for the white manufacturers and workers would have been total exclusion of Eastern import(s) in addition to the exclusion of the Chinese. To do so California would have had to secede from the union. (Chiu: 1963, 102)

Thus Chinese and white shirt manufacturers in San Francisco fought a losing battle to hold on to a diminishing share of the market.

Chinese Immigration's Impact on the California Economy

Chiu maintains that class differences helped structure different views on the effects of Chinese labor on California's economy. Underlying diverse responses to Chinese labor were diverse notions of "the proper limits of property ownership." (Chiu: 1963, 129) Employers tended to argue, according to Chiu, that they possessed unrestricted rights as owner to manage their property as they saw fit. If this included hiring Chinese workers, then so be it. Euroamerican workers, conversely, often insisted that white bosses were morally bound to hire whites; especially during economic downturns.

A related issue was the role of government in all this. Employers tended to argue for a laissez-faire economics and against significant, if any, government intervention on behalf of workers. On the other hand, workers declared that the government, whether national, state, or local, possessed a duty to help out the working class in time of need.

Once again, the bosses were not necessarily the good guys in this debate. Chiu states that "few employers were prepared to take a stand on racial equality, or to denounce discrimination as contrary to Christian ethics and the American sense of justice." Rather, they were in a market for a certain kind of worker; a market best fulfilled by Chinese.

Indeed, large-scale employers asserted that the presence of Chinese labor in their trade not only was necessary to the trade's survival, but

> that the employment of Chinese labor in certain industries had not replaced white workers but had in reality induced expansion and growth in many other industries and thereby created new jobs for white

workers. They stressed the idea that the increase in wealth resulting from employment of Chinese would benefit the community far more than any alternative. (Chiu: 1963, 131)

In terms of the low wages paid the Chinese, large-scale employers claimed that low wages attracted investment; investment which would only improve California competitive niche in a trade and thereby create more jobs for whites. Moreover, the low wages paid Chinese workers would actually result in a higher real income for Californians as a whole. Prices, it was argued, would decline' thus "stimulating consumption, accelerating economic growth in prosperity, hastening recovery during a recession." (Chiu: 1963, 132)

White workers, however, refused to let the market dictate employment. They "based their arguments upon primacy of the human rights of the white workers." (Chiu: 1963, 132) They added that the employment of Euroamerican as opposed to Chinese workers enhanced consumption, which would, in turn, stimulate production. The reason why was that whites possessed a "higher standard of living" than the Chinese; hence their demand for commodities would be greater.

To large-scale employers wages were related to the price of commodities produced. The lower the price of a pair of shoes produced in a particular shoe factory the lower the wages for the workers in that factory. Hence workers would have to pay attention to the competitiveness in a trade before they sought wage increases. Workers, however, viewed the size of the labor market as a key determinant of wages. The more workers available, the more wages will drop. So it was in their interest to exclude certain groups such as Chinese immigrants from the work place.

Many small-time, white entrepreneurs also demanded Chinese exclusion. Some of these entrepreneurs owned custom-shops, from which hand-made goods were sold. Others ran sweat-shops, which attempted to produce standardized goods with a minimum amount of technology. In either case, they argued that Chinese operated firms provided unfair competition; thus lowering prices and profits throughout a trade.

Chiu contends none of these divergent views of the impact of Chinese labor on the California economy possessed a firm grasp of the economic forces at play. However, he does argue that white industrialists were probably right to point out that paying high wages to white California workers would not make them competitive with Eastern manufacturers. At the same time, Chiu asserts that white industrialists' stress on low wages as an inducement to investment lacked foundation given their inadequate control of credit, raw material, and the market compared to Eastern industry.

White workers and small-time producers also harbored a narrow view of what was happening to them. Workers couldn't see that excluding Chinese would have little affect upon Eastern industrialists who would go on manufacturing and shipping consumer goods like shoes and cigars. As for small time producers:

> Technological changes led as well to a hierarchy of profits. Large capital was concentrated in trades enjoying a high rate of investment returns, as in railroads and factory manufacturing. Small capital was crowded into fields where profit was low and diminishing. Caught in this process, apprehensive over the loss of their status as independent producers, lacking any understanding of the workings of "economic forces," small manufacturers of cigars, shoes, and clothing rose to vent their anger upon a scapegoat. . . . (Chiu: 1963, 136)

Despite class differences, whites were able to form a basis for calling upon the federal government to exclude the Chinese. Industrialists were generally not willing to risk political isolation to defend the Chinese. White supremacy evoked little antagonism from them. Workers and small-producers agreed that the Chinese were tools of big business. Nevertheless, given the prevailing class differences prevailing, Chiu argues that the anti-Chinese movement was unable to launch a social movement which would truly come to grips with the role of government in either easing or accentuating the problems facing post-Civil War California and America.

Critique

While important, Chiu's book contains some important flaws. Sucheng Chan, for example, claims that his chapter on agriculture is built too much on conjecture rather than evidence. Moreover, Chiu's emphasis on economic factors leads readers to ignore issues related to ideology and politics. This is especially glaring in regards to the development of the anti-Chinese movement in California.

Chiu tends to argue that anti-Chinese activities emerged from shifts in California's economic fortunes. When the economy suffered, whites discovered Chinese immigrants as handy scapegoats. When the economy improved, whites seemed blissfully at peace with the Chinese presence. Because Chiu's book tries to focus on economic developments, there is no problem in its claim that economic shifts affected racial and ethnic consciousness. Indeed, recessions and depressions do heighten racial and ethnic tensions, as many Americans have witnessed in the early 1990s.

Yet in understanding why racism erupts, it is necessary to examine what Alexander Saxton calls the "ideological baggage" people bring into a multiracial, multiethnic situation. By the 1870s, large numbers of Euroamericans were inclined to place Chinese immigrants on the same low level as Blacks and American Indians. An ideological pre-disposition to view whites as more capable of being good, manly, freedom-loving Americans undoubtedly merits our attention. And so does the role of the Democratic Party in California in using the anti-Chinese as a foundation for its political comeback after the Civil War. The point is not that economic change is unimportant. Rather, the point is to try to discover how economic change interacts with social, cultural, political and ideological forces.

Notes

1. To many Californians, whether in the city or the countryside, the rail-road represented monopoly. This was so because of the enormous wealth and political power such railroad operators as Mark Hopkins, Leland Stanford, Charles Crocker, and Collis P. Huntington accumulated.

References

Chan, Sucheng. 1986. *This Bittersweet Soil: The Chinese in California Agriculture, 1860–1910.* Berkeley and Los Angeles: University of California Press.

Chiu, Ping. 1963. *Chinese Labor in California, 1850–1880: An Economic Study.* Madison: The State Historical Society of Wisconsin.

Saxton, Alexander. 1971. *The Indispensable Enemy: Labor and the Anti-Chinese Movement in California.* Berkeley and Los Angeles: University of California Press, 1971.

3.4
James H. Okahata (Ed)
Excerpt from *A History of Japanese in Hawaii*

Topical Introduction

The arrival of Europeans and Americans to the Hawaiian Islands fundamentally altered its history and life. American and European merchants were attracted to the Hawaiian Islands because of the whaling industry and the China trade. They were able to obtain much needed supplies for their long voyages. American merchants also traded for Sandalwood which was highly sought after in China and sold for many times its cost.

However, with contact, the Hawaiian people died in large numbers. European and American sailors brought venereal diseases. The arrival of American missionaries also undermined the native subsistence economy by advising the King to convert land into public and private property.

American merchants and missionaries sought to advance their economic interests by developing a plantation agriculture, particularly sugar cane. Native Hawaiians and Polynesians were used as field laborers. However, the demand for laborers was so great that the planters sought to recruit laborers from all across the world. With the proximity to Asia, planters recruited laborers from China, Japan, and the Philippines.

Chapter 1. Sugar Prosperity and Labor

1. *Hawaii's Need for Laborers*

Estimates of the native population when Captain James Cook discovered the Hawaiian Islands, or the Sandwich Islands as he christened them in 1778, vary anywheres from 220,000 to 400,000. Contact with Western civilization, however, brought on a steady decline of the native population. The first official census in 1832 showed the figure at

The United Japanese Society of Hawaii, *A History of Japanese in Hawaii*, Honolulu, 1971, p. 69

130,313, which had dwindled to 57,000 in 1866, and by 1872 it had declined to less than 50,000.

The Hawaiian Islands were still divided into several small kingdoms when Captain Cook first arrived and it was not until 1796 that the islands were united into a single kingdom under King Kamehameha. It passed through a short-lived period of prosperity during its 'sandalwood' and 'whale' economies, but by the 1850's sugar had become the hope and mainstay of its economy. However, sugar cultivation on any scale called for field laborers, which by nature and in numbers, the natives were unable to meet. But Hawaii had to have laborers for her cane fields in order to sustain her economy.

This brought about the enactment of the Master and Servants Act of 1850* which gave the planters the legal basis for the shipping and control of laborers into the islands. The first to be imported under this Act were 153 Chinese coolies in 1852, followed by 500 more in 1865. In 1867 the Hawaiian Immigration Bureau was established to regulate the import of laborers.

1. Penal Code of the Hawaiian Islands Passed by the House of Nobles and Representatives*

An Act for the Government of Masters and Servants

. . . 22. Any person who has attained the age of twenty years, may bind himself or herself, by written contract to serve another in any art, trade, profession, or other employment, for any term not exceeding five years.

23. All engagements of service contracted in a foreign country to be executed in this, unless the same be in contravention of the laws of this, shall be binding here: Provided, however, that all such engagements made for a longer period than ten years, shall be reduced to that limit, to count from the day of the arrival of the person bound in this kingdom.

24. If any person lawfully bound to service, shall wilfully absent himself from such service, without the leave of his master, any district or police justice of the kingdom upon complaint made under oath by the master, or by any one on his behalf, may issue a warrant to apprehend such person and bring him before the said justice; and if the complaint shall be sustained, the justice shall order such offender to be restored to his master, and he shall be compelled to serve double the time of his absence, unless he shall make satisfaction to the master for the loss and injury sustained by such absence: Provided,

*On the 21st of June, A.D. 1850 Honolulu, Oahu

always, that such additional term of service shall not extend beyond one year next after the end of the original term of service.

25. If any such person shall refuse to serve according to the provisions of the last section, or the terms of his contract, his master may apply to any district or police justice, where he may reside, who shall be authorized by warrant, or otherwise, to send for the person so refusing, and if such refusal be persisted in, to commit such person to prison, there to remain at hard labor until he will consent to serve according to law.

26. The justice's warrant or order, mentioned in the twenty-fourth section of this act, when directed to any officer or other person by name, shall authorize him to convey the offender to the place of residence of the master, although it may be in any other island in the kingdom.

27. All the costs incurred in any process against a servant under either the twenty-fourth or twenty-fifth sections of this act shall be paid in the first instance by the complainant; and if the complaint shall be sustained the master shall have judgment and execution therefor against the offending servant.

2. Memorandum of Agreement

This Memorandum of Agreement between the Hawaiian Government, represented by R. W. Irwin, Special Commissioner and Special Agent of the Bureau of Immigration, and Suyenaga Toranosuke voluntary passenger per Steamship City of Tokio from Yokohama to Honolulu. Witnesseth:

1st. The Hawaiian Government agrees to furnish steerage passage from Yokohama to Honolulu, free of expense to T. Suyenaga and Saka his wife, they having expressed a desire to go to Honolulu as voluntary passengers. This free passage includes ordinary food on the voyage.

2nd. On arrival at Honolulu the Hawaiian Government agrees to obtain employment for the said T. Suyenaga as an agricultural laborer for 3 years and also similar employment for Saka his wife if desired. Until such employment has been obtained, the Hawaiian Government will give the said T. S. and his wife lodging commodious enough to secure health and a reasonable degree of comfort and an allowance for food of six Dollars per month to the said T. S. and of four Dollars per month to the said Saka his wife.

The Hawaiian Government will furnish to the said T. S. and his family as aforesaid cleaned rice at a price not to exceed five cents per pound, and fuel for cooking free of expense.

3rd. The Hawaiian Government guarantees to the said T. S. wages at the rate of nine Dollars per month, and to the said Saka his wife, at the rate of six Dollars per month, payable in Hawaiian or United States Gold or Silver coin, with allowance for food and lodging as in Art. 2. But the said T. S. must furnish blankets and bed clothing for himself and his family.

4th. The Hawaiian Government agrees to furnish the said T. S. and his family good medical attendance and medicines free of cost to them.

5th. The Hawaiian Government guarantees that twenty-six days of ten (10) hours each in the field or twelve hours each in the sugar house, shall, within the meaning of this agreement constitute one month's service as an agricultural laborer. The hour of service shall be counted from the regularly established moment for departure to work in the field or in the sugar house and shall include the time occupied in going to and from work.

6th. The said T. S. and his family shall be exempted from all and every kind of personal tax for 3 years from the date of arrival at Honolulu.

7th. Twenty-five per cent of the sum received by the said T. S. and Saka his wife as wages shall be handed over to the Japanese Consul at Honolulu who will duly receipt therefore and deposit the same in the name of the said T. S. in the Hawaiian Government Postal Savings Bank, to be kept on interest at the rate of 5% per annum, and not to be withdrawn, except the Japanese Consul recognizes the absolute necessity of such withdrawal and signifies his approval in writing of the application of the said T. S. therefore.

Signed and sealed in triplicate at Yokohama this 26th day of January 1885. One copy to be retained by each of the parties hereto, and one to be left in the custody of the Kanagawa Ken Rei.

R. W. Irwin
His Hawaiian Majesty's Special Commissioner and Special Agent of the Bureau of Immigration.

I hereby certify that the above Agreement has been signed and sealed by both parties in my presence.

Suyenaga Toranosuke (Seal)
Volunteer Passenger

Oki Morikata (Seal)
KANAGAWA KEN REI
Canceled February 21st/88

3. Treaty of Friendship and Commerce Between the Kingdom of Hawaii and the Empire of Japan (1871)

His Majesty the King of the Hawaiian Islands, and His Imperial Japanese Majesty the Tenno being equally animated by the desire to establish relations of friendship between the two countries, have resolved to conclude a Treaty, reciprocally advantageous, and for that purpose have named for their Plenipotentiaries, that is to say His Majesty the King of the Hawaiian Islands, His Excellency C. E. DeLong appointed and commissioned by His Majesty, Envoy Extraordinary and Minister Plenipotentiary of the Kingdom of Hawaii near the Government of His Majesty the Tenno of Japan, and His Imperial Japanese Majesty the Tenno, His Excellency Sawa Jusanme Kiyowara Nobuyoshi Minister of Foreign Affairs, and His Excellency Terashima Jusee Fujiwara Munemori, First Assistant Minister for Foreign Affairs, who, having communicated to each other their respective full powers which are found in good order, and in proper form have agreed upon the following articles.

Article 1st

There shall be perpetual peace and friendship between His Majesty the King of the Hawaiian Islands and His Imperial Japanese Majesty the Tenno their heirs and successors and between their respective subjects.

Article 2nd

The subjects of each of the two high contracting parties, respectively, shall have the liberty freely and securely to come with their ships and cargoes to all places, ports and rivers in the territories of the other where trade with other nations is permitted, they may remain and reside in any such ports and places respectively, and hire and occupy houses and warehouses, and may trade in all kinds of produce, manufactures and merchandise of lawful commerce, enjoying at all times the same privileges as may have been, or may hereafter be granted to the citizens or subjects of any other nation, paying at all times such duties and taxes as may be exacted from the citizens or subjects of other nations, doing business or residing within the territories of each of the high contracting parties.

Article 3rd

Each of the high contracting parties shall have the right to appoint, if it shall seem good to them, a Diplomatic Agent, who shall reside at the seat of the government of the respective countries, and Consuls, and Consular Agents who shall reside in the ports or places within the territories of the other, where trade with other nations is permitted. The Diplomatic Agents and Consuls of each of the high contracting parties shall exercise all the authority and jurisdiction, and shall enjoy within the territories of the other, all the rights, privileges, exemptions and immunities which now appertain, or may hereafter appertain to agents of the same rank of the most favored nations.

Article 4th

It is hereby stipulated that the Hawaiian Government and its subjects, upon like terms and conditions, will be allowed free and equal participation in all privileges, immunities and advantages that may have been, or may hereafter be granted by His Majesty the Tenno of Japan, to the government, or citizens, or subjects of any other nation.

Article 5th

The Japanese government will place no restrictions whatever upon the employment by Hawaiian subjects of Japanese in any lawful capacity. Japanese in the employ of foreigners may obtain Government passports to go abroad, on application to the Governor of any open port.

Article 6th

It is hereby agreed that such revision of this Treaty, on giving six months previous notice, to either of the high contracting parties, may be made by mutual agreement as experience shall prove necessary.

Article 7th

The present treaty shall be ratified by His Majesty the King of the Hawaiian Islands, and by His Imperial Majesty the Tenno, and the ratifications exchanged at Yedo, the same day as the date of this Treaty, and shall go into effect immediately after the date of such exchange of ratifications.

In token whereof the respective Plenipotentiaries have signed this Treaty. Done at the City of Yedo this 19th day of August, A.D. one thousand eight hundred and seventy one, corresponding in Japanese date to the fourth day of the 7th Month of the 4th year of Meiji.

3.5

John A. Whitney

One Contemporary View of the Status of Chinese Labor in the United States

Topical Introduction

In 19th century America, most, but not all, of the Euroamerican commentators on Chinese immigrant labor were unflattering. Typical is the following written by a John A. Whitney in the 1880s. In the following passage, Whitney refers to an incident in Rock Springs, Colorado. Actually, the incident took place in Wyoming and what happened was that at least twenty-eight Chinese miners were killed by Euroamericans. From John A. Whitney, *The Chinese and the Chinese Question*, (New York: Tibbals Book Company, 1888), 117–122.

XXIII. True Status of Chinese Labor in this Country

I am aware that it is sometimes claimed that Chinese labor is not servile, but free. In a subject so important, we need hardly tolerate a quibble on words or a balancing of technical phrases. A people is servile when it becomes an inert mass, directed solely by the will of others, and repelled by fear from exercising the ordinary prerogatives of freemen. That this is the case with the Chinese in California is apparent when we consider, never so briefly, the circumstances under which they are brought into the country, and the tenure by which their stay is determined. The real masters of the Chinese in California are those of their own countrymen who compose the Six Companies, the Sam Yup, Kong Chow, Wing Yung, Hop Wo, Young Wo, and Yang Wo. These enforce their authority partly as creditors of the laborers, and partly by combinations with the steamship companies. A contractor desiring any given number of Chinese makes an agreement with one or the other of the companies, which undertakes to furnish the desired number, to be selected in China. A Chinaman wishing to emigrate from his own country to California will, in most cases, borrow money for his expenses, paying interest at from four to eight per cent a month; giving a mortgage on his wife and children for security, and until this money is repaid he is bound to the company, and goes hither and thither at its beck and call. In addition to the cost of his voyage, he is required to pay seventy-five dollars to the company as its commission. In return for this commission, the company exercises a general supervision and care over each individual, not only finding him employment, but caring for him in sickness and misfortune.

When the company is fully repaid, the immigrant is presumably free, but is not so in fact. Every Chinaman hopes to return sooner or later to his own country, or at least to have his remains laid beside those of his ancestors; but the Six Companies have made arrangements with the steamship companies by which no Chinaman, alive or dead, can be transshipped without their consent. More than this, the great majority, being directly indebted to the companies, work for the interests, real or imagined, of their creditors, and a Chinaman fares hard indeed at the hands of his own people, if he is found to be recalcitrant. Whatever name, therefore, may be given to the relation of the Chinese to their employers, they are neither more nor less than servile to the last degree.

Another result that has been observed to flow from this is the constantly increasing arrogance on the part of employers, a fault cultivated and encouraged by the patient and absolute servility of the Chinese laborer.

It is no wonder, therefore, that with wages depressed below the point of comfortable living, and with labor debased to the social depths of an Asiatic community, California has not increased in white population in anything like the ratio of other States less favored in climate and natural productions, and has materially diminished in that distributive wealth which is the only solid foundation for the material prosperity of a commonwealth. I know that it is claimed that the aggregate wealth of the State has been increased by Chinese labor, but the evidence does not bear out the assertion. On the contrary, it is not difficult to prove that the State is actually poorer to-day than she would have been had the Chinese never passed the Golden Gate. More than this, it is easy to show that the wealth of the State, even apart from that included in the land, has been principally accumulated in the hands of a few, while the mass of the people has been impoverished.

Nor is this all: the low rates of wages required by the Chinese, combined by their docility under authority, render them facile instruments of indirect coercion in differences between labor and capital. Thus introduced as an abnormal element into a problem sufficiently difficult of solution without it, Chinese cheap labor too often renders impossible the normal and proper adjustment of such difficulties; and the evil effects are felt, not merely in special industries but to a great extent throughout the body politic. Frequently, indeed, it has led to results which, however regrettable in themselves as separately considered, are but the tokens of a righteous indignation over a condition of affairs which a sound and well-regulated public policy would not permit to exist. For ten years past not less than one thousand Chinese have been employed in the coal mines of the Union Pacific Railroad, and the employment that would have sustained a thousand Caucasian families has been kept beyond their reach. Prior to the occurrences at Rock Springs, Colorado, in 1885, hundreds of white men sought in vain for work, while Chinamen were imported by the carload.

We may go further, and assert with perfect truth that even the cities of the Atlantic seaboard are poorer by many millions than they would have been had California been dependent upon white labor alone. That State has lost for the past quarter of a century the increase of white population that would have inured to her had she presented the attraction of high wages to the thrifty mechanics, farmers and laboring men of the Eastern States. And during the same period she has lost the refinements in tillage and the enterprise in commercial undertakings that she would have experienced had her immense ranches been divided into smaller farms, as they would have been had not the Chinese furnished vassals for their wholesale cultivation.

If agriculture has lost from cheap labor, commerce has not gained. It has been asserted that our trade with China has been promoted by the presence of the Chinese. But if we analyze this we shall find it as delusive as the others. Out of perhaps twenty millions of dollars of imports, thirteen millions are in tea and silk which would be imported to the same degree if there were no Chinese on the coast; and the same remark applies to most of the other imports, a very large proportion of which is consumed by the Chinese themselves, as, for example, two million dollars of rice, three hundred thousand of firecrackers, and one million dollars, more or less, of opium. Of the balance, some three or four millions of dollars, it is difficult to see in what respect it owes its existence to Chinese immigration. It consists of such items as oil of aniseed, cassia-buds, china ware, camphor and cassia, all of which find a considerable, if not their greatest, market in the Eastern States, and would be called for regardless of the character of the population on the Pacific coast. On the other hand, our exports amount to between ten and eleven millions, leaving a balance of trade against us of apparently about nine and a half millions, but which in reality is about seventeen millions; for more than seventenths of our so-called exports to China consist of treasure which is listed with the merchandise. This seventeen millions in coin and its equivalent passes to China, and thence, in payment for opium, to the British, to form part of the fund with which their power is maintained in the East. About one million dollars of our exports consist of quick-silver, and another million of sundries. The export of flour, about which so much has been said, amounts to only thirteen or fourteen thousand barrels per annum; of coal, about fifteen thousand tons; and of lumber, about two million feet, having a value of some fifty thousand dollars. There is not enough in this showing to indicate any great or permanent advantage to this country from the continuance of commerce with China.

Indeed, the impossibility, in the very nature of things, of any profitable market for American products in China is manifest. We cannot sell flour to a population that prefers rice to wheat and which raises rice in kind and quantity unexcelled anywhere in the world. We cannot sell improved machinery to a country whose people and government foresee that its introduction would destroy established industrial usages and throw tens of millions of already half-starving laborers wholly out of employment. We cannot sell leather to a population that makes its foot-gear with cloth uppers and wooden soles. We cannot export sugar to distant countries while we import it for ourselves, nor can we sell the products of the dairy, or of the shambles, to a people to whom the price of four ounces of either is more than the value of a whole day's work from dawn to sunset. It has been said that China affords a market for our cotton goods. The averment is a fair illustration of the utter rot that has been inculcated with reference to our commercial relations with that country. If China could purchase to any material extent the ''brown sheetings'' and other cotton fabrics of other countries, the cheaper looms of Great Britain would supply them. But as a matter of fact these have been unable to compete with the cheap labor and the rude hand-looms in the cottages of the Chinese operatives. In the words of a British consul at Shanghai: ''Roughly speaking, the working classes all over China are still clothed entirely with native fabrics manufactured from native grown cotton. . . . The great obstacle to China's becoming a consumer of English fabrics to the extent that the enormous size of the country and its swarming population would lead one to anticipate is . . . the fact that she herself can produce an article of more durable quality, and better suited to the wants of the people, at an equal or lower cost. . . . So long as the native looms continue to produce cloth at the same cost as at present, our manufacturers cannot seriously enter into competition with it for the supply of the wants of the million.'' Another consular report sets forth, of the cotton manufacture in Tsze Chuen, ''As the people count nothing for their time or labor, everything which the cotton cloth realizes over the cost of the raw material is reckoned profit.'' No greater fallacy was ever whispered into the ear of a credulous public than the idea that China may afford, to any material degree, a market for the productions of American labor or skill.

But the story is not yet fully told. There are in San Francisco fifteen or twenty Chinese firms through whom the most of the trifling commerce which we have with China is transacted, and its profit goes not to our people, but to the Chinese, whose allegiance is to their own country, and whose wealth is part of the wealth of China. The riches that have been accumulated through Chinese labor have been amassed by the few, and have contributed nothing to the prosperity of the masses. It is not twenty years since the Pacific Railway was built with subsidies from the Federal and the State governments, and even of counties along the line. The cost of building the road was based upon estimates of the ruling rates of white labor. Upon these estimates the appropriations and subscriptions were made. When the work was undertaken, instead of employing the workingmen of the country, the projectors, through the Six Companies, obtained ten thousand coolies direct from China, and with these the road was built. But the profits went, not to the community, but to the few bold business men, whose wealth dazzles the eye and inflames the imagination. And this wealth, obtained in this manner, and concentrated in a mere fraction of the population, has been prejudicial to the best interests of the State, for it has been used from the beginning to perpetuate the abnormal conditions through which it was first obtained.

3.6

Joel Franks

Chinese Shoemakers
in Industrializing San Francisco

Topical Introduction

The contributions of Chinese immigrant labor to the industrialization of the United States were remarkable. The role of Chinese railroad workers is now attaining its deserved attention. However, Chinese wage workers in places like San Francisco remain largely outside the pages of U.S. History text books. Thousands of Chinese workers labored in work places manufacturing consumer goods such as cigars, garments, and foot wear. Their presence aroused Euroamerican working class hostility and little support, in the long run, from white employers, who were eagerly looking for an inexpensive, reliable, and controllable labor force, regardless of race, ethnicity, and gender. Below is a description of Chinese shoemakers in industrializing San Francisco, revised from Joel S. Franks', "Boot and Shoemakers in Nineteenth Century San Francisco, 1860–1892,: A Study in Class, Culture, Ethnicity, and Popular Protest in an Industrializing Community," unpublished dissertation, University of California, Irvine.

Before the Civil War, the residents of the new city of San Francisco were largely dependent upon East Coast manufacturers to supply them with ready made footwear. Some boot and shoemaking establishments existed in the city. However, they were small shops, presumably doing custom, hand crafted work.

The Civil War, apparently, offered some inducement to the growth of boot and shoe manufacturing in San Francisco as the conflict interrupted the supply of East Coast manufactured goods to California. One problem faced by potential boot and shoe manufacturers in San Francisco was the nature of the available labor force. San Francisco Boot and shoemakers before the late 1860s were, like many other laboring people in the city, militant in their demand for high wages and quite willing to seek other alternatives when their demands were not met. Industrialization of the boot and shoe trade, some feared, could not proceed unless manufacturers asserted control over the work force and cut labor costs in order to compete with East Coast goods transported increasingly to California after the Civil War; needs which grew greater with the completion of the Transcontinental Railroad in 1869.

In the East, American industrialists could ultimately replace militant craftsmen with lesser skilled, relatively inexpensive women, European immigrant, and juvenile labor. In as yet a less populated California, Chinese immigrants were perceived by many as vital to industrial development. In 1869, the San Francisco *Chronicle* described one San Francisco firm employing Chinese workers:

> The factory on Sacramento is an open store, level with an opening to the street, about twenty feet wide and forty feet deep. In this room are three rows of benches; one row on each side, the other in the center. On these benches are seated about 40 Chinamen, or rather, lads, who sew on the soles and do the coarse work. At the upper end of the room are three Wheeler and Wilson sewing machines, on which other Chinamen stitch the uppers, while near the outer doors are half a dozen finishers who color and trim the finished goods.

What is noticeable about this description is, in the first place, the firm possesses the kind of division of labor and mechanization unlikely to attract the labor of skilled, Euroamerican boot and shoemakers. The use of the term "coarse work" suggests that Chinese shoemakers would be used to help manufacture "low end", inexpensive products.

By the early 1870s, the trickle of Chinese immigrants into San Francisco's boot and shoe trade had turned into a flood. As a result, Euroamerican manufacturers more confidently faced a future in which they no longer had to concern themselves with accommodating a too scarce and expensive white, male labor force. Compared to San Francisco's Euroamerican, male workers, Chinese immigrant labor was inexpensive. Manufacturers could pay a nominal fee to Chinese labor contractors, who represented Chinatown's dominant institutions—the Six Companies. Kin and familial based associations, the Six Companies offered a manufacturer a seemingly endless supply of labor, while, at the same time, supplying Chinese workers with housing and food; thus relieving white employers of any concern that the pay their Chinese hands received was below the standard wages paid skilled, Euroamerican workers. Euroamerican employers, meanwhile, expected that Chinese immigrants would quietly conform to the demands of industrial capital. Behind this expectation was the widely held, inaccurate notion that the Chinese lacked anything remotely resembling a trade union tradition or, for that matter, any interest in fighting for just treatment. Euroamerican employers, moreover, assumed that the Chinese merchant class, as represented by the Six Companies in San Francisco, held the complete loyalty of Chinese workers; thus guaranteeing that any agreement made between white boot and shoe manufacturers would be honored by their Chinese employees.

Accordingly, Euroamerican employers effectively broke the backbone of white boot and shoemaker militancy in San Francisco in the late 1860s and early 1870s by hiring greater numbers of Chinese workers. The white union, the Knights of St. Crispin, investigated the employment of Chinese boot and shoemakers before its demise in the early 1870s. The results of the investigation undoubtedly supported the union's racist argument that Euroamerican must resume control of the boot and shoe trade in San Francisco. Still, the investigation was confirmed in the 1880s by John S. Hittell, a generally pro-business historian of economic development on the West Coast. Hittell wrote that "in 1872 all the San Francisco factories employed more or less Mongolian labor."

What the Crispins found was that while the smaller shops and Euroamerican worker cooperatives were safely white, the three largest firms contained significant contingents of Chinese laborers. Over 40% of Buckingham and Hecht's employees were Chinese. In I. M. Wentworth's factory, 75% of the work force was Chinese. And Wolf and Company operated with nearly all Chinese workers. The Crispin investigation, moreover, pointed out the existence of one presumably Chinese run factory on Battery Street in San Francisco and another on Front Street, employing 200 and 100 Chinese immigrants respectively.

During the 1870s, Chinese boot and shoeworkers proved to be more difficult to live with than Euroamerican manufacturers expected. First, their employment helped inspire a bitter and popular anti-Chinese movement in California that throughout the 1870s was largely based in San Francisco and was, as well, significantly targeted at the city's boot and shoe trade. Second, Chinese shoemakers displayed a certain reluctance to meekly accept their Euroamerican and Chinese employers' demands. Consequently, when business turned sour in San Francisco and the rest of the American economy in the mid-1870s, the Chinese shoemaker became somewhat more expendable. Yet, to the dismay of Euroamerican employers and workers, many Chinese shoemakers did not necessarily leave San Francisco nor its boot and shoe trade upon discharge from white run firms. Rather, they went to work for Chinese employers or even ran shops on a cooperative basis with other Chinese immigrants. While the capitalization necessary for large-scale enterprise was growing dearer with the years, at least Chinese immigrants could lease the sewing machine primarily used in boot and shoe manufacturing, the McKay stitcher. Thus, it was quite possible for a Chinese shoemaker to learn enough of the trade while working for Euroamericans to set up a business on his own or help form a cooperative. Moreover, since the labor services of Chinese often cost a third those paid skilled, Euroamerican male workers, Chinese manufacturers could afford to put out relatively inexpensive shoes. John S. Hittell reported that Chinese firms sold shoes at two to three dollars a dozen below the price set for footwear manufactured by Euroamericans.

With their militancy broken by the introduction of Chinese labor into the trade and their spirit mangled by growing unemployment during the recessions of the 1870s, Euroamerican workers demonstrated a willingness to labor for cheaper wages. Yet employers failed to surrender entirely their access to the Chinese labor pool. Euroamerican manufacturers insisted upon their right to hire whomever they pleased—that the anti-Chinese movement was a radical assault upon employers' property rights. One manufacturer even felt compelled to secretly operate a half-dozen shops exclusively employing Chinese shoemakers. Others publicly maintained that they needed to hire cheap labor to remain competitive. If they were furnished with white females and boys, as well as less demanding Euroamerican males, they would no longer look enviously toward Chinatown.

The 1880 U.S. census provides a glimpse of what life was like for Chinese shoemakers in San Francisco. Hue Kai & Co. was probably the largest Chinese run shoe firm in the city. It employed an average of seventy-five workers during the census year. The work day was ten hours, which was typical of a boot and shoe manufacturing firm, whether Chinese or Euroamerican. Hue Kai paid its skilled workers $1.25 a day and its unskilled hands, $.50 a day. By the same token, a Euroamerican firm, Porter, Oppenheimer, and Col, paid its skilled white workers $3.50 daily and its unskilled, probably Euroamerican females, $2.50 daily. The justification for such a remarkable gap between Euroamerican and Chinese wages was that Chinese capitalists housed and fed their workers, often at the work place. Euroamerican workers, conversely, had to provide for their own shelter and food. Nevertheless, anti-Chinese Euroamericans preferred to consider Chinese workers as coolies, who quietly acquiesced to their own exploitation and the ruin of white labor.

Discrimination and
Anti-Asian Movements

Part 4. Discrimination and Anti-Asian Movements

4.1.   Joel Franks. "Republicanism, Producerism, and the Origins of the Anti-Asian Movement in the United States"

4.2.   Joel Franks. "The Democratic Party and the Anti-Chinese Movement in California"

4.3.   Alexander Yamato. "Institutionalized Discrimination in California"

4.4.   The United States Constitution and Slavery

4.5.   Thomas Benton. Oregon Question

4.6.   Robert F. Heizer and Alan F. Alkmquist. Making California a White Man's Paradise: 1849 California Constitutional Convention

4.7.   Native American during the Early Years of California Statehood

4.8.   John Bigler. To the Senate and Assembly of the State of California, 1852

4.9.   Foreign Miner's Tax, California, 1853

4.10.   Report of the Committee on Mines and Mining Interests, 1853

4.11.   Supreme Court of the State of California: People v Hall, 1854

4.12.   The Mexican Californian and the New State: 1855

4.13.   Dred Scott v. Sandford, 1856

4.14.   Report of Joint Select Committee Relative to the Chinese Population of the State of California, 1862

4.15.   San Francisco, Cubic Air Ordinance, 1870

4.16.   An Address to the People of the United States Upon the Evils of Chinese Immigration, 1877

4.17.   Constitution of the State of California, Article XIX, 1879

4.18.   Henry George. Henry George and the Workingmen's Party of California

4.19.   Chinese Exclusion Act of 1882

Very early upon the arrival of Asian Americans, discrimination was institutionalized. Chinese Americans found that laws which were established to curtail the rights of African Americans, Mexican Americans, and Native Americans on the basis of race were expanded to include them. Other laws in the 19th century were passed specifically against the Chinese.

Joel Franks, in "Republicanism, Producerism, and the Origins of the Anti-Asian Movement in the United States," identifies the ideology based on republicanism and producerism which created a "dual society," one society in which Euroamerican men would protect their interests and another society in which women and people of color would be excluded on the basis of race and gender in order to protect the privilege of those who feared that women and people of color threatened those rights.

Alex Yamato provides an overview of the discriminatory laws in California which prevented racial minorities from assimilating into American society. Although racial minorities were accused of not being able to assimilate into American society, the basic assumptions of individuals in American society as outlined by Franks reveal the extent to which discrimination was embedded in America's very structure. These assumptions of the inferiority of peoples of color was institutionalized in the United States Constitution, in Article I, Section 2, also called the "Three-fifths Compromise," and Article IV, Section 2 which supported fugitive slave laws.

In the selection from *The Congressional Globe*, Senator Thomas Benton from Missouri articulates notions of racial hierarchy many Americans had at the time. Benton was a slave owner and encouraged the settlement of the West. The selection, "Making California a White Man's Paradise," demonstrates the fact that from California's inception, racism, particularly towards African Americans was institutionalized in California's Constitution.

Governor John Bigler of California proposes in 1852 to press Congress to pass legislation to prevent Chinese contract labor from coming into California. In addition, Bigler recommends that California pass a tax to limit Chinese immigration. Bigler points out that the Chinese are not likely to be eligible to become naturalized citizens because of the naturalization law of 1790 limiting naturalization to "free white persons." Bigler points out that California would be breaking new ground in passing immigration legislation limiting the arrival of Chinese immigrants.

On March 30, 1853, the California Legislature passed the Foreigner Miners Tax which requires miners who are noncitizens to be licensed. The tax was directed against Chinese miners as evidenced by the fact that an act was passed less than two weeks later to translate the statute into Chinese.

The 1853 report of the Committee on Mines and Mining Interests opposed the exclusion of Chinese from mining. The Committee acknowledges the importance that the Chinese and the China trade have in increasing the investment capital in San Francisco and thus limit the power of capitalists in controlling markets. In addition, Americans, according to the Committee, have nothing to fear from the Chinese since Caucasians are racially superior to Asians.

As Chinese miners flocked to the mining regions, many became targets of white miners. The California Supreme Court decision, People v. Hall in 1854 extended the prohibition of testimony given by African

Americans, mulattos, and Native Americans against whites in court action to also include Chinese.

As the section, "The Mexican Californian and the New State," describes, Mexican Americans in the 1850s were treated as foreigners even though they were indigenous peoples. The United States Supreme Court in the Dred Scott decision in 1856 ruled that the rights of African Americans were not protected under the United States Constitution.

In 1862, the Joint Select Committee of the California Legislature found no evidence of Chinese immigrants used as "coolies." In addition, they report the tremendous benefit that Chinese laborers and trade with China would bring to California.

Reflective of the hostility against the Chinese, a number of laws were passed to harass or to restrict their rights at the local, state, and federal levels. San Francisco Board of Supervisors passed the "Cubic Air" ordinance in 1870. Although the ordinance did not mention the Chinese it was specifically enforced against Chinese residents of San Francisco. California in the 1879 Constitution banned Chinese employment in civil service. The United States Congress passed the 1882 Chinese Exclusion Act which prevented Chinese laborers from coming to the United States. The law was renewed in the Geary Act of 1892.

The selection, An Address to the People of the United States upon the Evils of Chinese Immigration," from a California Senate Committee in 1877 reflect the fears of white Californians toward the Chinese. Henry George in 1880 pointed out that it was a popular outcry, particularly among the political parties, to condemn the Chinese.

4.1

Joel Franks

"Republicanism, Producerism, and the Origins of the Anti-Asian Movement in the United States"

Benjamin B. Ringer's argument that racism in the United States can, to a significant extent, be discovered within the very fabric of American political life and thought deserves our attention. One of the major contradictions of American history is that American political institutions and the ideologies which shaped and justified them contain elements which push humanity closer to liberation and elements which push humanity closer to oppression.

The creation of a vital, yet stable, republic in North America during the late 1700s was no small accomplishment. Americans of different class, ethnic, and regional backgrounds believed they shared in a great, unique experiment; the development and defense of a representative form of government with sovereignty over a relatively substantial land mass and, more than that, very diverse groups of people and interests. Some European observers predicted the eventual collapse of the United States. But what had prevented this collapse, in the minds of many Americans, was the Republicanism practiced in the United States.

Historian Sean Willentz describes Republicanism in terms of "four interlocking concepts."

first, that the ultimate goal of any political society should be the preservation of the public good, or commonwealth; second, that in order to maintain the commonwealth, the citizens of a republic had to be able and willing to exercise virtue, to subordinate private ends to the legislation of the public good when they conflicted; third, that in order to be virtuous, citizens had to be independent of the public will of other men, lest they lose sight of the common good; fourth, that in order to guard against the encroachments of would-be tyrants, citizens had to be active in politics, to exercise their citizenship. To these concepts, eighteenth century Americans, above "middling" merchants and artisans added equality, the liberal idea that all citizens should be entitled to their natural civil and political rights under a representative, democratic system of laws. (Willentz, 1984: 14)

The philosophy of Republicanism had much to recommend it. It sought to advance the public good without diminishing individual rights. It encouraged an active, informed citizenry, a citizenry whose notion of patriotism was not mindless support of a government action, but a patriotism which also valued the contributions of responsible dissent. It supported the respectability of democracy and equality at a time when more than a few Americans regarded democracy and equality as allies of disorder, subversion, and mob rule. Finally, it helped justify the sacrifices of millions of Americans to keep the Republic alive through times of bewildering, even devastating crises such as the Civil War.

Nevertheless, Republicanism too easily lent itself to an unflattering American chauvinism. Quite rightly, United States citizens were proud of much of what they had accomplished. But many considered people of other lands incapable of performing the republican feats of Americans. They looked from Europe to Asia to Africa and back to Americans and what they saw were tyrants and pawns of tyrants—aristocratic, servile, unmanly people. They regarded American Indians as tyranized by their own savage, childlike emotions, when they were not captivated by some brutal, dictatorial chief. Women, Euroamerican women that is, could contribute to the republic, but as domestic protectors of its morality. They were, however, perceived as largely dependent upon the manly provider, political leader, and soldier.

Advocates of Republicanism might disagree as to the precise social characteristics of the useful citizen. Some, for example, possessed a class bias for and against the wealthy. But they generally agreed that the useful citizen was independent in status and thought. That citizen, moreover, possessed the presumed manly characteristics of rationality, maturity, and physical courage. Thus, in trying to rally Americans around the republic, Republicanism excluded the majority of Americans and future Americans from active participation in political life. Only Euroamerican, propertied males could, according to Republicanism, attain the necessary virtue to support the Republic.

A complementary philosophy to Republicanism was producerism, which emerged most fully during the early stirrings of industrial capitalism during the first half of the nineteenth century. During this time, class differences erupted over the future of the republic. Artisans, mechanics, and small farmers often condemned what they saw as a conspiracy of monopolists to deprive them of the fruits of hard work. They argued along the lines of a labor theory of value—that labor, not capital, produces wealth. Accordingly, they divided Americans into producers and non-producers. The former were artisans, mechanics, and small farmers. These people possessed the characteristics of republican independence, ownership of property or skill, a trust in the dignity of labor, manliness, public commitment intermingled with a strong sense of individual freedom, and a belief in a democracy and equality, limited, by and large, to white males. The latter were seen as parasites by producerism. They might be landlords, speculators in stock or land, capitalists, Southern plantation owners, or lawyers—people perceived as fully capable of prospering off the misery of others. But they might also be unskilled laborers, African American slaves, women, Native Americans, and Chinese "coolies"; people perceived as dependent, unmanly, or servile.

Producerism, therefore, expressed the understandable fear of small-scale businessmen and farmers, as well skilled workers that the expanding market economy was eliminating them as a powerful force in American life, let alone threatening their very existences. They asserted the valuable lesson that ordinary people who worked hard for a living deserved not only respect in American society, but political power. Yet they saw enemies not only from above in capitalists and wealthy slave owners, but they also saw enemies from below in African Americans and Chinese immigrants.

That the anti-Chinese movement in 19th century California was fueled, in large part, by Euroamerican laboring people is not really surprising. In the name of democracy and equality, workers and small farmers proved quite enthusiastic about denying the fruits of democracy, equality, and liberty to people of color, such as the Chinese and subsequent groups of Asian immigrants. As some of the documents in this reader will reveal, too many decent Americans, led by Republicanism and Producerism, had come to the inescapable conclusion that democracy, equality, and liberty could only prosper in a land that was a white man's land.

4.2

Joel Franks

"The Democratic Party and the Anti-Chinese Movement in California"

Topical Introduction

The Democratic Party in California at the end of the Civil War seemed doomed. There, like in many other union states, the party was associated with treachery and appeasement of the Confederacy. Nevertheless, it possessed a base among urban, Euroamerican workers, especially immigrants and children of immigrants who always found the party of Jefferson and Jackson more responsive than its various rivals.

What the Democratic Party in California needed was an issue to rally laboring class votes against the Republican Party? Fortunately for the party's fortunes, it could look back to a generation or more of race baiting as a way to mobilize voters. Just as the Democratic Party in the South and the North had raised a horrible spectre of free Blacks roaming white neighborhoods, taking white jobs, and marrying white daughters, the post-Civil War Democratic Party in California hitched its fortunes to a vicious anti-Chinese movement. Linking up with anti-Chinese trade unions and the many anti-coolies formed after the Civil War, the Democratic Party regained much, if not all, of its former power.

Below is an excerpt from a victory speech given by Democratic Governor-Elect Henry Haight in 1867. Quoted in Alexander Saxton, *The Indispensable Enemy: Labor and the Anti-Chinese Movement in California,* (Berkeley and Los Angeles: University of California Press, 1971), 91.

I will simply say that in this result we protest against corruption and extravagance in our State affairs—against populating this fair State with a race of Asiatics—against sharing with inferior races the Government of the country—against the military despotism which now exists at the South under the late acts of Congress; and this protest of ours, echoing the voice of Connecticut and Kentucky, will be re-echoed in thunder tones by the great central states until the Southern States are emancipated from negro domination, and restored to their proper places as equals and sisters in the great Federal family.[58]

4.3

Alexander Yamato

"Institutionalized Discrimination in California"

Native Americans

Decades before California became a state in 1850, Indians were seen as an impediment to civilization. No less than President Jackson was to justify the extermination of the Indians as the price of progress (Takaki, 1979:103).

From the beginning of statehood in 1850 until 1863, it was legal to sell Indians into coerced labor as indentured servants (Almaguer, 1979:93–95). However, Native Americans were not seen as a convenient source of labor, and were not viewed as economic competition as were Blacks and Asians (Almaguer, 1979:97).

The framers of the California Constitution viewed Indians as a serious political problem. One of the fears raised by some delegates to the Constitutional Convention was that if Indians were granted the right to vote, the Indian votes would be used by large ranch owners to manipulate the polls (Almaguer, 1979:98). As a result, Indians in California were not allowed to vote until 1879 (Almaguer, 1979:100).

In addition, in 1851, Indians could not testify in court in cases involving white persons (Almaguer, 1979:99). Beginning in 1863, Indians could not attend public school but by 1870, Indians could attend school but only under segregated conditions (Almaguer, 1979:99). Also, Indians had lost the right to gain title to land which they had lived on but had not claimed under the 1851 Land Law (Almaguer, 1979:99).

In the later part of the 19th Century, state sanctioned raids on Indian villages were made as well as the establishment of reservations through federal support (Almaguer, 1979:101). As a result of disease, starvation, and physical attacks, the Indian population which was about 100,000 in 1850 had dropped to only 16,000 by 1880 (Almaguer, 1979:104).

Mexican Americans

Mexican Americans, as the Indians, were not seen as economic competition and a threat to the livelihood to the white working class or organized labor. The Mexican population was small numerically after statehood, when it constituted only 11% of the state's population (Almaguer, 1979:110). The gold rush attracted 100,000 new arrivals to California in 1849 alone (Pitt, 1966:52). In 1850, there were only 15,000 Californios or Mexican Americans (Pitt, 1966:53). The major issue after statehood was title over land between the Mexican elite or ranchero class and white land owners (Almaguer, 1979:105). Over a period of thirty years, much of the land once held by the Mexican American elite was taken over by Eastern capitalists (Almaguer, 1979:107).

Unlike other minority groups, Mexican Americans gained citizenship rights, established through the Treaty of Guadalupe Hildago in 1848, whereby those living in the state one year after passage of the Treaty would become citizens of the United States (Almaguer, 1979:114). At the 1849 Constitutional Convention, many references by delegates were made to the effect that for all intents and purposes Mexicans would be considered as white (Almaguer, 1979:114–115).

However, very quickly in the first years of statehood, the diverse groups of people who were Spanish speaking became lumped together in the minds of the white Americans who settled in California. Thus, the historian Leonard Pitt stated: " . . . angry Yankees simply refused to recognize any real distinctions between Latin Americans. Whether from California, Chile, Peru, or Mexico, whether residents of twenty years' standing or immigrants of one week, all the Spanish-speaking were lumped together as 'interlopers' and 'greasers' " (Pitt, 1966:53).

The working class Mexican Americans were stereotyped as undesirable. They were persecuted by various laws, such as the Vagrancy Act of 1855 which allowed for the arrest and forced labor of those unable to pay the fine (Almaguer, 1979:118). Unlike the Chinese, Mexican workers could not be found in urban manufacturing areas and were not hired in industrial employment until the 1880s (Almaguer, 1979:110–111). Mexican workers were employed to build the Southern Pacific Railroad line from Los Angeles to the Valley in 1875 but were not hired to work in the railroad yard just across from Mexican community in downtown Los Angeles (Pitt, 1966:156). Members of the Mexican working class were seen as inherently lazy and unable to assimilate into American culture. In contrast, some members of the landholding class were allowed to participate with whites on an equal basis, attending college and intermarrying with the white settlers (Almaguer, 1979:119–122).

There were three processes at work in the 1850s with respect to the Mexican American experience as a minority group which had parallels in the Chinese experience. One process was the lumping together of the Spanish-speaking groups as though they were one people. The second process was the association of immigrant Spanish-speaking groups with enslaved Blacks as though all the immigrant Mexicans or Chileans were peons bonded to patrons (Pitt, 1966:57). The third process was the creation of a lower caste, particularly in the mining regions, such that the Chinese were to take the places of the Mexicans. The only options open to the Mexican miner and later the Chinese miner was to pay an oppressive foreign miner's tax or to work for a mining company (Pitt, 1966:69).

Black Americans

In 1849, a convention was called at Monterey to work on a constitution for California. At the constitutional convention the issues of the status of Blacks and whether they should be allowed to migrate to California were debated (Thurman, 1945:27). Although California's first governor, P. H. Burnett, in his inaugural address, announced the need for laws to exclude Blacks who were indentured, attempts in 1850, 1851, and 1857 to exclude free Blacks from coming into the state failed (Eaves, 1910:89–91, 103). In addition, it was proposed and considered that Blacks be denied the right to vote as well as denied admission into the state, the motions were not adopted by the Convention (Almaguer, 1979:36; Goode, 1974:48). In contrast, when California was part of Mexico, Blacks were allowed to enjoy the rights of other citizens (Goode, 1974:73; Thurman, 1945:28). In 1849, the California Constitution specified the eligible voters as white men who were American or Mexican citizens (Wong, 1977:2). Blacks did not gain the right to vote in California until 1869, with the passage of the Fifteenth Amendment to the Constitution, stating that citizens cannot be denied the right to vote on the basis of "race, color, or previous condition of servitude" (Goode, 1974:81).

In 1850, although California declared itself to be a free state, in actuality forms of slavery were condoned. In some cases, slave owners would indenture their slaves and then bring them to California to work in the mines (Goode, 1974:49–52; Thurman, 1945:31). In 1852, the California legislature passed the Fugitive Slave Law which permitted Blacks to be arrested on the claim that they were slaves and further that they be either returned to their masters or be forced to work to repay their debts (Almaguer, 1977:34; Thurman, 1945:32). The real intent of the Fugitive Slave Law was to institutionalize forced labor (Eaves, 1910:95–96). From 1850 to 1856, it was legal for slave owners to maintain possession of slaves who were in California prior to 1850, as well as engage in transactions for or with these slaves (Almaguer, 1979:34). Enslaved Blacks were even leased out by their owners to others to serve as domestics (Almaguer, 1979:35).

In 1851, the state legislature passed an act prohibiting the testimony of Blacks and Indians in a court of law. According to the Civil Practice Act, "No Indian, or Negro, or persons having one-half or more Indian blood, and Negroes or persons having one-half or more of Negro blood, shall be allowed to testify as a witness in an action in which a white person is a party" (Thurman, 1945:41). In 1863, after a number of petitions from Blacks and the support of a number of legislators, the restriction against the submission of testimony from Blacks was withdrawn.

Unlike the situation with the Native Americans, Blacks were perceived as potential economic competitors who needed to be kept from entering the state (Almaguer, 1979:30–31). Thus, the issue of the migration of Black people was tied to the fear of "cheap labor." However, the initial protests and proposed measures to prohibit the free migration of Blacks into the state were overshadowed by immediate political issues such as gaining statehood (Almaguer, 1979:30). The working class perceived Blacks as an economic threat because of the fear that large business interests would employ many Black workers, making it impossible for free white workers to compete. Legislation which attempted to forbid the entrance of Blacks into the state continued to be proposed from 1850 to 1857 (Almaguer, 1979:38). As a result, numbers of Blacks did leave the state in 1858 for Canada, reducing the state population of Blacks by fifteen percent (Almaguer, 1979:38).

In addition, Blacks found themselves at a disadvantage when they were interested in establishing roots by homesteading. When Blacks bought land, the laws allowed whites to claim the land as their own. Laws passed in 1851 and 1860 stated: "Whenever any white man or female resident in this state shall desire to avail himself or herself of the benefits of this act, such person shall make a written application to the county judge in which the land is situated" (Thurman, 1945:42, 45). These laws had the effect of discouraging Blacks from purchasing land and thereby establishing roots in California.

Blacks experienced social ostracism in San Francisco in certain places such as the city's Opera House where they could sit only in one section along with the Chinese. Blacks were excluded from three private libraries. (Lapp, 1977:268–269). Blacks were also denied access to streetcars, denied service at restaurants, and admission to theaters. For example, Blacks were not able to use the city's streetcars until 1866 (Goode, 1974:87).

As the Indian children, Black children were similarly excluded from attending the public schools in 1863. From 1870, Black students were allowed to attend only segregated schools. However, as early as 1872, the Oakland schools allowed Black children to attend the public schools without being segregated; and in 1875, the San Francisco schools also established an integrated racial policy with respect to Blacks (Goode, 1974:85). Finally, in 1880 the law allowing school districts to segregate Black and Indian students was revoked (Almaguer, 1979:37).

Chinese Americans

It was the Chinese who provided much of the early California labor. It has been estimated that one out of every four wage workers in California in the 1870s was Chinese (Saxton, 1975:7). The Chinese arrived in California during the controversy over the slavery issue and the issue over the free migration of Blacks into the state. It was during this period that doubts concerning the desirability of Blacks became fused with images of Chinese (Caldwell, 1971). As Blacks were defined as non-white and inferior, so were the Chinese similarly defined (Almaguer, 1979:48). However, the Chinese as "coolies" under contract labor were perceived as more of a threat than Blacks or slaves. A State Senate bill was proposed by George Tingley to make contract labor legal in California in 1852, but was defeated through the efforts of various groups, labor among them (Almaguer, 1979:50). However, a similar bill allowing for contract labor was passed by the State Assembly (Paul, 1938:186). A minority report in the Assembly responding to the contract labor bill passed by the Assembly articulated a theme which would frame later opposition to the Chinese. It reported that the Chinese were unfair economic competition because of their lower standard of living. Philip Roach, the author of the report stated: "We are called upon to enact a law by which the surplus and inferior population of Asia may be brought into competition with the labor of our own people" (Paul, 1938:187). Roach, however, recognized the usefulness of "cheap labor" for certain needs such as the clearing and draining of swamp lands. This kind of labor would not threaten the jobs of others as long as the Chinese were prevented from becoming citizens (Paul, 1938:187–188). Thus, although the Chinese had only arrived in 1848, by 1852, the issue of Chinese as contract laborers initiated a heated debate about the desirability of the Chinese. In fact, in debates that were to follow, the Chinese were to be associated with indentured labor (Paul, 1938:188). In attempts to maintain a status quo, the California legislature and the judicial system developed laws to restrict the rights of the Chinese in three main ways: through the extension of laws directed towards one non-white group to the Chinese; the creation of laws singling out the Chinese; and the passage of laws which lumped non-white groups together.

Examples of the extension of laws discriminating against one non-white minority group being applied to the Chinese were the Foreign Miner's Tax and the California Supreme Court decision, People v. Hall. Public sentiment towards exclusion was centered particularly in the mining areas but was tempered by the revenues from the Foreign Miners Tax which provided revenue to the counties as well as to the state (Paul, 1977:194). First passed in 1850, the Foreign Miner's Tax was initially intended to discourage Mexican miners who would have had to pay twenty dollars a month (Chen, 1980:48). In 1853, a new Foreign Miner's Tax of four dollars a month was passed. It was estimated that the tax supplied up to 50% of the state revenue. Counties also benefited from the tax, which went to fund schools and hospitals. When the tax was ruled unconstitutional in 1870, the amount collected from the Chinese was five million dollars out of a total of almost six million dollars during the operation of the tax (Chen, 1980:48).

The fact that the Chinese were considered to be non-white in California was made clear in the California Supreme Court decision, People v. Hall in 1854. The decision established that testimony by Chinese persons could not be admissible in a court of law in an action against Whites, since the Chinese were considered non-white under the legal statutes and non-white persons could not testify in a court of law against White persons (Wong, 1977:2). The decision stated: "Held that the words, Indian, Negro, Black, and White, are generic terms, designating race. That, therefore, Chinese and all other people not white are included in the prohibition from being witnesses against whites" (Heizer and Almquist, 1971:229). The court argued that the term Indian was a generic term for Asians, that since the time of Columbus, the term was used in that way, and that the intent of the law was to include Asians as well as Indians in the North American continent (Heizer and Almquist, 1971:230–231). The court, in another line of reasoning, also decided that "the words 'Black person' . . . must be taken as contradistinguished from White, and necessarily includes all races other than the Caucasian" (Heizer and Almquist, 1971:233). Although the legal issue was one of the admissibility of the testimony of Chinese persons, the California Supreme Court was also concerned with upholding public policy. "The same rule which would admit them to testify, would admit them to all the equal rights of citizenship, and we might soon see them at the polls, in the jury box, upon the bench, and in our legislative halls. This is not a speculation which exists in the excited and overheated imagination of the patriot and statesman, but it is an actual and present danger" (Heizer and

Almquist, 1971:233). Thus, the People v. Hall decision established quite early in the arrival of the Chinese to America that the Chinese were to be considered non-white and to be treated as unworthy of holding citizenship privileges. Although Blacks were later removed from the prohibition in 1863, the law continued to be applied to Indians and Chinese until it was negated in 1872 with the enactment of the Federal Civil Rights Act (Almaguer, 1979:59–60).

Other laws were passed with the Chinese in mind. Many state laws from the 1860s to the 1880s were passed to restrict the rights and access to job opportunities of the Chinese immigrants. For example, in 1860, only Chinese were required to pay a fishing tax of $4 a month. In 1879, the California Constitution contained four sections singling out the Chinese, specifically giving cities and towns the right to expel them if found to be "detrimental to the well-being or peace of the state," denying corporations the right to employ Chinese or Mongolians, prohibiting the employment of Chinese by any local or state government, and, by equating Chinese with coolie labor, directed the legislature to prevent the Chinese from entering the state as well as discourage Chinese immigration (Daniels, 1962:18).

The third way laws were utilized in restricting the rights of the Chinese was the passage of laws treating all non-whites alike, such as the segregation of non-white children. As early as 1858, it was suggested by the State Superintendent of Public Instruction that "Africans, Chinese, and Diggers" be prohibited from attending the public schools. By the early 1860s, the state legislature did determine that Black, Chinese, and Indian children attend segregated schools. However, when the state law governing public education was revised in 1870, no provision was made for the education of Chinese children. The Mamie Tape v. Jennie Hurley case challenged the denial of the right to education of Chinese children and the State Supreme Court ruled in 1885 that Chinese children should be allowed to attend public schools (Chen, 1980:185). The Chinese Public School was established in 1885 in Chinatown as a result of the Tape v. Hurley ruling. In 1906, the school was called the Oriental Public School. That year, the School Board decided that children of Japanese and Korean descent living in San Francisco could only attend the segregated school for Asians. The state educational code allowing school districts the power to maintain segregated schools was not changed until 1947 (Lai and Choy, 1971:101).

Federal laws had the most decisive impact on Chinese Americans. In addition to denial of citizenship, for the first time in immigration law in the United States, a group was discriminated against on the basis of race. With the passage of the Chinese Exclusion Act in 1882, laborers of Chinese ancestry were excluded from immigrating to the

United States, as well as declaring foreign born Chinese ineligible for naturalization.

Rodman Paul's assessment of the Chinese experience is that the major issues of the conflict over Asian Americans as a racial minority could be traced to the early 1850s (Paul, 1938:196). Merchants and businessmen supported the Chinese because of concerns that restrictive legislation would hinder trade as well as sources of "cheap labor" while workers, especially miners feared displacement by Chinese workers (Paul, 1938:194–195). Furthermore, the Governor of California, John Bigler, in 1852 accused the Chinese of removing wealth from the state without reciprocating in any way as would citizens and, in addition, they were of "questionable morality" (Paul, 1938:189–190).

However, no mention was made over the issue of assimilability of Asians (Paul, 1938:190). The issue of assimilation arose in the 1870s and came at the time when pseudo-scientific ideas of social and physical differences between white and non-white races began to emerge (Miller, 1969:158–159). The New York World argued in 1876 that the Chinese were not part of the "melting pot" of America because of cultural and biological differences, but it made sense to use their labor power since they were a population which would return to their native land (Miller, 1969:159). Stuart Creighton Miller's study of attitudes of Chinese in the United States shows the importance of understanding the conflict over the acceptance of Chinese in America as not merely an issue occurring in California or the West Coast but involving the whole country. Miller documents the fact that there were well established attitudes towards Chinese before the first large group of Chinese ever set foot in the United States dating from the 1780s and attributable to merchants, missionaries and diplomats (Miller, 1969:201). According to Miller, 1870 was the crucial year in coalescing anti-Chinese sentiment on the East Coast as well as on the West Coast (Miller, 1969:200). Thus, by that time, there were well established prejudices towards the Chinese such that it was believed that the Chinese were dishonest, sly, cruel, and heathen in nature (Miller, 1969:201). These unfavorable images were given wide dissemination in the United States in the 1830s and 1840s during the wars in China, the Taiping Rebellion and the Opium Wars.

The passage of the Chinese Exclusion Act of 1882 by Congress indicated the strength of prejudice towards Chinese by diverse segments of the national population. A Congressman from Delaware stated: "They [Chinese] are of a different race and possess an entirely different civilization, and in my opinion are incapable of being brought into assimilation in habits, customs, and manners with the people of this country" (Miller, 1969:159). The importance of the passage of the Chinese Exclusion Act is that it clearly indicated that the notion of the melting pot had its limits and that the American public and its elected representatives supported the belief that the Chinese as an immigrant group could not be absorbed into America without danger to its social and cultural foundations (Miller, 1969:192). Up to this point in the American ethnic experience, Blacks and Indians were excluded from participation in American society. The notion of a melting pot meant that the various immigrant groups contribute the best from their cultures to create a unique American hybrid. But the Chinese as a non-white immigrant group challenged this notion, and the emphasis became one of Anglo conformity (Miller, 1969:193).

The Chinese Exclusion Act of 1882, the first immigration law to discriminate on the basis of race, defined the rights of the Chinese in America. The Act excluded the immigration of skilled and semi-skilled workers for a period of ten years; specifically declared that the Chinese could not become naturalized citizens; denied the immigration of wives of Chinese workers living in America at the time; and defined an acceptable group who could enter the United States, the "exempt classes" which included students and scholars, merchants, government officials, and tourists (Chen, 1980:148). The impact of the Chinese Exclusion Act was bar the Chinese working class from immigrating to the United States, becoming citizens, and establishing families.

The Chinese, while being defined as non-white and accorded treatment similar to other non-white groups such as Blacks, Mexican Americans, and Indians, were also affected by the international relations between the two countries. Thus, the immigration of the Chinese in large numbers was made possible through the passage of the Burlingame Treaty of 1868 which was passed due to the demand for labor in California (Tsai, 1983:13). With the denial of naturalization and basic rights and privileges coupled with laws that harassed the Chinese, their only source of protection was to turn to the sovereignty of China. However, China, being a weak nation at that time, needed an ally to protect itself from the imperialistic acts of Japan as well as European nations (Tsai, 1983:143–144). Thus, the Ching government did very little to intervene in the acts of discrimination experienced by the Chinese in America. However, the Burlingame Treaty was important in protecting the rights of the Chinese, and the courts would refer to the treaty in addressing anti-Chinese laws or restrictions (Chen, 1980:129).

In California, laws were passed which prevented the integration of the different racial groups, and the Chinese found themselves legislated against as had other minority groups. For instance, in 1854, an anti-miscegenation law was passed preventing the intermarriage between Chinese and Whites following the precedent of the anti-miscegenation statute between Blacks and Whites (Modell, 1977:5).

The experience of the Chinese reflects their arrival in a context where ethnic stratification of racial minorities of Indians, Mexican Americans and Blacks existed. As a result, the Chinese were placed in a status similar to that of other non-white groups. While the other minority groups were declining in population or discouraged from entering the state, the Chinese were actively recruited and their presence made possible by treaty. Thus, in reality, the Chinese did not have the rights of an immigrant group, since the larger society had no desire or intention of allowing the Chinese to become a permanent, settled population. The Chinese Exclusion Act made that clear stating that the Chinese were not eligible to become naturalized citizens.

4.4
The United States Constitution and Slavery

Topical Introduction

As originally written, the United States Constitution provides some evidence to support Benjamin Ringer's conceptualization of a dual society. While attempting to secure the "blessings of liberty" for the people, the Constitution denies those blessing to the "others." Indeed, the two sections below clearly define slavery as a legal system of labor in the United States.

The "Three-fifths Compromise", Article 1, Section 2, resulted from a debate in the U.S. Constitutional Convention over how slaves should be counted for representation and taxation purposes. Delegates from Southern states believed that slaves should be counted toward representation of individual states, but not counted in determining a state's tax burden. Northern states, in which there were relatively few slaves, countered that just the opposite would be appropriate. The compromise arranged maintained that three fifths of the slaves would be counted toward both representation and taxation.

The next section, Article IV, Section 2, contains a passage which stipulates that any "person held to service or labor in one state" and has escaped to another state must be returned to his or her status of servitude. This meant that the Constitution did not recognize that slaves possessed a legal right to escape their bondage; to attain the "blessings of liberty."

Representatives and direct Taxes shall be apportioned among the several States which may be included within this Union, according to their respective Numbers, which shall be determined by adding to the whole Number of free Persons, including those bound to Service for a Term of Years, and excluding Indians not taxed, three fifths of all other Persons.

Section 2. The citizens of each State shall be entitled to all privileges and immunities of citizens in the several States.

A person charged in any State with treason, felony, or other crime, who shall flee from justice, and be found in another State, shall on demand of the executive authority of the State from which he fled, be delivered up, to be removed to the State having jurisdiction of the crime.

No person held to service or labor in one State, under the laws thereof, escaping into another, shall, in consequence of any law or regulation therein, be discharged from such service or labor, but shall be delivered up on claim of the party to whom such service or labor may be due.

4.5
Thomas Benton
Oregon Question

The effect of the arrival of the Caucasian, or White race, on the western coast of America, opposite the eastern coast of Asia, remains to be mentioned among the benefits which the settlement of the Columbia will produce; and that a benefit, not local to us, but general and universal to the human race. Since the dispersion of man upon earth, I know of no human event, past or to come, which promises a greater, and more beneficent change upon earth than the arrival of the van of the Caucasian race (the Celtic-Anglo-Saxon division) upon the border of the sea which washes the shore of the eastern Asia. The Mongolian, or Yellow race, is there, four hundred millions in number, spreading almost to Europe; a race once the foremost of the human family in the arts of civilization, but torpid and stationary for thousands of years. It is a race far above the Ethiopian, or Black—above the Malay, or Brown, (if we must admit five races)—and above the American Indian, or Red: it is a race far above all these, but still, far below the White; and, like all the rest, must receive an impression from the superior race whenever they come in contact. It would seem that the White race alone received the divine command, to subdue and replenish the earth! for it is the only race that has obeyed it—the only one that hunts out new and distant lands, and even a New World, to subdue and replenish. Starting from western Asia, taking Europe for their field, and the Sun for their guide, and leaving the Mongolians behind, they arrived, after many ages, on the shores of the Atlantic, which they lit up with the lights of science and religion, and adorned with the useful and the elegant arts. Three and a half centuries ago, this race, in obedience to the great command, arrived in the New World, and found new lands to subdue and replenish. For a long time it was confined to the border of the new field, (I now mean the Celtic-Anglo-Saxon division;) and even fourscore years ago the philosophic Burke was considered a rash man because he said the English colonists would top the Alleganies, and descend into the valley of the Mississippi, and occupy without parchment if the Crown refused

to make grants of land. What was considered a rash declaration eighty
years ago, is old history, in our young country, at this day. Thirty
years ago I said the same thing of the Rocky Mountains and the Columbia: it was ridiculed then: it is becoming history to-day. The ven-
erable Mr. Macon has often told me that he remembered a line low
down in North Carolina, fixed by a royal governor as a boundary between the whites and the Indians: where is that boundary now? The
van of the Caucasian race now top the Rocky Mountains, and spread
down to the shores of the Pacific. In a few years a great population
will grow up there, luminous with the accumulated lights of European
and American civilization. Their presence in such a position cannot be
without its influence upon eastern Asia. The sun of civilization must
shine across the sea: socially and commercially, the van of the Caucasians, and the rear of the Mongolians, must intermix. They must talk
together, and trade together, and marry together. Commerce is a great
civilizer—social intercourse as great—and marriage greater. The
White and Yellow races can marry together, as well as eat and trade
together. Moral and intellectual superiority will do the rest: the White
race will take the ascendant, elevating what is susceptible of improvement—wearing out what is not. The Red race has disappeared from
the Atlantic coast: the tribes that resisted civilization, met extinction.
This is a cause of lamentation with many. For my part, I cannot mur-
mur at what seems to be the effect of divine law. I cannot repine that
this Capitol has replaced the wigwam—this Christian people, replaced
the savages—white matrons, the red squaws—and that such men as
Washington, Franklin, and Jefferson, have taken the place of Powhat-
tan, Opechonecanough, and other red men, howsoever respectable
they may have been as savages. Civilization, or extinction, has been
the fate of all people who have found themselves in the track of the
advancing Whites, and civilization, always the preference of the
Whites, has been pressed as an object, while extinction has followed
as a consequence of its resistance. The Black and the Red races have
often felt their ameliorating influence. The Yellow race, next to themselves in the scale of mental and moral excellence, and in the beauty
of form, once their superiors in the useful and elegant arts, and in
learning, and still respectable though stationary; this race cannot fail
to receive a new impulse from the approach of the Whites, improved
so much since so many ages ago they left the western borders of
Asia. The apparition of the van of the Caucasian race, rising upon
them in the east after having left them on the west, and after having
completed the circumnavigation of the globe, must wake up and reani-
mate the torpid body of old Asia. Our position and policy will commend us to their hospitable reception: political considerations will aid
the action of social and commercial influences. Pressed upon by the
great Powers of Europe—the same that press upon us—they must in

our approach hail the advent of friends, not of foes—of benefactors, not of invaders. The moral and intellectual superiority of the White race will do the rest: and thus, the youngest people, and the newest land, will become the reviver and the regenerator of the oldest.

4.6

Robert F. Heizer and Alan F. Almquist

Making California a White Man's Paradise: 1849 California Constitutional Convention

Topical Introduction

The state of California is significant, because of its relatively high concentration of residents of Asian background. Although California has something of a reputation for cultural tolerance, it's important to point out that from the beginning of the state's history, it was substantially unfriendly to people of color.

The delegates to the first California constitutional convention in 1849 had a difficult job to do in that they had to deal with the very controversial issue of whether the state would enter the union free or slave. The delegates eventually decided to ban slavery from California, but not necessarily because they believed in human equality, for the constitution also banned free Blacks from the new state. A major reason why was that Blacks, whether free or slave, were perceived as threats to the dignity of free white labor. In a passage from the Constitutional proceedings, delegate Wozencraft supports the ban. From Robert F. Heizer and Alan F. Almquist, *The Other Californians: Prejudice and Discrimination Under Spain, Mexico, and the United States to 1920*, (Berkeley and Los Angeles: University of California Press, 1971), 106.

"I desire to protect the people of California against all monopolies—to encourage labor and protect the laboring class. Can this be done by admitting the negro race? Surely not; for if they are permitted to come, they will do so—nay they will be brought here. Yes, Mr. President, the capitalists will fill the land with these living laboring machines, with all their attendant evils. Their labor will go to enrich the few, and impoverish the many; it will drive the poor and honest laborer from the field, by degrading him to the level of the negro. The vicious propensities of this class of population will be a heavy tax on the people. Your officers will have to be multiplied; your prisons will

167

have to be doubled; your society will be corrupted. Yes, sirs, you will find when it is too late that you have been saddled with an evil that will gall you to the quick, and yet it cannot be thrown off.

4.7
Native American during the Early Years of California Statehood

Topical Introduction

After annexation, Americans in California were, for some reason, disappointed that many California Indians lacked interest in working for white people. Somewhat in contradiction with the notion of producerism, the new state government passed an act in 1850 to guarantee, one way or another, that Native Americans would provide useful services to white employers. From *Statutes of California,* chapter 133, April 22, 1850; *Statutes of California,* chapter 232, April 18, 1860.

20. Any Indian able to work and support himself in some honest calling, not having wherewithal to maintain himself, who shall be found loitering and strolling about, or frequenting public places where liquors are sold, begging, or leading an immoral or profligate course of life, shall be liable to be arrested on the complaint of any resident citizen of the county, and brought before any Justice of the Peace of the proper county, Mayor or Recorder of any incorporated town or city, who shall examine said accused Indian, and hear the testimony in relation thereto, and if said Justice, Mayor or Recorder shall be satisfied that he is a vagrant, as above set forth, he shall make out a warrant under his hand and seal, authorizing and requiring the officer having him in charge or custody, to hire out such vagrant within twenty-four hours to the best bidder, by public notice given as he shall direct, for the highest price that can be had, for any term not exceeding four months; and such vagrant shall be subject to and governed by the provisions of this Act, regulating guardians and minors, during the time which he has been so hired. The money received for his hire, shall, after deducting the costs, and the necessary expense for clothing for said Indian, which may have been purchased by his employer, be, if he be without a family, paid into the County Treasury, to the credit of the Indian fund. But if he have a family, the same

shall be appropriated for their use and benefit: *Provided,* that any such vagrant, when arrested, and before judgment, may relieve himself by giving to such Justice, Mayor, or Recorder, a bond, with good security, conditioned that he will, for the next twelve months, conduct himself with good behavior, and betake to some honest employment for support. [Chapter 133 of the *Statutes of California,* enacted into law on April 22, 1850.]

Amendments in 1860 to the Act of April 1850

Chap. CCXXXI—An Act amendatory of an Act entitled "An Act for the Government and Protection of Indians," passed April twenty-second, one thousand eight hundred and fifty. [Approved April 18, 1860.]

The People of the State of California, represented in Senate and Assembly, do enact as follows:

Section 1. Section third of said act, is hereby amended so as to read as follows:

Sec. 3. County and District Judges in the respective counties of this State, shall, by virtue of this act, have full power and authority, at the instance and request of any person having or hereafter obtaining any Indian child or children, male or female, under the age of fifteen years, from the parents or person or persons having the care or charge of such child or children, with the consent of such parents or person or persons having the care or charge of any such child or children, or at the instance and request of any person desirous of obtaining any Indian or Indians, whether children or grown persons, that may be held as prisoners of war, or at the instance and request of any person desirous of obtaining any vagrant Indian or Indians, as have no settled habitation or means of livelihood, and have not placed themselves under the protection of any white person, to bind and put out such Indians as apprentices, to trades, husbandry, or other employments, as shall to them appear proper, and for this purpose shall execute duplicate articles of indenture of apprenticeship on behalf of such Indians, which indenturess shall also be executed by the person to whom such Indian or Indians are to be indentured; one copy of which shall be filed by the County Judge, in the Recorder's office of the county, and one copy retained by the person to whom such Indian or Indians may be indentured; such indentures shall authorize such person to have the care, custody, control, and earnings, of such Indian or Indians, as shall require such person to clothe and suitably provide the necessaries of life for such Indian or Indians, for and during the term for which such Indian or Indians shall be apprenticed, and shall contain the sex, name, and probable age, of such Indian or Indians; such indentures may be for the following terms of years: Such children as are under fourteen years of age, if males, until they attain the age of twenty-five years; if females, until they attain the age of twenty-one years; such as are over fourteen and under twenty years of age, if males, until they attain the age of thirty years; if females, until they attain the age of twenty-five years; and such Indians as may be over the age of twenty years, then next following the date of such indentures, for and during the term of ten years, at the discretion of such Judge; such Indians as may be indentured under the provision of this section, shall be deemed within such provisions of this act, as are applicable to minor Indians.

Sec. 2. Section seventh of said act is hereby amended so as to read as follows:

Sec. 7. If any person shall forcibly convey any Indian from any place without this State, to any place within this State, or from his or her home within this State, or compel him or her to work or perform any service, against his or her will, except as provided in this act, he or they shall, upon conviction thereof, be fined in any sum not less than one hundred dollars, nor more than five hundred dollars, before any court having jurisdiction, at the discretion of the court, and the collection of such fine shall be enforced as provided by law in other criminal cases, one-half to be paid to the prosecutor, and one-half to the county in which such conviction is had. [Chapter 231 of the *Statutes of California,* enacted into law on April 18, 1860.]

4.8

John Bigler

To the Senate and Assembly of the State of California, 1852

Executive Department,
Sacramento City, April 23d, 1852.

The subject which I deem it my duty to present for your consideration before our final separation, is the present wholesale importation to this country, of immigrants from the Asiatic quarter of the globe. I am deeply impressed with the conviction that, in order to enhance the prosperity and to preserve the tranquility of the State, measures must be adopted to check this tide of Asiatic immigration, and prevent the exportation by them of the precious metals which they dig up from our soil without charge, and without assuming any of the obligations imposed upon citizens. I allude, particularly, to a class of Asiatics known as "Coolies," who are sent here, as I am assured, and as is generally believed, under contract to work in our mines for a term; and who, at the expiration of the term, return to their native country. I am sensible that a proposition to restrict international intercourse, or to check the immigration of even Asiatics, would appear to conflict with the long cherished benevolent policy of our Government. That Government has opened its paternal arms to the "oppressed of all nations," and it has offered them an asylum and a shelter from the iron rigor of despotism. The exile pilgrim and the weary immigrant, have been recipients of its noble hospitalities. In this generous policy, so far as it effects Europeans, or others capable of becoming citizens under our laws, I desire to see no change; nor do I desire to see any diminution of that spirit of liberality which pervades the naturalization laws of the United States.

A question around which there has been thrown some doubt, is whether Asiatics could, with safety, be admitted to the enjoyments of all the rights of citizens in our Courts of Justice. If they are ignorant of the solemn character of the oath or affirmation, in the form prescribed by the Constitution and Statutes, or if they are indifferent to the solemn obligation which an oath imposes to speak the truth, it would be unwise to receive them as jurors or permit them to testify in courts of law, more especially in cases affecting the rights of others than Asiatics.

Congress, possessing the exclusive power to establish a uniform rule of naturalization, has enacted that "every alien, being *a free white person,* may become a citizen of the United State," by complying with certain conditions. Of the construction of this law, Chancellor Kent remarks, that "the Act of Congress confines the description of Aliens capable of naturalization to *free white persons.*" "I presume," continues the learned writer, that "this excludes the inhabitants of Africa and their descendants; and it may become a question, to what extent persons of mixed blood are excluded, and what shades and degrees of mixture of color disqualify an alien from application for the benefits of the Act of naturalization. Perhaps there might be difficulties, also, as to the copper-colored natives of America, or the yellow or tawny races of the Asiatics; and it may be well doubted whether any of them are white persons in the purview of the law. It is the declared law of New York, South Carolina, Tennessee, (and other States,) that Indians are not citizens, but distinct tribes, living under the protection of the Government, and consequently they never can be citizens under the Act of Congress."

It is certain that no Asiatic has yet applied for, or has received the benefits of this Act. Indeed, I am not aware that a single subject of the Chinese Empire ever acquired a residence or a domicil in any of the States of the Union, except, perhaps, in this. In this State their habits have been migratory; and so far as I can learn, very few of them have evinced a disposition to acquire a domicil, or, as citizens, to identify themselves with the country. Gold, with a talismanic power, has overcome these national habits of reserve and non-intercourse which the Chinese and their neighbors have hitherto exhibited; and under the impulse which the discovery of the precious metals in California has given to their cupidity, vast numbers of them are immigrating hither, not, however, to avail themselves of the blessings of a free Government. They do not seek our land as "the asylum for the oppressed of all nations." They have no desire (even if permitted by the constitution and laws) to absolve themselves from allegiance to other powers, and, under the laws of the United States, become American citizens. They come to acquire a certain amount of the precious metals, and then return to their native country.

I invite your attention, for a moment, to results which may ensue, if by inaction we give further encouragement to the mania for emigration which pervades several of the Asiatic States, and which it may be presumed, is being rapidly diffused throughout all continental Asia. The area of Asia is 17,865,000 English square miles, and the total population is computed by the best authorities at three hundred and seventy-five millions two hundred and thirty thousand. The population of the Chinese Empire and dependant States alone is 168,000,000. It will be readily perceived that millions might be detached from such myriads, without any perceptible diminution of the aggregate population; and that vast numbers may be induced, under contracts, to emigrate to a country which they are told contains inexhaustible mines of gold and silver. The facilities afforded them for emigration are rapidly increasing, and few vessels now enter our ports from Asiatic countries which are not crowded with these peculiar people. I have received intelligence, from reliable sources, that the average rate charged an Asiatic from China to California, is forty dollars; that over two thousand of their number have arrived at San Francisco, within the last few weeks, and that at least five thousand are now on their way hither. Letters from Canton to the end of January, estimate the immigration from that port to California, for 1852, at over twenty thousand, nearly all of whom will be hired by Chinese masters, to come here and collect gold under the direction and control of the master himself, who accompanies them, or of an agent.

I have mentioned in the preceding portion of this communication, that numbers of Asiatics have been and are being sent here, under contracts to labor for a term of years in our mines at merely nominal wages, and their families have been retained as hostages for the faithful performances of the contracts. If this intelligence is correct, it may well be doubted whether such contracts should be recognized or enforced within the limits of the State. Mr. Justice Story, in his Commentaries upon ''Conflict of Laws,'' and ''Foreign Contracts,'' contends with great force and clearness, that ''there is an exception to the rule as to the universal validity of contracts, which is, that *no nation is bound to recognize or enforce any contracts which are injurious to its own interest, or to those of its own subjects.*'' Mr. Justice Martin, has expressed it in the following terms: ''The exception applies to cases in which the contract is immoral or unjust, or in which the enforcing it in a State, WOULD BE INJURIOUS TO THE RIGHTS, THE INTEREST OR THE CONVENIENCE OF SUCH STATE OR ITS CITIZENS.''

''This exception results from the consideration that the authority of the acts and contracts done in other States, as well as the laws by which they are regulated, are not of any efficacy beyond the limits of that State; and whatever is attributed to them elsewhere, is from *comity,* and not of *strict right;* and every independent community will and ought to judge for itself, how far that *comity* ought to extend. The reasonable limitation is, that it shall not suffer prejudice by its comity.''

The cases which form an exception to the rule as to the universal validity of contracts, have been classified by eminent legal authorities. Among those enumerated are contracts to corrupt or evade the due administration of justice; contracts to cheat public agents, or to defeat the public rights; contracts which are opposed to the national policy and institutions; and, in short, all contracts which, in their own nature are founded in moral turpitude, and *are inconsistent with the good order and solid interests of society.* All such contracts, even though they might be held valid in the country where they are made, would be held void elsewhere, or at least ought to be, if the dictates of Christian morality, or even of natural justice, are allowed to have their due force and influence in the administration of international jurisprudence. There cannot be a reasonable doubt that contracts made in China, with the subjects of that Empire, by their own countrymen, or by resident foreigners, for the performance of work and labor within the State of California, come within the class of contracts here enumerated, as exceptions to the rule in respect to the universal validity of contracts. This question will form an appropriate subject for the consideration of Courts of Law; but I cannot forbear to express the opinion that such contracts ought not to be recognized or enforced within the limits of this State, either upon the score of international comity or law.

If it be admitted that the introduction of one hundred thousand, or a less number of ''Coolies'' into this State, under such contracts with nonresidents, may endanger the public tranquility and injuriously affect the interests of our people, then we are bound to adopt measures to avert such evils. I therefore respectfully submit for your consideration two distinct propositions:

1st. Such an exercise of the taxing power by the State as will check the present system of discriminate and unlimited Asiatic immigration.

2d. A demand by the State of California for the prompt interposition of Congress, by the passage of an Act prohibiting ''Coolies'' shipped to California under contracts, from laboring in the mines of this State. With the consent of the State, Congress would have the clear right to interpose such safeguards as in their wisdom might be deemed necessary. The power to tax as well as to entirely exclude this class of Asiatic immigrants, it is believed, can be constitutionally exercised by the State. As the subject is one of great magnitude, I have deemed it my duty to examine the opinions of eminent writers on international law, as well as the written opinions of the Judges of the Supreme Court of the United States.

It might be urged, as an objection to the imposition of a tax, that such a statute would be a regulation of commerce, and that the power to regulate commerce is exclusively reposed in Congress. I am aware that a majority of the Judges composing the Supreme Court of the United States, have decided that statutes passed by the Legislatures of New York and Massachusetts, imposing a tax on passengers of a ship from a foreign port, were regulations of foreign commerce; and that the power to regulate commerce being exclusively reposed in Congress, the statutes were void. But the whole Court were understood to concede the right of the State to tax immigrants after they were on shore. The power of States to exclude immigrants is also shown by the best writers on international law, as well as by the decisions of the Supreme Court of the United States. Mr. Justice Woodbury remarked, in his opinion given in the case of Norris *vs.* the City of Boston, that "it having been, both in Europe and America, a matter of municipal regulation whether aliens shall or shall not reside in any particular State, or even cross its borders, it follows that if a sovereign State pleases, it may, as a matter of clear right, exclude them entirely;" and, "as further proof and illustration that this power exists in the States, and has never been parted with, it was clearly exercised by Virginia, as to others than paupers; and it is now exercised in one form or another, as to various persons, by more than half the States of the Union."

In the case above referred to, involving the question whether the statute of New York, imposing taxes upon alien passengers arriving in the ports of that State, was contrary to the Constitution of the United States, five of the Judges of the Supreme Court delivered opinions in the affirmative and four in the negative. In delivering his dissenting opinion, Chief Justice Taney remarked, that "the first enquiry suggested by these cases, was whether, under the Constitution of the United States, the Federal Government has the power to compel the several States to receive, and suffer to remain in association with its citizens, every person or class of persons whom it may be the policy or pleasure of the United States to admit;" and he proceeded to say that he thought it "very clear, both upon principle and the authority of adjudged cases, that the several States have a right to prevent from entering the State, any person, or class or description of persons, whom it may deem dangerous or injurious to the interests or welfare of its citizens, and that the State has the exclusive right to determine, in its sound discretion, whether the danger does or does not exist, free from the control of the General Government."

But, without further reference to the able opinion delivered in this case by Mr. Justice Taney, I will remark that the principle involved in the recommendation which I have made, does not appear to me to be entirely analogous to that contained in the statutes of New York and Massachusetts, and declared to be unconstitutional by the Supreme Court of the United States. In those cases it was proposed to impose a tax upon "free white persons," who could acquire the rights of American citizens. But, in the present instance, it is proposed to tax persons who, it is believed, cannot assume the obligations imposed upon, nor acquire the civil or political privileges of citizens of the United States. In those cases, the public health merely was endangered; but it is believed that in this instance the most vital interests of the State and people—and, perhaps, the public peace are at stake.

Whether the objection raised by the Supreme Court to the statute of New York, that it was a regulation of commerce, and that, therefore, it was void, would apply to a statute of this State, imposing a similar tax upon Asiatics, I must leave it to you and to other tribunals, to determine.

There is no official information in this department, touching the nature of the contracts said to have been made with Asiatics, by their own countrymen, or by foreign residents in the Chinese Empire, to work in our mines. It is not officially known to this department whether those persons are here in a state of voluntary or involuntary servitude. But if it be ascertained that their immigration and servitude is voluntary, I am still of the opinion that the Legislature may enact laws to prevent or discourage shipments of vast bodies of "Coolies" into this State. I am convinced not only that such a measure is necessary, but I am also convinced that there is nothing in the Federal Constitution which forbids the enactment of such laws.

It is a remarkable fact that the treaty concluded at Waug Hiya, on the 3d of July, 1845, between the United States and China, contains no provisions in relation to the civil or political privileges which the subjects of the Chinese Empire, immigrating to the United States, shall enjoy. It is true that this treaty guarantees important commercial privileges to our citizens; but in the exercise of these privileges no encroachments are made upon the rights or the property of the subjects of China. The measures which I have now recommended you to enact, would not, of course, justify any retaliation by Chinese upon Americans residing in that country. Indeed, in view of the fact that in all the Governments of Europe and Asia, foreigners are excluded from mines, and in view of the further fact that in those countries the precious metals are commonly retained by the Government, to the exclusion even of their own citizens, it is not easy to believe that the Chinese will urge objections to the measures which I have here presented, if adopted.

It must be conceded that the extraordinary wants of this State will demand novel if not extraordinary legislation. The history and condition of California is peculiar—it is without parallel. Her resources, like her exigencies, are without precedent. In framing laws, therefore, to meet such exigencies, it is clear that we cannot be guided entirely by precedents which have been established in the common course of events in other States. But, though our condition may sometimes require departures from precedents in the enactment as well as in the execution of laws, we should not fail to follow the Constitution, both as our chart and as the palladium of our liberties.

Having thus performed one of the most important duties which will perhaps devolve upon me during my term of office, I commit this subject to your care, and entreat for it your careful consideration.

John Bigler.

4.9

Foreign Miner's Tax, California, 1853

An Act to Provide for the Protection of Foreigners, and to Define Their Liabilities and Privileges. [Approved March 30, 1853]

The People of the State of California, represented in Senate and Assembly, do enact as follows:

Section 1. That from and after the passage of this Act, no person, not being a citizen of the United States (California Indians excepted) shall be allowed to take gold from the mines of this State, unless he shall have a license therefor, as hereafter provided.

Sec. 2. It shall be the duty of the Comptroller of State to procure a sufficient number of blank licenses, which shall be substantially in the following form and numbered consecutively, and a record thereof be filed in his office. He shall deliver said licenses to the Treasurer of State and take his receipt for the same upon the books of his office:

Form of License

To be renewed upon expiration of term.

No.

    County (date)

                 185

has paid four dollars mining license, which entitles him to work in the mines one month.

No. _____   County, (date).
  This certifies that . . . . has this day paid the Sheriff of . . . . County, four dollars, which entitles him to work in the mines of this State for one month from date.

         Comptroller of State.

   By . . . . *Sheriff.*

To be renewed upon expiration of term.

Every subsequent license after the first, shall be dated from the expiration of the former license issued by the Sheriff or his Deputy to any foreign miner who shall have been engaged in mining, from the expiration of such former license.

Sec. 3. The Sheriff of each County shall be the Collector of License Tax, under the provisions of this Act, who, before entering upon the duties herein provided for, shall enter into bond to the State, with two or more sureties, to be approved by the Board of Supervisors, if any such Board exists in his county; if there be no such Board, then by the County Judge, in the sum of fifteen thousand dollars, conditioned for the faithful performance of the duties required of him by this Act, which bond shall be filed in the office of the Clerk of said county.

Sec. 4. The Treasurer of State shall fill the blanks for the numbers and counties which have been left in the printed form, and shall be liable on his bond for all licenses delivered to him by the Comptroller, except for such as he may have issued to the Recorders of counties, under the provisions of the following section.

Sec. 5. The Treasurer of State shall issue, as soon as practicable, to the Recorder of each mining county, and thereafter previous to the fifteenth of December of each year, such number of licenses as may be deemed sufficient for the use of said county, taking a receipt therefor, which receipt shall be recorded by the Treasurer, in a book to be provided for that purpose, and shall stand as a charge against said Recorder; and said Recorder shall execute a bond to the State, conditioned for the faithful performance of all the duties required of him by this Act, in the sum of ten thousand dollars; said bond to be approved by the Governor and Comptroller.

Sec. 6. The amount to be paid for each license shall be at the rate of four dollars per month, and said license shall in no case be transferable.

Sec. 7. The Recorder shall deliver to the Sheriff of his County such number of licenses as said Sheriff may require, charging him therewith, and taking his receipt therefor. The Sheriff shall make monthly returns to the Recorder of his County, of the number of licenses issued, and to whom, and the amount of money received. The first returns shall be made to the Recorder on the first Monday of May next, and thereafter, a return shall be made on the first Monday of each succeeding month as herein specified.

Sec. 8. It is hereby made the duty of the Treasurer of each County to which licenses have been issued, to report to the Treasurer of State on the first Monday of August next, and on the first Monday of every third month thereafter, the amount of money received by him on account of foreign miners' licenses.

Sec. 9. Fifty percent of the net proceeds of all moneys collected under the provisions of this Act, shall be paid into the State Treasury, and shall constitute a part of the General Fund; the remaining fifty percent of the net proceeds shall be paid into the General Fund of the County; and it shall be the duty of the Sheriff to pay over to the County Treasurer, monthly, the amounts specified in this section.

Sec. 10. The collector may seize the property of any person liable to, and refusing to pay such tax, and sell at public auction, on one hour's notice, by proclamation, and transfer the title thereof to the person paying the highest price therefor, and after deducting the tax and necessary expenses incurred by reason of such refusal and sale of property, the collector shall return the surplus of the proceeds of the sale, if any, to the person or persons whose property was sold: *Provided,* That should any person liable to pay such tax in any County of this State escape into any other County with intent to evade the payment of such tax, then and in that event it shall be lawful for the collector to pursue such person, and enforce the payment of such tax in the same manner as if no such escape had been made. Any foreigner representing himself to be a citizen of the United States, shall, in absence of his certificate to that effect, satisfy the collector of the correctness of his statement by affidavit, or otherwise, and that the collector be and is empowered to administer such oath or affirmation. All foreigners residing in the mining districts of this State shall be considered miners under the provisions of this Act, unless they are directly engaged in some other lawful business avocation.

Sec. 11. Immediately preceding the time provided by law for the final settlement of the County Treasurer with the Treasurer of State, it shall be the duty of each Recorder to whom licenses have been issued to report to the Comptroller of State the number of licenses on hand in his office, as also the number in the hands of the Sheriff, who is hereby required to report to said Recorder the number of licenses not disposed of, for which he has receipted to the said Recorder.

Sec. 12. The Treasurer and Comptroller of State shall, as soon as practicable, compare the returns of the Sheriff with the reports of the County Recorder, and if there shall be any discrepancy in the statements, it shall be the duty of the Comptroller to immediately inform the prosecuting Attorney of the county in which such delinquent resides, who shall commence suit against such delinquent and his sureties forthwith.

Sec. 13. Any Sheriff or his Deputy who shall neglect or refuse to pay over the money collected by him or them, under the provisions of this Act, or shall appropriate any part thereof to his or their use, other than the percentage they are entitled to retain by the provisions of this Act, shall be deemed guilty of embezzlement, and upon conviction thereof shall be punished by imprisonment in the State Prison any time not less than one year, nor more than ten years.

Sec. 14. Any officer charged with the collection of the tax provided to be collected by this Act, who shall give any receipt other than the receipt prescribed in this Act, or receive money for such license without giving the necessary receipt, shall be deemed guilty of a misdemeanor, and upon conviction shall be fined in a sum not exceeding one thousand dollars, and be imprisoned in the county jail not exceeding six months.

Sec. 15. It shall be the duty of the different Sheriffs to return all unsold licenses to the County Recorder prior to the fifteenth day of December of each year, and receive new licenses, and the County Recorders shall immediately transmit to the Comptroller of State said licenses, who shall deliver them to the Treasurer of State. Such licenses so returned shall be placed to the credit of the different County Recorders on the books of the Treasurer, and the licenses destroyed in presence of the Comptroller of State, who shall also make a record of the same.

Sec. 16. Any person who shall make any alteration, or cause the same to be made, in any license, shall be deemed guilty of a misdemeanor, and upon conviction shall be fined in a sum not exceeding one thousand dollars, and imprisonment in the State Prison not exceeding six months.

Sec. 17. Any person or company hiring foreigners to work in the mines of this State shall be liable for the amount of the licenses for each person so employed.

Sec. 18. The Sheriff shall have power, and it is hereby made his duty to appoint a sufficient number of Deputy Collectors to assist him in the collection of the tax provided to be collected by this Act, said Deputy Collectors to be paid not less than fifteen (15) percent on all sums collected by them; and the Sheriff shall be responsible for the acts of said Deputy Collectors, and may require from them such bond and surety as he may deem proper for his own indemnification, and for such service he shall be entitled to receive three percent on all sums collected by them. Should the Board of Supervisors, or in the event of there being no such Board, then the County Judge, deem the percentage to be paid to Deputy Collectors by the provisions of this section to be insufficient, an order may be entered by the Board of Supervisors or the County Judge providing that an additional sum shall be paid such Deputy Collector, not to exceed in all twenty-five percent to be paid as herein provided. The County Recorder of each County shall receive three percent on all sums collected under the provisions of this Act.

Sec. 19. That the Sheriff be required to receive good clean gold dust when tendered at seventeen dollars per ounce in payment for licenses, and be required to pay the same into the Treasury at the same rate.

Sec. 20. That the Act entitled "An Act to Provide for the Protection of Foreigners, and to Define their Liabilities and Privileges," approved May fourth, one thousand eight hundred and fifty-two, and all laws or parts of laws conflicting with the provisions of this Act be and the same are hereby repealed. (From *California Statutes,* 1853).

4.10

Report of the Committee on Mines and Mining Interests, 1853

Mr. Speaker:

The Committee on Mines and Mining Interests, to whom were referred several bills amendatory of the ''Act to provide for the protection of Foreigners, and to define their liabilities and privileges,'' approved May 4th, 1852, ask leave to report:

Your committee have given to these several bills the care and attention their provisions merit, and find their objects two-fold: First, to increase the State revenue, and secondly, to exclude certain Foreigners from the mines.

The Assembly could not have regarded the revenue objects as the striking features of the proposed amendments to the existing law; otherwise they would have been referred to the Committee on Ways and Means.

So far as revenue is concerned, we are satisfied the present law needs change.

A larger per centage should be given to the collector of Foreign Miners' tax, and the means for enforcing the payment of the license money should be more stringent; twenty-five per cent would probably reward the collector, and secure a faithful performance of the duties of the office; and payment of the tax might be enforced by giving the collector authority to assess the amount due from the foreigner, with power to sell under the assessment as under execution; these amendments, together with an increase of the tax to four dollars a month, would make the revenue objects of the law, attainable.

But the second object of these proposed amendments—the exclusion of certain foreigners from the mines, presents a more difficult subject for our consideration.

In this are involved questions of right and justice, as well as of convenience and policy, requiring for their solution numerous facts and enlarged views of political economy.

The difficulty of attaining the ends sought for by the advocates of the exclusive policy may be seen in the language of the bills proposed: Thus, one of the bills would enact that ''no Asiatic, or person

of Asiatic descent, nor Chileno shall be permitted to work in any of
the mines of this State under the provisions of this Act.'' Such a
clause would unfortunately exclude the whole Caucasian race, of
which the American people is almost entirely composed.

And as to the Chileno, why single him out for special reprobation?
What has he done to deserve such signal reproof?

And even if the Chileno were excluded by law, how could he be
distinguished from the kindred race of Mexico and Peru? Under such
a statute, Chilenos would be as scarce as Jewish treasure in the middle ages, and the State would have to provide an ethnologist to accompany the Sheriff in his tour through the mining districts.

Another bill, drawn apparently with more care, and essaying to be
more definite, would have us, after demanding and receiving license
money from all foreigners, provide ''That nothing contained in the
provisions of this Act, shall secure Foreign miners, who from their
color, nature, and education can never become citizens of the United
States, against the liability of being ousted from any mining claim by
citizen miners of this State who may be present at such claim, and
desirous and prepared to work it immediately, and who shall first pay
or offer to pay to such Foreigner, Miner or Miners the cash value of
any improvements they may have made thereon—such cash value to
be determined by two disinterested citizens, duly sworn, to be selected by each party.''

The injustice of such a provision is at once apparent; we do not
release from the payment of the tax, those foreigners, who, in the peculiar language of the bill, ''from their color, nature, and education
can never become citizens of the United States,'' we only take away
the property they have paid us to protect.

Then, too, the vagueness of the language, pardonable in an essay,
is inconsistent with the strictness and precision we require in a law.
Who are the persons that from their color, nature, and education can
never become citizens of the United States?

What nature and what education unfit a man for American citizenship?

The Greenlander who dozes away existence over fish-oil and fire,
and the Laplander whose intellect is benumbed by six months night,
may become citizens of the United States.

Therefore, we presume it is not brutality of nature or savageness of
education which work corruption in the blood of a foreigner, and render him incapable of naturalization.

We are constrained to believe the clause we have quoted means
nothing at all, and that it was inserted for the purpose rather of round-
ing a period than of giving force, and clearness, and precision to a law.

It is said, however, that these provisions—indefinite as they are—
intend to apply principally, if not entirely, to the Chinese.

If this be so, let us inquire whether the policy they aim at establishing is wise and proper.

Some persons advocate the exclusion of the Chinese, because they fear the immigration of this people will become too large, and thus crowd out our own citizens and other white races. On this ground we have no apprehensions.

Independent of the peculiar influences which operate to keep the Chinese in their own country, the intensity of their attachment to old customs and old opinions, their strong feeling of family and reverence for the government which discourages immigration, we do not think it probable that they will ever be found in the way of Caucasian races. Physiologists tell us that whenever two races meet on the same soil, the weaker is bound to succumb and give way before the stronger.

The superior energy of the Caucasian will always conquer the sullen industry of the Mongal, and the latter can never, either in the struggle of commerce or of arms, compete successfully with the former.

And if all the Caucasian tribes, the American—last in its formation, but destined, undoubtedly, to be most perfect in its development—fears least to meet the other races.

If the American has maintained his place amidst the immense immigrations of Celt and Saxon, Sclave and Dane, which have for the last fifty years been pouring into the country, surely he can stand against a people who for centuries have been tyrannized over by a band of Tartars.

It appears to us derogatory to the national spirit and the national character to express a fear of being overrun by any number of Chinese who may choose to land on our shores.

Instead of discouraging immigration of the Chinese, it would better become us to encourage the important trade which is the result of their coming hither.

For a long time European nations have been endeavoring to open the trade of the Chinese and Japanese Empires; and we have also been aiming at the same object for a number of years. With this policy the Federal Government has lately fitted out an expedition with the view of opening trade with the Japanese; and it would ill become the State of California to do aught in contravention of such a wise and beneficial policy.

And how are we to enlarge our trade with China?—surely not by annihilating the Chinese themselves.

The trade between San Francisco and China has been rapidly increasing ever since the discovery of the gold mines; but last year when the exclusion of the Chinese from the minds was spoken of, the Chinese trade languished, and only revived after it was understood that all foreigners would be permitted to work in the mines on the payment of a certain license tax.

The products of China will certainly be cheaper in our markets if we do not close our ports to the Chinese themselves; and a larger market for our own goods will be created by permitting the Chinese to come among us and acquire the same habits and customs, and therefore the same wants, as we ourselves have. Every Chinese who returns from California to his own country is a missionary for the propagation of American tastes, and an agent for increasing the demand and the sale of American products.

A necessary consequence of an enlarged commerce between San Francisco and the Chinese ports, will be an increase of the fixed capital in San Francisco. And the more capital there is in our commercial centre, the less opportunity will there be for combinations of capitalists to command the markets and monopolize the trade in the necessaries of life.

It is only where capital is small and limited, that such combinations are able to accomplish their selfish purpose.

Enlarge the amount of capital, and the flour and provision markets will no longer be under the control of men who do not scruple to sacrifice their fellow-beings on the altar of mammon. Let us, then, by all the means in our power, allure to our shores the vast accumulations of Asiatic capital which are the result of ages of labor and economy. Let us invite to our State the hoarded treasures of a people who fear, in their own country, to expose all their wealth to the eyes of greedy Tartars and impoverished mandarins. Thus will we secure benefit to ourselves, and at the same time elevate the inferior race which are to live and trade among us.

We cannot therefore sanction the exclusive policy contemplated by two of the bills referred to us. In addition to the amendments we have already suggested to the Act of 1852, the first section of it should be amended by striking out the clause acknowledging the right of Congress to assume the control of the mining lands of California.

It is not necessary for us at this time, to examine the rights of the Federal Government over the mines; we only ask that the right of Congress to control them may not be hastily or inconsiderately acknowledged.

We beg leave to report back the several bills referred to us, and to recommend the passage of the bill for ''an Act to revise the Act to provide for the protection of Foreigners and to define their liabilities and privileges,'' with amendments thereto annexed.

James H. Gardner, Chairman.
T. T. Cabaniss,
Benj. B. Redding,
R. G. Reading,
Patrick Canney.

4.11
Supreme Court of the State of California: People v Hall, 1854

Topical Introduction

In 1850, the California state legislature passed an act prohibiting African-Americans, mulattos, and Native Americans from testifying for or against whites in court. One reason why was that Native Americans conspicuously sued employees for failing to live up to labor agreements. The overall thinking was that people of color lacked the integrity to be trustworthy.

Meanwhile, thousands of Chinese immigrants had migrated to California gold fields. Euroamerican miners believed that their Chinese counterparts posed unfair competition and threatened the dignity of white labor in the gold country. It seems that Chinese miners working a claim in cooperative teams were wrongly perceived as members of coolie or slave labor gangs. The Foreign Miner's Tax was one way in which California whites fought Chinese immigrant miners. But outright violence was another alternative; an alternative encouraged by People v. Hall, a decision rendered by the California Supreme Court which almost declared open season on Chinese immigrants in the state of California.

The People, Respondent, v. George W. Hall, Appellant.

Mr. Ch. J. Murray delivered the opinion of the Court. Mr. J. Heydenfeldt concurred.

The appellant, a free white citizen of this State, was convicted of murder upon the testimony of Chinese witnesses.

The point involved in this case is the admissibility of such evidence.

The 394th section of the Act Concerning Civil Cases provides that no Indian or Negro shall be allowed to testify as a witness in any action or proceeding in which a white person is a party.

The 14th section of the Act of April 16th, 1850, regulating Criminal Proceedings, provides that "No black or mulatto person, or Indian, shall be allowed to give evidence in favor of, or against a white man."

The true point at which we are anxious to arrive is, the legal signification of the words, "black, mulatto, Indian, and white person," and whether the Legislature adopted them as generic terms, or intended to limit their application to specific types of the human species.

Before considering this question, it is proper to remark the difference between the two sections of our statute, already quoted, the latter being more broad and comprehensive in its exclusion, by use of the word "black," instead of Negro.

Conceding, however, for the present, that the word "black," as used in the 14th section, and "Negro," in 394th, are convertible terms, and that the former was intended to include the latter, let us proceed to inquire who are excluded from testifying as witnesses under the term "Indian."

When Columbus first landed upon the shores of this continent, in his attempt to discover a western passage to the Indies, he imagined that he had accomplished the object of his expedition, and that the Island of San Salvador was one of those Islands of the Chinese Sea, lying near the extremity of India, which had been described by navigators.

Acting upon this hypothesis, and also perhaps from the similarity of features and physical conformation, he gave to the Islanders the name of Indians, which appellation was universally adopted, and extended to the aboriginals of the New World, as well as of Asia.

From that time, down to a very recent period, the American Indians and the Mongolian, or Asiatic, were regarded as the same type of the human species.

In order to arrive at a correct understanding of the intention of our Legislature, it will be necessary to go back to the early history of legislation on this subject, our statute being only a transcript of those of older States.

At the period from which this legislation dates, those portions of Asia which include India proper, the Eastern Archipelago, and the countries washed by the Chinese waters as far as then known, were denominated the Indies, from which the inhabitants had derived the generic name of Indians.

Ethnology, at that time, was unknown as a distinct science, or if known, had not reached that high point of perfection which it has since attained by the scientific inquiries and discoveries of the masterminds of the last half century. Few speculations had been made with regard to the moral or physical differences between the different races of mankind. These were general in their character, and limited to those visible and palpable variations which could not escape the attention of the most common observer.

The general, or perhaps universal opinion of that day was, that there were but three distinct types of the human species which, in their turn, were subdivided into varieties of tribes. This opinion is still held by many scientific writers, and is supported by Cuvier, one of the most eminent naturalists of modern times.

Many ingenious speculations have been resorted to for the purpose of sustaining this opinion. It has been supposed, and not without plausibility, that this continent was first peopled by Asiatics, who crossed Behring's Straits, and from thence found their way down to the more fruitful climates of Mexico and South America. Almost every tribe has some tradition of coming from the North, and many of them, that their ancestors came from some remote country beyond the ocean.

From the eastern portions of Kamtschatka, the Aleutian Islands form a long and continuous group, extending eastward to that portion of the North American Continent inhabited by the Esquimaux. They appear to be a continuation of the lofty volcanic ranges which traverse the two continents, and are inhabited by a race who resemble, in a remarkable degree, in language and appearance, both the inhabitants of Kamtschatka (who are admitted to be of the Mongolian type), and the Esquimaux, who again, in turn, resemble other tribes of American Indians. The similarity of the skull and pelvis, and the general configuration of the two races; the remarkable resemblance in eyes, beard, hair, and other peculiarities, together with the contiguity of the two continents, might well have led to the belief that this country was first peopled by the Asiatics, and that the difference between the different tribes and the parent stock was such as would necessarily arise from the circumstances of climate, pursuits, and other physical causes, and was no greater than that existing between the Arab and the European, both of whom were supposed to belong to the Caucasian race.

Although the discoveries of eminent archeologists, and the researches of modern geologists, have given to this continent an antiquity of thousands of years anterior to the evidence of man's existence, and the light of modern science may have shown conclusively that it was not peopled by the inhabitants of Asia, but that the Aborigines are a distinct type, and as such claim a distinct origin, still, this would not in any degree alter the meaning of the term, and render that specific which was before generic.

We have adverted to these speculations for the purpose of showing that the name of Indian, from the time of Columbus to the present day, has been used to designate, not alone the North American Indian, but the whole of the Mongolian race, and that the name, though first applied probably through mistake, was afterward continued as appropriate on account of the supposed common origin.

That this was the common opinion in the early history of American legislation cannot be disputed, and, therefore, all legislation upon the subject must have borne relation to that opinion.

Can, then, the use of the word "Indian," because at the present day it may be sometimes regarded as a specific, and not as a generic term, alter this conclusion? We think not; because at the origin of the legislation we are considering, it was used and admitted in its common and ordinary acceptation, as a generic term, distinguishing the great Mongolian race, and as such, its meaning then became fixed by law, and in construing statutes the legal meaning of words must be preserved.

Again: the words of the Act must be construed in *pari materia*. It will not be disputed that "white" and "Negro" are generic terms, and refer to two of the great types of mankind. If these, as well as the word "Indian," are not to be regarded as generic terms, including the two great races which they were intended to designate, but only specific, and applying to those whites and Negroes who were inhabitants of this continent at the time of the passage of the Act, the most anomalous consequences would ensue. The European white man who comes here would not be shielded from the testimony of the degraded and demoralized caste, while the Negro, fresh from the coast of Africa, or the Indian of Patagonia, the Kanaka, South Sea Islander, or New Hollander, would be admitted, upon their arrival, to testify against white citizens in our courts of law.

To argue such a proposition would be an insult to the good sense of the Legislature.

The evident intention of the Act was to throw around the citizen a protection for life and property, which could only be secured by removing him above the corrupting influences of degraded castes.

It can hardly be supposed that any Legislature would attempt this by excluding domestic Negroes and Indians, who not unfrequently have correct notions of their obligations to society, and turning loose upon the community the more degraded tribes of the same species, who have nothing in common with us, in language, country, or laws.

We have, thus far, considered this subject on the hypothesis that the 14th section of the Act Regulating Criminal Proceedings and the 394th section of the Practice Act were the same.

As before remarked, there is a wide difference between the two. The word "black" may include all Negroes, but the term "Negro" does not include all black persons.

By the use of this term in this connection, we understand it to mean the opposite of "white," and that it should be taken as contradistinguished from all white persons.

In using the words "no black or mulatto person, or Indian shall be allowed to give evidence for or against a white person," the Legislature, if any intention can be ascribed to it, adopted the most comprehensive terms to embrace every known class or shade of color, as the apparent design was to protect the white person from the influence of all testimony other than that of persons of the same caste. The use of these terms must, by every sound rule of construction, exclude everyone who is not of white blood.

The Act of Congress, in defining what description of aliens may become naturalized citizens, provides that every "free white citizen," etc., etc. In speaking of this subject, Chancellor Kent says that "the Act confines the description to 'white' citizens, and that it is a matter of doubt, whether, under this provision, any of the tawny races of Asia can be admitted to citizenship." (2 Kent's Com. 72.)

We are not disposed to leave this question in any doubt. The word "white" has a distinct signification, which *ex vi termini*, excludes black, yellow, and all other colors. It will be observed, by reference to the first section of the second Article of the Constitution of this State, that none but white males can become electors, except in the case of Indians, who may be admitted by special Act of the Legislature. On examination of the constitutional debates, it will be found that not a little difficulty existed in selecting these precise words, which were finally agreed upon as the most comprehensive that could be suggested to exclude all inferior races.

If the term "white," as used in the Constitution, was not understood in its generic sense as including the Caucasian race, and necessarily excluding all others, where was the necessity of providing for the admission of Indians to the privilege of voting, by special legislation?

We are of the opinion that the words "white," "Negro," "mulatto," "Indian," and "black person," wherever they occur in our Constitution and laws, must be taken in their generic sense, and that, even admitting the Indian of this continent is not of the Mongolian type, that the words "black person," in the 14th section, must be taken as contradistinguished from white, and necessarily excludes all races other than the Caucasian.

We have carefully considered all the consequences resulting from a different rule of construction, and are satisfied that even in a doubtful case, we would be impelled to this decision on grounds of public policy.

The same rule which would admit them to testify, would admit them to all the equal rights of citizenship, and we might soon see them at the polls, in the jury box, upon the bench, and in our legislative halls.

The anomalous spectacle of a distinct people, living in our community, recognizing no laws of this State, except through necessity, bringing with them their prejudices and national feuds, in which they indulge in open violation of law; whose mendacity is proverbial; a race of people whom nature has marked as inferior, and who are incapable of progress or intellectual development beyond a certain point, as their history has shown; differing in language, opinions, color, and physical conformation; between whom and ourselves nature has placed an impassable difference, is now presented, and for them is claimed, not only the right to swear away the life of a citizen, but the further privilege of participating with us in administering the affairs of our Government.

These facts were before the Legislature that framed this Act, and have been known as matters of public history to every subsequent Legislature.

There can be no doubt as to the intention of the Legislature, and that if it had ever been anticipated that this class of people were not embraced in the prohibition, then such specific words would have been employed as would have put the matter beyond any possible controversy.

For these reasons, we are of opinion that the testimony was inadmissible.

The judgment is reversed and the cause remanded. (From *Reports of Cases Argued and Determined in the Supreme Court of the State of California, 1854*).

4.12

Robert F. Heizer and Alan F. Almquist

The Mexican Californian and the New State: 1855

Topical Introduction

One of the great ironies of recent American history is that in California people of Mexican descent are treated as unwelcome, even illegal strangers in a land that once belonged to Mexico. In 1848, the Treaty of Guadalupe Hidalgo ended the Mexican War and California was a part of the vast territory ceded to the United States by Mexico. California residents of Mexican descent were guaranteed their land holdings and U.S. citizenship. However, with the Gold Rush and the trek by thousands of Americans and Europeans into California the property and rights of Mexican people, often called Californios, were open to question.

Legal and not so legal means were devised to deprive people of Mexican and Latin American descent of their livelihoods and property. Even Mexican culture was subject to political attack during the 1850s as the following excerpt from Heizer and Almquists' *The Other Californians* points out. From Robert F. Heizer and Alan F. Almquist, *The Other Californians: Prejudice and Discrimination Under Spain, Mexico, and the United States to 1920,* (Berkeley: University of California Press, 1971), 151.

There were a number of laws that directly or indirectly were aimed at restricting the freedom of Mexican Californian citizens. These included a law prohibiting operation of any "bull, bear, cock or prize fights, horserace, circus, theatre, bowling alley, gambling house, room or saloon, or any place of barbarous or noisy amusements on the Sabbath," the penalty being a fine of ten to five hundred dollars.[23] Others were a special act controlling gambling;[24] a head tax of fifty dollars imposed on immigrants, aimed primarily at Chinese, but incidently including Mexicans; and a renewal of the foreign miners' tax set at five dollars per month. The most direct slap at Mexicans was the refusal of the legislature to provide funds for translation of laws into Spanish, and the passage of the antivagrancy act, called the "Greaser Act"[25] because section 2 specified "all persons who are commonly known as 'Greasers' or the issue of Spanish or Indian blood . . . and who go armed and are not peaceable and quiet persons." Even though the legislature removed the objectionable reference to "greasers" in an amendment to the act in 1856, the law so read and was applied for a full year.

4.13
Dred Scott v. Sandford, 1856

December Term 1856

Mr. Chief Justice Taney delivered the opinion of the court.

This case has been twice argued. After the argument at the last term, differences of opinion were found to exist among the members of the court; and as the questions in controversy are of the highest importance, and the court was at that time much pressed by the ordinary business of the term, it was deemed advisable to continue the case, and direct a re-argument on some of the points, in order that we might have an opportunity of giving to the whole subject a more deliberate consideration. It has accordingly been again argued by counsel, and considered by the court; and I now proceed to deliver its opinion.

There are two leading questions presented by the record:

1. Had the Circuit Court of the United States jurisdiction to hear and determine the case between these parties? And

2. If it had jurisdiction, is the judgment it has given erroneous or not?

The plaintiff in error, who was also the plaintiff in the court below, was, with his wife and children, held as slaves by the defendant, in the State of Missouri; and he brought this action in the Circuit Court of the United States for that district, to assert the title of himself and his family to freedom.

The declaration is in the form usually adopted in that State to try questions of this description, and contains the averment necessary to give the court jurisdiction; that he and the defendant are citizens of different States; that is, that he is a citizen of Missouri, and the defendant a citizen of New York.

The defendant pleaded in abatement to the jurisdiction of the court, that the plaintiff was not a citizen of the State of Missouri, as alleged in his declaration, being a negro of African descent, whose ancestors

From *U.S. Reports,* 1856. Opinion of the Supreme Court, December Term, 1856.

were of pure African blood, and who were brought into this country and sold as slaves.

To this plea the plaintiff demurred, and the defendant joined in demurrer. The court overruled the plea, and gave judgment that the defendant should answer over. And he thereupon put in sundry pleas in bar, upon which issues were joined; and at the trial the verdict and judgment were in his favor. Whereupon the plaintiff brought this writ of error.

Before we speak of the pleas in bar, it will be proper to dispose of the questions which have arisen on the plea in abatement.

That plea denies the right of the plaintiff to sue in a court of the United States, for the reasons therein stated.

If the question raised by it is legally before us, and the court should be of opinion that the facts stated in it disqualify the plaintiff from becoming a citizen, in the sense in which that word is used in the Constitution of the United States, then the judgment of the Circuit Court is erroneous, and must be reversed.

It is suggested, however, that this plea is not before us; and that as the judgment in the court below on this plea was in favor of the plaintiff, he does not seek to reverse it, or bring it before the court for revision by his writ of error; and also that the defendant waived this defence by pleading over, and thereby admitted the jurisdiction of the court.

But, in making this objection, we think the peculiar and limited jurisdiction of courts of the United States has not been adverted to. This peculiar and limited jurisdiction has made it necessary, in these courts, to adopt different rules and principles of pleading, so far as jurisdiction is concerned, from those which regulate courts of common law in England, and in the different States of the Union which have adopted the common-law rules.

In these last-mentioned courts, where their character and rank are analogous to that of a Circuit Court of the United States; in other words, where they are what the law terms courts of general jurisdiction; they are presumed to have jurisdiction, unless the contrary appears. No averment in the pleadings of the plaintiff is necessary, in order to give jurisdiction. If the defendant objects to it, he must plead it specially, and unless the fact on which he relies is found to be true by a jury, or admitted to be true by the plaintiff, the jurisdiction cannot be disputed in an appellate court.

Now, it is not necessary to inquire whether in courts of that description a party who pleads over in bar, when a plea to the jurisdiction has been ruled against him, does or does not waive his plea; nor whether upon a judgment in his favor on the pleas in bar, and a writ of error brought by the plaintiff, the question upon the plea in abatement would be open for revision in the appellate court. Cases that may have been decided in such courts, or rules that may have been laid down by common-law pleaders, can have no influence in the decision in this court. Because, under the Constitution and laws of the United States, the rules which govern the pleadings in its courts, in questions of jurisdiction, stand on different principles and are regulated by different laws.

This difference arises, as we have said, from the peculiar character of the Government of the United States. For although it is sovereign and supreme in its appropriate sphere of action, yet it does not possess all the powers which usually belong to the sovereignty of a nation. Certain specified powers, enumerated in the Constitution, have been conferred upon it; and neither the legislative, executive, nor judicial departments of the Government can lawfully exercise any authority beyond the limits marked out by the Constitution. And in regulating the judicial department, the cases in which the courts of the United States shall have jurisdiction are particularly and specifically enumerated and defined; and they are not authorized to take cognizance of any case which does not come within the description therein specified. Hence, when a plaintiff sues in a court of the United States, it is necessary that he should show, in his pleading, that the suit he brings is within the jurisdiction of the court, and that he is entitled to sue there. And if he omits to do this, and should, by any oversight of the Circuit Court, obtain a judgment in his favor, the judgment would be reversed in the appellate court for want of jurisdiction in the court below. The jurisdiction would not be presumed, as in the case of a common-law English or State court, unless the contrary appeared. But the record, when it comes before the appellate court, must show, affirmatively, that the inferior court had authority, under the Constitution, to hear and determine the case. And if the plaintiff claims a right to sue in a Circuit Court of the United States, under that provision of the Constitution which gives jurisdiction in controversies between citizens of different States, he must distinctly aver in his pleading that they are citizens of different States; and he cannot maintain his suit without showing that fact in the pleadings.

This point was decided in the case of *Bingham v. Cabot,* (in 3 Dall., 382,) and ever since adhered to by the court. And in *Jackson v. Ashton,* (8 Pet., 148,) it was held that the objection to which it was open could not be waived by the opposite party, because consent of parties could not give jurisdiction.

It is needless to accumulate cases on this subject. Those already referred to, and the cases of *Capron v. Van Noorden,* (in 2 Cr., 126) and *Montalet v. Murray,* (4 Cr., 46,) are sufficient to show the rule of which we have spoken. The case of *Capron v. Van Noorden* strikingly illustrates the difference between a common-law court and a court of the United States.

If, however, the fact of citizenship is averred in the declaration, and the defendant does not deny it, and put it in issue by plea in abatement, he cannot offer evidence at the trial to disprove it, and consequently cannot avail himself of the objection in the appellate court, unless the defect should be apparent in some other part of the record. For if there is no plea in abatement, and the want of jurisdiction does not appear in any other part of the transcript brought up by the writ of error, the undisputed averment of citizenship in the declaration must be taken in this court to be true. In this case, the citizenship is averred, but it is denied by the defendant in the manner required by the rules of pleading, and the fact upon which the denial is based is admitted by the demurrer. And, if the plea and demurrer, and judgment of the court below upon it, are before us upon this record, the question to be decided is, whether the facts stated in the plea are sufficient to show that the plaintiff is not entitled to sue as a citizen in a court of the United States. . . .

We think they are before us. The plea in abatement and the judgment of the court upon it, are a part of the judicial proceedings in the Circuit Court, and are there recorded as such; and a writ of error always brings up to the superior court the whole record of the proceedings in the court below. And in the case of the *United States v. Smith,* (11 Wheat., 172) this court said, that the case being brought up by writ of error, the whole record was under the consideration of this court. And this being the case in the present instance, the plea in abatement is necessarily under consideration; and it becomes, therefore, our duty to decide whether the facts stated in the plea are or are not sufficient to show that the plaintiff is not entitled to sue as a citizen in a court of the United States.

This is certainly a very serious question, and one that now for the first time has been brought for decision before this court. But it is brought here by those who have a right to bring it, and it is our duty to meet it and decide it.

The question is simply this: Can a negro, whose ancestors were imported into this country, and sold as slaves, become a member of the political community formed and brought into existence by the Constitution of the United States, and as such become entitled to all the rights, and privileges, and immunities, guaranteed by that instrument to the citizen? One of which rights is the privilege of suing in a court of the United States in the cases specified in the Constitution.

It will be observed, that the plea applies to that class of persons only whose ancestors were negroes of the African race, and imported into this country, and sold and held as slaves. The only matter in issue before the court, therefore, is, whether the descendants of such slaves, when they shall be emancipated, or who are born of parents who had become free before their birth, are citizens of a State, in the sense in which the word citizen is used in the Constitution of the United States. And this being the only matter in dispute on the pleadings, the court must be understood as speaking in this opinion of that class only, that is, of those persons who are the descendants of Africans who were imported into this country, and sold as slaves.

The situation of this population was altogether unlike that of the Indian race. The latter, it is true, formed no part of the colonial communities, and never amalgamated with them in social connections or in government. But although they were uncivilized, they were yet a free and independent people, associated together in nations or tribes, and governed by their own laws. Many of these political communities were situated in territories to which the white race claimed the ultimate right of dominion. But that claim was acknowledged to be subject to the right of the Indians to occupy it as long as they thought proper, and neither the English nor colonial Governments claimed or exercised any dominion over the tribe or nation by whom it was occupied, nor claimed the right to the possession of the territory, until the tribe or nation consented to cede it. These Indian Governments were regarded and treated as foreign Governments, as must so as if an ocean had separated the red man from the white; and their freedom has constantly been acknowledged, from the time of the first emigration to the English colonies to the present day, by the different Governments which succeeded each other. Treaties have been negotiated with them, and their alliance sought for in war; and the people who compose these Indian political communities have always been treated as foreigners not living under our Government. It is true that the course of events has brought the Indian tribes within the limits of the United States under subjection to the white race; and it has been found necessary, for their sake as well as our own, to regard them as in a state of pupilage, and to legislate to a certain extent over them and the territory they occupy. But they may, without doubt, like the subjects of any other foreign Government, be naturalized by the authority of Congress, and become citizens of a State, and of the United States; and if an individual should leave his nation or tribe, and take up his abode among the white population, he would be entitled to all the rights and privileges which would belong to an emigrant from any other foreign people.

We proceed to examine the case as presented by the pleadings.

The words "people of the United States" and "citizens" are synonymous terms, and mean the same thing. They both describe the political body who, according to our republican institutions, form the sovereignty, and who hold the power and conduct the Government through their representatives. They are what we familiarly call the "sovereign people," and every citizen is one of this people, and a constituent member of this sovereignty. The question before us is, whether the class of persons described in the plea in abatement compose a portion of this people, and are constituent members of this sovereignty? We think they are not, and that they are not included, and were not intended to be included, under the word "citizens" in the Constitution, and can therefore claim none of the rights and privileges which that instrument provides for and secures to citizens of the United States. On the contrary, they were at that time considered as a subordinate and inferior class of beings, who had been subjugated by the dominant race, and, whether emancipated or not, yet remained subject to their authority, and had no rights or privileges but such as those who held the power of the Government might choose to grant them.

It is not the province of the court to decide upon the justice or injustice, the policy or impolicy, of these laws. The decision of that question belonged to the political or law-making power; to those who formed the sovereignty and framed the Constitution. The duty of the court is, to interpret the instrument they have framed, with the best lights we can obtain on the subject, and to administer it as we find it, according to its true intent and meaning when it was adopted.

In discussing this question, we must not confound the rights of citizenship which a State may confer within its own limits, and the rights of citizenship as a member of the Union. It does not by any means follow, because he has all the rights and privileges of a citizen of a State, that he must be a citizen of the United States. He may have all of the rights and privileges of the citizen of a State, and yet not be entitled to the rights and privileges of a citizen in any other State. For, previous to the adoption of the Constitution of the United States, every State had the undoubted right to confer on whomsoever it pleased the character of citizen, and to endow him with all its rights. But this character of course was confined to the boundaries of the State, and gave him no rights or privileges in other States beyond those secured to him by the laws of nations and the comity of States. Nor have the several States surrendered the power of conferring these rights and privileges by adopting the Constitution of the United States. Each State may still confer them upon an alien, or any one it thinks proper, or upon any class or description of persons; yet he would not be a citizen in the sense in which that word is used in the Constitution of the United States, nor entitled to sue as such in one of its courts, not to the privileges and immunities of a citizen in the other States. The rights which he would acquire would be restricted to the State which gave them. The Constitution has conferred on Congress the right to establish a uniform rule of naturalization, and this right is evidently exclusive, and has always been held by this court to be so. Consequently, no State, since the adoption of the Constitution, can by naturalizing an alien invest him with the rights and privileges secured to a citizen of a State under the Federal Government, although, so far as the State alone was concerned, he would undoubtedly be entitled to the rights of a citizen, and clothed with all the rights and immunities which the Constitution and laws of the State attached to that character.

It is very clear, therefore, that no State can, by any act or law of its own, passed since the adoption of the Constitution, introduce a new member into the political community created by the Constitution of the United States. It cannot make him a member of this community by making him a member of its own. And for the same reason it cannot introduce any person, or description of persons, who were not intended to be embraced in this new political family, which the Constitution brought into existence, but were intended to be excluded from it.

The question then arises, whether the provisions of the Constitution, in relation to the personal rights and privileges to which the citizen of a State should be entitled, embraced the negro African race, at that time in this country, or who might afterwards be imported, who had then or should afterwards be made free in any State; and to put it in the power of a single State to make him a citizen of the United States, and endue him with the full rights of citizenship in every other State without their consent? Does the Constitution of the United States act upon him whenever he shall be made free under the laws of a State, and raised there to the rank of a citizen, and immediately clothe him with all the privileges of a citizen in every other State, and in its own courts?

The court think the affirmative of these propositions cannot be maintained. And if it cannot, the plaintiff in error could not be a citizen of the State of Missouri, within the meaning of the Constitution of the United States, and, consequently, was not entitled to sue in its courts.

It is true, every person, and every class and description of persons, who were at the time of the adoption of the Constitution recognised as citizens in the several States, became also citizens of this new political body; but none other; it was formed by them, and for them and their posterity, but for no one else. And the personal rights and privileges guarantied to citizens of this new sovereignty were intended to embrace those only who were then members of the several State communities, or who should afterwards by birthright or otherwise become members, according to the provisions of the Constitution and the principles on which it was founded. It was the union of those who were at that time members of distinct and separate political communities into one political family, whose power, for certain specified purposes, was to extend over the whole territory of the United States. And it gave to each citizen rights and privileges outside of his State which he did not before possess, and placed him in every other State upon a perfect equality with its own citizens as to rights of person and rights of property; it made him a citizen of the United States.

It becomes necessary, therefore, to determine who were citizens of the several States when the Constitution was adopted. And in order to do this, we must recur to the Governments and institutions of the thirteen colonies, when they separated from Great Britain and formed new sovereignties, and took their places in the family of independent nations. We must inquire who, at that time, were recognised as the people or citizens of a State, whose rights and liberties had been outraged by the English Government; and who declared their independence, and assumed the powers of Government to defend their rights by force of arms.

In the opinion of the court, the legislation and histories of the times, and the language used in the Declaration of Independence, show, that neither the class of persons who had been imported as slaves, nor their descendants, whether they had become free or not, were then acknowledged as a part of the people, nor intended to be included in the general words used in that memorable instrument. . . .

4.14

Report of Joint Select Committee Relative to the Chinese Population of the State of California, 1862

Report

Mr. President:—The Joint Select Committee of the Legislature, which was appointed to confer with the Chinese merchants of this State, and to report the result of said conference to the Legislature, together with such views as bear upon the legality of admitting and the influence of a permanent Chinese population amongst us, beg leave to submit the following report:

Your Committee has had several interviews with the leading Chinese merchants of this city, and found them to be men of intelligence, ability, and cultivation, who kindly and promptly met our many inquiries in a spirit and with an urbanity that left upon our minds favorable impressions.

They placed us in possession of a mass of statistics respecting the industry and the value of the labors of their countrymen to this State, which we here present.

These statements surprised us, and we feel confident they will deeply interest you and our constituents, and it will be well to ponder them before any action shall be proposed that will have a tendency to disturb so important an interest, and drive from our State a class of foreigners so peaceful, industrious, and useful.

From the information which we derived from the merchants, and from examining their data, we put down the Chinese population in the State at this time at about fifty thousand. The merchants, from their books, where they keep an accurate account of arrivals, departures, and deaths, of their countrymen, say there are forty-eight thousand three hundred and ninety-one; that there are engaged in mining, about thirty thousand; in farming, about twelve hundred—hired as laborers principally; in washing and ironing, and as servants, they could not tell; that there are about two thousand traders. The number of Chinese prostitutes they say they cannot tell, as they have nothing to do with them. There are about one hundred families of respectability here, that is, married females having families. They say they think that about two hundred Chinese are employed in the manufacture of cigars in this city.

Their estimates of the numbers in the various branches of industry in the State, they say may not be correct, as they have no control over the Chinese—they pursue whatever calling they choose and are as free as any persons in the State.

Upon this head, your Committee examined them at great length and in the most minute and careful manner, and your Committee is satisfied that there is no system of slavery or coolieism amongst the Chinese in this State. If there is any proof, going to establish the fact that any portion of the Chinese are imported into this State as slaves or coolies, your Committee have failed to discover it.

The present laws in force in regard to this class of our population, in the opinion of your Committee, impose upon them quite as heavy burdens as they are able to bear, and, in many instances, far beyond their ability to stand up under.

Your Committee trust that no more legislation will be had, calculated to oppress and degrade this class of persons in our State.

The truth of many of the statements we have been able to verify from other and independent sources confirming their reliability.

Statistics for Eighteen Hundred and Sixty-one.

Amount of Duties paid by Chinese importers into the Custom House at this port, was	$500,000 00
Freight money paid to ships from China	180,683 00
Passage money paid to ships from China	382,000 00
Head Tax	7,556 00
Boat Hire	4,767 00
Rents for Stores and Storage	370,000 00
Licenses, Taxes, etc., in State	2,164,273 00
Commissions paid Auctioneers and Brokers	20,396 00
Drayage in San Francisco	59,662 00
Teaming in interior of State	360,000 00
Paid for American Products in San Francisco	1,046,613 00
Paid for American Products in the State	4,953,387 00
Paid for Fire Insurance in the city	1,925 00
Paid for Marine Insurance in the city	33,647 00
Paid for Steamboat Fare to Sacramento City and Stockton	50,000 00
Paid for Stage Fare to and from the mines	250,000 00
Paid for steamboat up-river Freights	80,000 00
*Water Rates for Chinese miners	2,160,000 00
†Mining Claims bought by Chinese miners	1,350,000 00
Total	$13,974,909 00

*Twenty thousand miners buy water at thirty cents per man per day.

†Fifteen thousand miners buy claims at twenty-five cents per man per day.

The data of many of these estimates of expenditure are kept by several of the Chinese companies with great minuteness and particularity, so that from these accounts we have been enabled to deduce average expenditures per head per annum.

From the above remarkable statistics, amounting to fourteen millions of dollars nearly, you will be able to form an idea of the value which this Chinese population and industry confers upon the State.

Dissect these various items, and see what employment this "scourged race" gives to our ship-owners, our watermen, our real estate men, our merchants, draymen, teamsters, steamboat men, our stage-owners, with their hostlers and horses, and blacksmiths, and carriage makers, our farmers and cattle men—in short, to nearly every branch of human industry in the State.

These departments of labor are carried on by white men, independent of Chinese labor; but largely indebted for its recompense to Chinese industry and patronage.

And for this fourteen millions of dollars which we gather from the Chinese population, what do we give in exchange? Mainly, thus far, the privilege to work in the mines, on bars, beds and gulch claims, which have been abandoned by our countrymen and other white men, because, by their intelligence and skill, they could find other diggings where they could do better. Such claims to all but the patient, moderate Chinese, would otherwise have remained idle and unproductive.

In towns and cities, we have washmen and cooks, who, to some extent, compete with imported servants from Europe; and this is about the only competition which some fifty thousand peaceable, patient and industrious Chinese immigrants have, thus far, produced in California. Surely, is this declared evil were doubled or magnified tenfold, it need not create alarm in the breasts of cautious and fearful citizens.

We have about eighty Chinamen working in the Mission woollen factory, which, by reason of their cheap labor, is able to find employment for some seventy white men. With high rates of labor, this valuable enterprise could not be prosecuted in this State. Woollen manufacturers should be specially encouraged by generous legislation.

Our climate is highly favorable to sheep raising, and it should be our study to find a home market for all the wool that can be grown here. Coarse blankets and coarse cloths are consumed upon this coast in unlimited quantities, and we shall soon find customers for stuffs of finer quality. The rearing of sheep and raising of wool could soon become an interest of vast value to the State. This interest, yet to *be* created, infringing upon no existing class of labor, would afford occupation for thousands of Chinamen, associated with as many or more whites, and prove a mutual and public blessing.

With cheap labor we could supply all our own wines and liquors, besides sending large quantities abroad. The wine crop of France, in eighteen hundred and forty-nine, was nine hundred and twenty-five million gallons, valued at one hundred millions of dollars. In eighteen hundred and fifty-three, she had in vineyards, four million eight hundred and seventy-three thousand nine hundred and thirty-four acres, (giving less than two hundred gallons to the acre,) making about eight thousand one hundred and seven square miles, or an area of two hundred and fifty miles in length by thirty-two in breadth. California contains one hundred and eighty-eight thousand nine hundred and eighty-one square miles, which would give one hundred and twenty million nine hundred and forty-seven thousand eight hundred and forty acres; so that if only one twenty-fifth of her area should be planted with vineyards, she would have an amount equal to France.

We have a fresher soil, better climate for grape culture, than France; and we could produce quantities of better quality than is grown in worn out lands.

This cannot be done without the aid of cheap labor from some quarter; but a portion of Chinese, with white labor, would add incalculably to the resources of the State in this particular branch. It would also diminish drunkenness and consequent pauperism, thereby greatly diminishing crime and misery.

To the wine produced, add the cost of pipes and bottles, the transportation and commissions on sales, and this wine and liquor interest would become second only to the mining and farming interests.

Turning from the grape, let us dwell a moment upon the production of rice, tea, sugar, tobacco, and dried fruits of every description, such as figs, raisins, etc., etc., all of which can be easily grown within the State, and soon will be commenced, if we encourage cheap labor from abroad to cultivate our waste luxuriant soil. It is industry which makes a people great, and rich, and powerful; and to our enterprise and resources, we need but the willing hand of patient labor to make our young and giant State the glory of our country, and the marvel of the world.

To develop her latent resources, and vitalize all her powers, we need sound, liberal, far-seeing Legislators; men who can mould and harness *all* inferior races to work out and realize our grand and glorious destiny.

It is charged that the Chinese demoralize the whites. We cannot find any ground for the allegation. We adopt none of their habits; form no social relations with them; do not intermarry with them; but keep them separate and apart; a distinct, inferior race.

They work for us; they help us build up our State, by contributing largely to our taxes, to our shipping, farming, and mechanical interests, without, to any extent, entering these departments as competitors; they are denied privileges equal with other foreigners; they cannot vote nor testify in Courts of Justice, nor have a voice in making our laws, nor mingle with us in social life. Certainly we have nothing to fear from a race so contemned and restricted; on the contrary, those Chinamen who remain here are educated up to our standard.

When they leave us, they carry the knowledge of our improvements home to their countrymen, and although we must not look for miracles in a decade of years in changing the manners of *any* people, yet the business relations between California and Asia will do more to liberalize and Christianize those countries than the labors of all the missionaries throughout China. The Chinese are quick to see, and ready to adopt, any custom or thing that promises improvement.

The practice of Chinese prostitution by their women is as abhorrent to their respectable merchants as it is to us. They have made several attempts to send these abandoned women home to China, but their efforts have been frustrated under the plea that this is a free country, and these women can do as they please. These women generally live in boats on the rivers in China, and arrange for the payment of their own passages to this State. No companies of Chinese merchants encourage the importation of women to California.

The evil exists to a far greater extent in China than here, and the respectable Chinese here would be glad to have the most stringent restrictions placed upon this degraded and abandoned class of persons. Your Committee refer to the following letter, to show how the Chinese of this city stand in regard to crimes and punishments:

San Francisco, March 5, 1862.

Hon. R. F. Perkins—*Dear Sir:* In accordance with your request, I herewith give you a statement of the convictions and forfeitures of bail in the Police Justice's Court during the year eighteen hundred and sixty-one, *not* including the twenty-four hours sentences for drunks, in which only one Chinaman appeared during the entire year.

Months.	Convictions.	Chinese.
January	195	5
February	187	24
March	204	8
April	209	7
May	233	14
June	181	8
July	204	7
August	166	5
September	228	6
October	356	15
November	355	21
December	265	48
Totals	2,783	168

Average of Chinese about one in sixteen. The twenty-four hours sentences, as above, average about one hundred and thirty per month. About three fourths of the Chinese convictions are women, (prostitutes,) arrested from the alleys about Jackson and Pacific streets.

Yours,

John H. Titcomb

Clerk Police Judge's Court.

Your Committee were furnished with a list of eighty-eight Chinamen who are known to have been murdered by white people, eleven of which number are known to have been murdered by Collectors of Foreign Miner's License Tax—sworn officers of the law. But two of the murderers have been convicted and hanged. Generally they have been allowed to escape without the slightest punishment.

The above number of Chinese who have been *robbed and murdered,* compose, probably, a very small proportion of those which have been murdered, but they are all which the records of the different societies or companies in this city show. It is a well known fact that there has been a wholesale system of wrong and outrage practised upon the Chinese population of this State, which would disgrace the most barbarous nation upon earth.

Our relations with China are constantly increasing. Our exports to China were—

In 1859	$252,000 00
In 1860	623,000 00
In 1861	712,000 00
Total	$1,587,000 00

One seventh of our entire exports, (other than treasure,) go to China. One nineteenth of all the tonnage engaged in coming to or going from our port, is in the China trade.

In 1861, entered from all parts of the world, tons	600,000
Cleared	434,000
Total tons entered and cleared	1,034,000

Vessels in the China Trade.	**Tons.**
Entered	28,286
Cleared	28,092
Total	56,378

Our present principal exports to China consist of abalones, grain, bread, fish, flour, lumber, potatoes, and quicksilver.

Treasure shipped in eighteen hundred and sixty-one amounted to three million five hundred and forty-one thousand, two hundred and seventy-nine dollars and seventeen cents. Nearly the whole of this sum was gold bars. Until recently the Chinese would receive nothing but silver. The Chinese merchants here have, by carefully selected remittances, brought gold to be preferred to silver. This change will save to our State one million five hundred thousand dollars, which is now paid for remittances, and greatly enhance the value of our gold product to the miner.

A number of our large steamers are now going to China to find profitable employment upon those rich and extensive rivers that have recently been opened to the commerce of the world. Ship and steamboat building and machinery will hereafter become a large item of yearly California export. Our shipments of lumber are largely on the increase.

Lumber Shipped.	Feet.
In 1858	263,963
In 1859	
In 1860	1,321,565
In 1861	963,982

Of quicksilver we shipped—

Years.	Flasks.	Amount.
In 1858	4,132	
In 1861	13,788	
At $30 per flask it amounts to		$413,640

This carrying business to and from China, (the safest business in the world,) is nearly all our own. No Chinese capital or labor is here employed.

We have arrive and depart, annually, about thirty ships in the regular China trade, and these ships disburse in this port, at each arrival, from five thousand to ten thousand dollars each, for repairs and refitting. The ship Dictator, now in port, will need to disburse, before leaving, about twenty-five thousand dollars. These amounts aggregate very considerably, and afford active employment to many ship and house carpenters, ship chandlers, riggers, sailmakers, painters, and other laborers.

In the interior, like advantages arise from Chinese residents. In some of the mining counties the Chinese, forming less than one tenth of the population, pay one fourth of the entire county tax. Has the reflection occurred, what these counties would do without this useful people?

Your Committee are under obligations to Mr. T. A. Mudge, U. S. Customs, for the following letter, kindly furnished us by him:

SAN FRANCISCO, March 10, 1862.

T. MUDGE, Esq., U. S. Customs:

Dear Sir:—In reference to our conversation, regarding the trade between this port and Hongkong, we have to say, that since the first of January of this year, we paid the following charter moneys to vessels consigned to us, viz:

Name of Vessel.	Charter Money.	Disbursed.
White Swallow	$11,000 00	$10,000 00
Dictator	13,000 00	8,000 00
Dictator, repairs		25,000 00
Mary Whitridge	13,000 00	7,000 00
Benefactor	8,000 00	5,000 00
Swordfish	12,000 00	6,000 00
Consigned to Messsrs. W. T. Coleman & Co.—		
Fortuna (about)	13,000 00	
Charger (about)	18,500 00	
Consigned to S. C. Cary—		
George Lee	10,000 00	
Consigned to Messrs. D. Gibb & Co.—		
Therese	6,000 00	
The disbursements of these four, say		24,000 00
We expect daily from Hongkong:		
Moonlight, (charter money payable here,)	13,000 00	
Jos. Peabody, (charter money payable here,)	26,000 00	
Daphne, (charter money payable here,)	24,000 00	
Bald Eagle, (charter money payable here,)	16,000 00	

The Bald Eagle, we are afraid, must have foundered, with all on board, as we have had no accounts of her since her sailing, on tenth November last.

We are, yours truly,
Koopmanschap & Co.

4.15
San Francisco, Cubic Air Ordinance, 1870

Regulating Lodging Houses [Approved July 29, 1870]

Section 1. Every house, room, or apartment within the limits of the City and County of San Francisco, except such public prisons and hospitals as may have been already erected, which shall be used or occupied as lodging house, room, or apartment, and every building, house, room, or apartment in which persons live or sleep, shall contain within the walls of such houses, rooms, or apartments, at least five hundred cubic feet for each adult person dwelling or sleeping therein: and every owner or tenant of any house, room, or apartment, who shall lodge, or permit to be lodged, in such house, room, or apartment more than one person to each five hundred cubic feet of air in such house, room, or apartment, shall be deemed guilty of a misdemeanor, and for every offense shall be fined not less than ten nor more than five hundred dollars, or imprisoned in the city prisons not less than five days nor more than three months, or both such fines and imprisonment.

Sec. 2. No person or persons shall lodge, dwell, sleep, or have their abode in any room, house, building, or apartment which shall not contain at least five hundred cubic feet of air each, and every person lodging, dwelling, sleeping, or having their place of abode therein: and any person or persons who shall violate any provision of this Section shall be deemed guilty of a misdemeanor and punished as provided in the first section of this Order.

Sec. 3. It shall be the duty of the Chief of Police to detail a competent and qualified officer of the regular police force to examine into and arrest for all violations of any of the provisions of this Order all persons who may be guilty thereof. (San Francisco Board of Supervisors, Order No. 939).

4.16

An Address to the People of the United States Upon the Evils of Chinese Immigration, 1877

Prepared by a Committee of the Senate of the State of California. April 3, 1976. *To the People of the United States, other than those of the State of California.*

Fellow-citizens: On the third day of April, eighteen hundred and seventy-six, in the Senate of the State of California, the Hon. Creed Haymond, Senator from the Eighteenth Senatorial District, offered the following resolutions, which were unanimously adopted:

> *Be it resolved by the Senate of the State of California,* That a committee of five Senators be appointed, with power to sit at any time or place within the State, and the said committee shall make inquiry:
>
> 1. As to the number of Chinese in this State, and the effect their presence has upon the social and political condition of the State.
>
> 2. As to the probable result of Chinese immigration upon the country, if such immigration be not discouraged.
>
> 3. As to the means of exclusion, if such committee should be of the opinion that the presence of the Chinese element in our midst is detrimental to the interests of the country.
>
> 4. As to such other matters as, in the judgment of the committee, have a bearing upon the question of Chinese immigration. And be it further
>
> *Resolved,* That said committee * * * shall prepare a memorial to the Congress of the United States, which memorial must set out at length the facts in relation to the subject of this inquiry, and such conclusions as the committee may have arrived at as to the policy and means of excluding Chinese from the country. And be it further
>
> *Resolved,* That said committee is authorized and directed to have printed, at the State Printing Office, a sufficient number of copies of such memorial, and of the testimony taken by said committee, to furnish copies thereof to the leading newspapers of the United States, five copies to each member of Congress, ten copies to the Governor of each State, and to deposit two thousand copies with the Secretary of State of California for general distribution. And be it further

Resolved, That such committee shall * * * furnish to the Governor of the State of California two copies of said memorial, properly engrossed, and the Governor, upon receipt thereof, be requested to transmit, through the proper channels, one of said copies to the Senate and the other to the House of Representatives of the United States. And be it further

Resolved, That said committee have full power to send for persons and papers, and to administer oaths, and examine witnesses under oath, and that a majority of said committee shall constitute a quorum.

* * * * * * * * * * * * *

Resolved, That said committee report to the Senate, at its next session, the proceedings had hereunder.

To the investigation with which we were charged—*quasi judicial* in its character, and in the unsettled state of the country of the highest importance—we addressed ourselves, having but one object in view, the ascertainment of truth.

All must admit that the safety of our institutions depends upon the homogeneity, culture, and moral character of our people. It is true that the Republic has invited the people of foreign countries to our borders, but the invitation was given with the well founded hope that they would, in time, by association with our people, and through the influence of our public schools, become assimilated to our native population.

The Chinese came without any special invitation. They came before we had time to consider the propriety of their admission to our country. If any one ever hoped they would assimilate with our people that hope has long since been dispelled.

The Chinese have now lived among us, in considerable numbers, for a quarter of a century, and yet they remain separate, distinct from, and antagonistic to our people in thinking, mode of life, in tastes and principles, and are as far from assimilation as when they first arrived.

They fail to comprehend our system of government; they perform no duties of citizenship; they are not available as jurymen, cannot be called upon as a *posse comitatus* to preserve order, nor be relied upon as soldiers.

They do not comprehend or appreciate our social ideas, and they contribute but little to the support of any of our institutions, public or private.

They bring no children with them, and there is, therefore, no possibility of influencing them by our ordinary educational appliances.

There is, indeed, no point of contact between the Chinese and our people through which we can Americanize them. The rigidity which characterizes these people forbids the hope of any essential change in their relations to our own people or our government.

We respectfully submit the admitted proposition that no nation much less a republic, can safely permit the presence of a large and increasing element among its people which cannot be assimilated or made to comprehend the responsibilities of citizenship.

Mr. Ellis, Chief of Police for San Francisco, testifies as follows: (Evidence, p. 112).

Q.—What are the difficulties in the way of enforcing laws in cases where the Chinese are concerned?

A.—The Chinese will swear to anything, according to orders. Their testimony is so unreliable that they cannot be believed.

Q.—What is the greatest difficulty in the way of suppressing prostitution and gambling?

A.—To suppress these views would require a police force so great that the city could not stand the expense. It is difficult to administer justice, because we do not understand their language, and thus all combine to defeat the laws.

Q.—What is their custom of settling cases among themselves, and then refusing to furnish testimony?

A.—It is generally believed to be true that the Chinese have a Court of arbitration where they settle differences.

Q.—After this settlement is made, is it possible to obtain testimony from the Chinese?

A.—If in secret they determine to convict a Chinaman, or to acquit him, that judgment is carried out. In a great many cases I believe they have convicted innocent men through perjured evidence.

Mr. Davis Louderback, for several years past Judge of the Police Court of San Francisco, testifies as follows: (Evidence, p. 93.)

Q.—What do you know about the habits, customs, and social and moral status of the Chinese population of this city?

A.—I think they are a very immoral, mean, mendacious, dishonest, thieving people, as a general thing.

Q.—What are the difficulties in the way of the administration of justice where they are concerned?

A.—As witnesses, their veracity is of the lowest degree. They do not appear to realize the sanctity of an oath, and it is difficult to enforce the laws, where they are concerned, for that reason. They are very apt, in all cases and under all circumstances to resort to perjury and the subornation of perjury. They also use our criminal law to revenge themselves upon their enemies, and malicious prosecutions are frequent.

Mr. Alfred Clark, for nineteen years past connected with the police force of San Francisco, and for the last eight years Clerk of the Chief of Police, testifies as follows: (Evidence, p. 63.)

In regard to the vice of prostitution, I have here a bill of sale of a Chinawoman, and a translation of the same.

Witness submits a paper written in Chinese characters, and rends the translation, as follows:

An agreement to assist the woman Ah Ho, because coming from China to San Francisco she became indebted to her mistress for passage. Ah Ho herself asks Mr. Yee Kwan to advance for her six hundred and thirty dollars, for which Ah Ho distinctly agrees to give her body to Mr. Yee for service of prostitution for a term of four years. There shall be no interest on the money. Ah Ho shall receive no wages. At the expiration of four years Ah Ho shall be her own master. Mr. Yee Kwan shall not hinder or trouble her. If Ah Ho runs away before her time is out, her mistress shall find her and return her, and whatever expense is incurred in finding and returning her, Ah Ho shall pay. On this day of agreement Ah Ho, with her own hands, has received from Mr. Yee Kwan six hundred and thirty dollars. If Ah Ho shall be sick at any time for more than ten days, she shall make up by an extra month of service for every ten days' sickness. Now this agreement has proof—this paper received by Ah Ho is witness.

TUNG CHEE.

Twelfth year, ninth month, and fourteenth day (about middle of October, eighteen hundred and seventy-three).

The Chinese women are kept in confinement more by fear than by anything else. They believe the contracts to be good and binding, and fear the consequences of any attempt at escape.

Chinese Prostitution

We now come to an aspect of the question more revolting still. We would shrink from the disgusting details did not a sense of duty demand that they be presented. Their lewd women induce, by the cheapness of their offers, thousands of boys and young men to enter their dens, very many of whom are innoculated with venereal diseases of the worst type. Boys of eight and ten years of age have been found with this disease, and some of our physicians treat a half dozen cases daily. The fact that these diseases have their origin chiefly among the Chinese is well established.

The Hon. W. J. Shaw, a distinguished citizen of this State, whose opportunities for investigation have been ample, declares (Evidence, p. 16): "That prostitution in China is not regarded as a disgrace, but is regarded as a profession or calling. That the condition of the lower classes is as near that of brutes as can be found in any human society.'' Indeed, the Chinese appear to have very little appreciation of the weaker sex. Says Mr. Shaw (Evidence, p. 16): ''It is no rare occurrence when a girl is born to place it on the street and abandon it to its fate.'' And, again, (Evidence, p. 19): ''The women in China occupy the same position as in most parts of Asia—virtually slaves; mere creatures, to pander to the wishes of the males, and promote their happiness.'' And Mr. Charles Wolcott Brooks, who, from his position, opportunities and ability, is high authority upon this topic, observes (Evidence, p. 42): ''That the population of China has been decreasing lately, caused, in a great measure, by the scarcity of women. They drown their females as we drown kittens.''

Mr. David C. Woods testifies as follows: (Evidence, p. 113).

Mr. Haymond—How long have you resided in this State?

A.—Twenty-five years, off and on.

Q.—What position do you hold?

A.—Superintendent of the Industrial School.

Q.—How long have you occupied that position?

A.—Two years and three months.

Q.—Do you know anything about the effect the presence of a large Chinese population has upon the boys that are growing up here?

A.—I think it has a very bad effect. I find that the larger proportion of boys who come to the school, large enough to cohabit with women, are afflicted with venereal diseases.

Q.—How many boys are usually in that school?

A.—One hundred and eighty, on an average.

Q.—What proportion do you think are affected with that disease?

A.—I think that, during the time I have been there, fifty have come with venereal diseases.

Q.—Do you attribute that to the presence of Chinese prostitutes in this city?

A.—They tell me so themselves. I question them, and they say they got it in Chinatown?

Q.—What are the ages of those boys?

A.—We have had them as young as thirteen, with gonorrhea: they have all sorts of venereal diseases. There is not time that I have had less than two or four down with them.

Mr. Karcher testifies as follows: (Evidence, p. 131.)

Wong Ben, a Chinaman in the service of the San Francisco police force, testifies as follows: (Evidence, p. 100.)

Q.—Who bring the Chinese women here?

A.—Wong Fook Soí, Bi Chee, An Geo, and Wong Woon.

Q.—What do these men do?

A.—They keep gambling-houses and houses of prostitution.

Q.—To what company do these men belong?

A.—An Geo belongs to the See-yup Company; Wong Woon to the Sam-yup Company. That fellow has got lots of money. He buys women in China for two hundred dollars or three hundred dollars, and brings them out here and sells them for eight hundred or nine hundred dollars, to be prostitutes.

Q.—How do they get those women in China?

A.—In Tartary. They are "big feet" women, and are sometimes bought for ninety dollars. When they bring them out here they sell them for nine hundred dollars.

Q.—What do they do with them?

A.—They make them be prostitutes. If they don't want to be prostitutes they make them be.

Q.—Can they get away?

A.—No, sir.

Q.—What do they do with them when they get sick and cannot work any longer?

A.—They don't treat them well at all. They don't take as much care of them, whether they are sick or well, as white people do a dog. Chinawomen in China are treated first rate, but in California these "big feet" women are treated worse than dogs.

Mr. Bovee testifies as follows: (Evidence, p. 108.)

Q.—Are these prostitutes bought and sold and held in bondage?

A.—Yes: that has always been my idea.

Q.—How do they treat their sick and helpless?

A.—I have seen them thrown out on the street and on the sidewalk, and I have seen them put into little rooms without light, bedding, or food. They were left to die.

Q.—What opportunities have these women to escape, if they should desire?

A.—I don't see that they have any at all, for where a woman escapes a reward is offered and she is brought back. Where they can get her in no other way they use our Courts.

Q.—Would boys be able to visit the houses of white prostitutes?

A.—They would not be so liable.

Q.—Why is that?

A.—The prices are higher, and boys of that age will not take the liberties with white women that they do in Chinatown. In addition to that, it can be said on behalf of the white women that they would not allow boys of ten, eleven, or fourteen years of age to enter their houses. No such cases have ever been reported to the police, while the instances where Chinese women have enticed these youths are very frequent. Some three years ago two boys, one thirteen and the other fifteen, were taken from a Chinese house of prostitution and brought to the stationhouse. One belonged here and the other to San Francisco. I met the San Francisco boy about a month afterwards, and found him suffering from a loathsome disease, which he said he contracted in that house.

Criminal Propensities of the Chinese

Mr. D. J. Murphy, District Attorney of San Francisco, testifies: (Evidence, p. 83.)

That from seven-tenths to eight-tenths of the Chinese population of San Francisco belong to the criminal classes.

Chief of Police Ellis testifies: (Evidence, p. 111.)

Q.—It is in testimony that there are about thirty thousand Chinese living in this city (San Francisco) the most of them residing in seven or eight blocks. Do you know what proportion of that population is criminal?

A.—I should say that there are about one thousand five hundred or two thousand regular criminals.

Q.—Including those who violate the city ordinances in relation to fires and health, and those who live off the wages of the criminal classes, what is the proportion?

A.—I think almost the entire population.

Q.—Excluding from consideration the Chinese quarter, how are the laws and ordinances enforced in this city, as compared with other American cities?

A.—Favorably.

Sanitary Aspects of the Subject

Senator Lewis, a member of this Committee, who made a personal inspection of the Chinese quarter of San Francisco, testifies as follows: (Evidence, p. 45.)

"We went into places so filthy and dirty I cannot see how these people lived there. The fumes of opium, mingled with the odor arising from filth and dirt, made rather a sickening feeling creep over us. I would not go through that quarter again for anything in the world. The whole Chinese quarter is miserably filthy, and I think that the passage of an ordinance removing them from the city, as a nuisance, would be justifiable. I do not understand why a pestilence has not ere this raged there. It is probably owing to the fact that this is one of the most healthy cities in the world. The houses would be unfit for the occupation of white people, for I do not see how it would be possible to cleanse them, unless you burn up the whole quarter, and even then I doubt whether you can get rid of the filth.''

The Influence of Chinese Upon Free Labor

We not call attention to an aspect of the subject of such huge proportions, and such practical and pressing importance, that we almost dread to enter upon its consideration, namely, the effect of Chinese labor upon our industrial classes. We admit that the Chinese were, in the earlier history of the State, when white labor was not attainable, very useful in the development of our peculiar industries; that they were of great service in railroad building, in mining, gardening, general agriculture, and as domestic servants.

We admit that the Chinese are exceedingly expert in all kinds of labor and manufacturing; that they are easily and inexpensively handled in large numbers.

We recognize the right of all men to better their condition when they can, and deeply sympathize with the overcrowded population of China.

But our own people are the original settlers of California, their children, and recent immigrants from the East and Europe. They cannot compete with Chinese labor, and are now suffering because of this inability. This inability does not arise out of any deficiency of skill or will, but out of a mode of life hitherto considered essential to our American civilization.

Our people have families, a condition considered of vast importance to our civilization, while the Chinese have not, or if they have families they need but little to support them in their native land.

Our laborers cannot be induced to live like vermin, as the Chinese, and these habits of individual and family life have ever been encouraged by our statesmen as essential to good morals.

Our laborers require meat and bread, which have been considered by us as necessary to that mental and bodily strength which is thought to be important in the citizens of a republic which depends upon the strength of its people, while the Chinese require only rice, dried fish, tea, and a few simple vegetables. The cost of sustenance to the whites is four-fold greater than that of the Chinese, and the wages of the whites must of necessity be greater than the wages required by the Chinese. The Chinese are, therefore, able to underbid the whites in every kind of labor. They can be hired in masses; they can be managed and controlled like unthinking slaves. But, our laborer has an individual life, cannot be controlled as a slave by brutal masters, and this individuality has been required of him by the genius of our institutions, and upon these elements of character the State depends for defense and growth.

Mr. Shaw (Evidence, pp. 18 and 19,) testifies:

Q.—How is the condition of the laboring men in China to be compared with the condition of those who are here?

A.—It is undoubtedly going from misery to comfort. The amount of destitution in China is very serious. Pekin, in my opinion, is one of the filthiest cities to be found. There is what is called a Chinese City of Pekin and a Tarter city. The Chinese city is filthy to a degree almost beyond belief. I have seen tricks perpetrated in the streets of Pekin proper that would only be tolerated in brutes in a civilized country. When I was there I wondered how ladies could go into the street at all, and I was told that they hardly ever did; that they never attempted to walk in the streets, but when compelled to go out used the conveyances of that country. When they wanted exercise they were carried to the walls of the city, where they could walk without seeing sights that would be disgusting. Those streets are filthy beyond what should ever be seen among human beings. The great mass of the people, it seemed to me, were ignorant, and not in a position to be removed from ignorance. They have, it is true, a system of education, but that system of education is confined to certain books, written four thousand years ago. They think there is no knowledge anywhere that is not found in those books, and, as a consequence, their learning, from the highest to the lowest, must be very limited, according to our ideas."

Rev. Mr. Loomis testifies as follows: (Evidence, pp. 54 and 55.)

Q.—What wages are received in China?

A.—I think from three to five dollars a month.

Q.—And board themselves?

A.—Well, I don't know about that. I think servants in Hongkong, Canton, and Maeao receive three dollars or four dollars a month, where they are employed in families. Then they board with the families, I think. On the farms they board themselves.

Q.—How much will it take to support the family of a laboring man in China, where he has a wife and two or three children?

A.—Three or four dollars a month. Some live on less than that. Everything is very cheap. A man who acquires three hundred dollars or four hundred dollars is rich—esteemed comfortably well off. There are large land-holders and heavy merchants there who are very wealthy.

Mr. Altemeyer testifies: (Evidence, p. 51.)

Q.—Is the employment of Chinese labor here detrimental to the employment of white labor?

A.—Yes, sir: there is not question but that it keeps white men from coming here, while those who are here can not get work.

Q.—Is it not true that the lighter branches of trade and manufacturers, which in other places are filled by boys, are here filled by the Chinese?

A.—Yes, sir.

Q.—This deprives both boys and girls of occupations?

A.—Yes, sir.

Q.—Are they skillful?

A.—They are quick at imitation. They learn soon by looking on. Then they go off in business for themselves. For business men to employ Chinese, is simply putting nails in their coffins. Every Chinaman employed will be a competitor. The result must be the driving from the country of white business men and white laborers. White laborers could not live as they do, and the result would be a ruinous competition for the whites. The Chinese merchant can live as much cheaper than the white merchant as can the Chinese laborer live cheaper than the white laborer. When such a thing gets full headway the whites will be displaced. I have made this thing a very careful study, and my experience teaches me that these views are correct?

Mr. Duffy testifies as follows: (Evidence, pp. 125 and 126.)

Q.—Why can they (the Chinese) afford to do work cheaper than white men?

A.—They can work cheaper than the white man, because they have no families to support, and therefore live much cheaper. Their living does not cost them over fifteen cents per day. Take a laboring man here who has a wife and two children dependent upon him, and his expenses at the very least are two dollars and fifty cents a day, and he must live very economically to make that amount do. Where a laboring man has no family, his necessary expenses will be from one dollar and seventy-five cents to two dollars a day. He can board for twenty dollars a month, and his washing, clothing, etc., will make up the balance. Most of the Chinese here wear clothes of Chinese manufacture, consume goods imported from China, and all their dealings are against the American interests. Where they do not board themselves, they can be accommodated—boarded and lodged—at houses in Chinatown for one dollar and fifty cents a week, and less.

Loss to the Country from this Immigration

The effect of this immigration is to prevent that of a more desirable class. There, again, in the mere matter of dollars and cents, the country at large is loser. These people bring no money with them, while it is assumed, on the most credible evidence, that one hundred dollars at least is the average amount in possession of each European immigrant. A well known social economist estimates the capital value of every laborer that comes from Europe and settles in this country at fifteen hundred dollars. This value rests upon the fact that such laborer makes this country his home, creates values, and contributes to the support of the nation. The Chinese laborer, on the contrary, makes a draft upon the wealth of the nation; takes from instead of adding to its substance. Not less than one hundred and eighty million dollars in gold have been abstracted from this State alone by Chinese laborers, while they have contributed nothing to the State or national wealth.

Given in place of one hundred and twenty-five thousand Chinese laborers the same number of male European immigrants, and the result may be stated in figures, as follows:

Amount of money brought into the country, $100 each	$ 12,500,000
Capital value of 125,000 European male laborers, at $1,500 each	187,500,000
Add gold abstracted by Chinese laborers	180,000,000
	$380,000,000

Thus, it is beyond question that, from a purely financial point of view, the United States is loser nearly four hundred millions of dollars by Chinese immigration—a sum which, if distributed throughout the country, now would go far toward alleviating present want and misery.

If it was true that no real objection existed to the presence of a large Chinese population, if it was true that the wrong and injury to the whites existed only in the imagination of the people of this country, even then we would insist that this immigration be restricted. This is a republic, dependent for its existence, not upon force, but upon the will and consent of the people, upon their satisfaction with the government. When that satisfaction ceases, will and consent will be withdrawn. Therefore, it behooves the representatives of the people, charged, in part, with the administration of that government, to wisely consider not only real, but fancied causes of dissatisfaction. If it be found that the presence of the Chinese element is a constant source of irritation and annoyance to our people, that it is not here to assimilate and become part of the body politic, that no good, or but little, results from its presence, it does seem that the mere dissatisfaction of the people with its presence should be cause for grave concern on the part of the government.

Commercial Relations Will Not Be Affected by Restriction

But it is said that action on our part, tending to restrict Chinese immigration, would redound to the injury of commercial relations with that Empire. There is not the slightest foundation, in fact, for any such notion. The Government of China is opposed to the immigration. All of the witnesses agree upon this point.

The people of the Eastern States of the Union may not at present directly suffer from competition with these people, but they cannot but be sensible that State lines constitute no barrier to the movement of the Chinese—that as soon as the Pacific States are filled with this population it will overflow upon them. The Chinese Empire could spare a population far in excess of the population of the United States, and not feel the loss. Unless this influx of Chinese is prevented all the horrors of the immigration will in a few years be brought home to the people of the Eastern States. While the States east of the Mississippi do not directly feel the effects of Chinese immigration they are indirectly affected by it. The eastern manufacturer, for instance, of coarse boots and shoes, is driven out of the California market. He finds it stocked with the products of Chinese labor. The profits that would accrue to the manufacturer in the east, and his employés, have been diverted, and flow in a steady stream to China.

The Unarmed Invasion

Already, to the minds of many, this immigration begins to assume the nature and proportions of a dangerous unarmed invasion of our soil. Twenty years of increasing Chinese immigration will occupy the entire Pacific Coast to the exclusion of the white population. Many of our people are confident that the whole coast is yet to become a mere colony of China. All the old empires have been conquered by armed invasions, but North and South America, and the Continent of Australia, have been conquered and wrested from their native inhabitants by peaceable, unarmed invasions. Nor is this fear entirely groundless as to the Pacific Coast, for it is in keeping with the principles which govern the changes of modern dynasties, and the advance guard is already upon our shores. The immigration which is needed to offset and balance that from China is retarded by the condition of the labor question on this coast, and we have reason to expect that within ten years the Chinese will equal in number the whites. In view of these facts thousands of our people are beginning to feel a settled exasperation—a profound sense of dissatisfaction with the situation. Hitherto this feeling has been restrained, and the Chinese have had the full protection of our laws. It may be true that, at rare intervals, acts of violence have been committed toward them; but it is also true that punishment has swiftly followed. Our city criminal courts invariably inflict a severer punishment for offenses committed upon Chinese than for like offenses committed against whites. The people of this State have been more than patient—we are satisfied that the condition of affairs, as they exist in San Francisco, would not be tolerated without a resort to violence in any eastern city. It is the part of wisdom to anticipate the day when patience may cease, and by wise legislation avert its evils. Impending difficulties of this character should not, in this advanced age, be left to the chance arbitrament of force. These are questions which ought to be solved by the statesman and philanthropist and not by the soldier.

Adopted at a meeting of the Committee held in the City of San Francisco, August 13th, 1877.

Creed Haymond, Chairman.

Attest: Frank Shay, Secretary.

4.17
Constitution of the State of California, Article XIX, 1879

Topical Introduction

By the late 1870s, the anti-Chinese movement possessed widespread support throughout California. With some Chinese immigrants moving into manufacturing and farming, non-working class white Californians could feel the pinch of economic competition. While probably no less prejudiced than white workers, the white middle and upper class could always say before that Chinese immigration was good for business. Now, more and more of them were far less certain. One of the consequences of the popularity of the anti-Chinese movement can be found in these racist provisions written into the second California Constitution enacted in 1879.

Section 1. The Legislature shall prescribe all necessary regulations for the protection of the State, and the counties, cities, and towns thereof, from the burdens and evils arising from the presence of aliens, who are or may become vagrants, paupers, mendicants, criminals, or invalids afflicted with contagious or infectious diseases, and from aliens otherwise dangerous or detrimental to the well-being or peace of the State, and to impose conditions upon which such persons may reside in the State, and to provide means and mode of their removal from the State upon failure or refusal to comply with such conditions; provided, that nothing contained in this section shall be construed to impair or limit the power of the Legislature to pass such police laws or other regulations as it may deem necessary.

Section 2. No corporation now existing or hereafter formed under the laws of this State, shall, after the adoption of this Constitution, employ, directly or indirectly, in any capacity, any Chinese or Mongolian. The Legislature shall pass such laws as may be necessary to enforce this provision.

Section 3. No Chinese shall be employed on any State, county, municipal, or other public work, except in punishment for crime.

Section 4. The presence of foreigners ineligible to become citizens of the United States is declared to be dangerous to the well-being of the State, and the Legislature shall discourage their immigration by all the means within its power. Asiatic coolieism is a form of human slavery, and is forever prohibited in this State; and all contracts for coolie labor shall be void. All companies or corporations, whether formed in this country or any foreign country, for the importation of such labor, shall be subject to such penalties as the Legislature may prescribe. The Legislature shall delegate all necessary power to the incorporated cities and towns of this State for the removal of Chinese without the limits of such cities and towns, or for their location within prescribed portions of those limits; and it shall also provide the necessary legislation to prohibit the introduction into this State of Chinese after the adoption of this Constitution. This section shall be enforced by appropriate legislation.

4.18
Henry George
Henry George and the
Workingmen's Party of California

Topical Introduction

The Workingmen's Party of California emerged during the late 1870s; a time when California was suffering from a severe economic downturn and like much of the rest of the nation was seeing a growth in bitter class conflict. In a vacant lot (the sand lot) near what is now San Francisco city hall, unemployed and various other San Franciscans would gather on Sunday to listen to speeches, typically condemning the Monopolists and the Chinese for the problems besetting Euroamerican working people. One speaker, in particular, caught the imagination of aggrieved San Franciscans; an Irish teamster by the name of Denis Kearney. Eventually, Kearney would rise to the leadership of the party that was formed out of those sand lot meetings—the Workingmen's Party of California. And Kearneyism, a mixture of heated attacks on the wealthy and their supposed Chinese tools, was seen by some Californians as a new and diabolical form of Communism.

Radical social critic and political economist, Henry George knew better. A one time supporter of the anti-Chinese movement, George sympathized with the grievances felt by many Californian working people. However, by the1870s, he seemed aware that the Workingmen's Party of California was spending too much time worrying about the Chinese and not enough time seeking to understand the root cause of unemployment and poverty; the unequal distribution of land and political power among Californians and Americans in general. Below are excerpts from an article he wrote for Popular Science Monthly. Henry George, "The Kearney Agitation in California," *Popular Science Monthly,* vol. 17 (August, 1880), 435, 436, 442, 443.

———————

Contrary, too, to the reputation which she seems to have got, San Francisco is really an orderly city. Although the police force has been doubled within the past two years, it still bears a smaller proportion to population than in other large American cities. Chinamen go about the streets with far more security than I imagine they will go about any

Eastern city when they become proportionately as numerous; and, after all said of hoodlumism, there is little obtrusive rowdyism and few street fights—a fact which may in part result from the once universal practice of carrying arms.

Nor has communism or socialism (understanding by these terms the desire for fundamental social changes) made, up to this time, much progress in California, for the presence of the Chinese has largely engrossed the attention of the laboring classes, offering what has seemed to them a sufficient explanation of the fall of wages and difficulty of finding employment. Only the more thoughtful have heeded the fact that in other parts of the world where there are no Chinamen the condition of the laboring classes is even worse than in California. With the masses the obvious evils of Chinese competition have excluded all thought of anything else. And in this anti-Chinese feeling there is, of course, nothing that can properly be deemed socialistic or communistic. On the contrary, socialists and communists are more tolerant of the Chinese than any other class of those who feel or are threatened by their competition. For not only is there, at the bottom of what is called socialism and communism, the great idea of the equality and brotherhood of men, but they who look to changes in the fundamental institutions of society as the only means for improving the condition of the masses necessarily regard Chinese immigration as a minor evil, if in a proper social state it could be any evil at all. Nor is there in this anti-Chinese feeling anything essentially foreign. Those who talk about opposition to the Chinese being anti-American shut their eyes to a great many facts if they mean anything more than that it *ought* to be anti-American.

In short, I am unable to see, in the conditions from which this agitation sprang, anything really peculiar to California. I can not regard the anti-Chinese sentiment as really peculiar, because it must soon arise in the East should Chinese immigration continue; and because, in the connection in which we are considering it, its nature and effects do not materially differ from those which elsewhere are aroused by other causes. The main fact which underlies all this agitation is popular discontent; and, where there is popular discontent, if there is not one Jonah, another will be found. Thus, over and over again, popular discontent has fixed upon the Jews, and among ourselves there is a large class who make the "ignorant foreigner" the same sort of a scapegoat for all political demoralization and corruption.

There has been in California growing social and political discontent, but the main causes of this do not materially differ from those which elsewhere exist. Some of the factors of discontent may have attained greater development in California than in older sections, but I am inclined to think this is merely because in the newer States general tendencies are quicker seen. For instance, the concentration of the

whole railroad system in the hands of one close corporation is remarkable in California, but there is clearly a general tendency to such
concentration, which is year by year steadily uniting railroad manage-
ment all over the country.

The "grand culture" of machine-worked fields, which calls for
large gangs of men at certain seasons, setting them adrift when the
crop is gathered, and which is so largely instrumental in filling San
Francisco every winter with unemployed men, is certainly the form to
which American agriculture generally tends, and is developing in the
new Northwest even more rapidly than in California.

Nor yet am I sure that the characteristics of the press, to which San
Franciscans largely attribute this agitation, are not characteristics to
which the newspaper press generally tends. Certain it is that the development of the newspaper is in a direction which makes it less and
less the exponent of ideas and advocate of principles, and more and
more a machine for money-making.

These impotent attempts at repression produced their natural result.
The new party was fairly started, brought into prominence and importance by the intemperance which had sought to crush it.

The feeling on the Chinese question has long been so strong in
California as to give certain victory to any party that could fully util-
ize it. But the difficulty in the way of making political capital of this
feeling has been to get resistance, since all parties were willing to
take the strongest anti-Chinese ground. But the fear that the agitators
had evidently inspired, the effort to put them down, served as such
resistance; and, though all parties were anti-Chinese, the party they
were endeavoring to start became at once *the* anti-Chinese party in the
eyes of those who were bitterest and strongest in their feeling, while
it at the same time became an expression, though rudely and vaguely,
of all sorts of discontent. It was evident that it would be a political
power for at least one election. The lower strata of ward politicians
went rushing into it as a good chance for office; the "Chronicle,"
which, at the first symptom of reaction, had redoubled its services,
placarded the State with resolutions of the new party asking workingmen to stop the "Call." That paper, losing heavily in subscribers,
quietly began to outdo the "Chronicle" in its reports and its puffery.
Other papers, recognized as organs of interests popularly regarded
with dislike, did their utmost by denunciation to keep Kearney in the
foreground.

Kearney had quickly come to the head of the movement, changing
his first place of secretary for that of president shortly after taking to
the sand-lot, and having, by the time he and his companions emerged
from jail in triumph, got so well to the head as to become in the
popular eye its representative and embodiment. He showed great address in keeping the place. The organization which he managed to

give the new party was admirably designed for this purpose. The weekly assemblage on the sand-lot, where anybody could shout and vote, was recognized as the great parliament and plebiscitum, and in the State conventions, in which the country as well as the city clubs were represented, the supremacy of the city clubs was provided for by the interdiction of proxies. As president of the party (something new in American politics, but an idea probably borrowed from the Committee of Public Safety), Kearney was anything but a mere figurehead. He has seemed to see, as clearly as any philosophical student of history has seen, the true spring and foundation of arbitrary power— the connection between Caesar and the proletariate.

He appeared on all occasions in rough working-dress; he announced that he would take no office, but, as soon as he had led the people to a victory, he would go back to his dray, and must in the mean time be supported by collections, for which he passed around the hat at every meeting. These things, the style of his oratory, the prominence he had attained, his energy, tact, and temperance, gave him command of that floating element which will travel around to the most meetings and do the loudest shouting. And, commanding this, he commanded his party.

4.19
Chinese Exclusion Act of 1882

CHAP. 126.—An Act to Execute Certain Treaty Stipulations Relating to Chinese

Whereas, in the opinion of the Government of the United States the coming of Chinese laborers to this country endangers the good order of certain localities within the territory thereof: Therefore,

Be it enacted by the Senate and House of Representatives of the United States of America in Congress assembled, That from and after the expiration of ninety days next after the passage of this act, and until the expiration of ten years next after the passage of this act, the coming of Chinese laborers to the United States be, and the same is hereby, suspended; and during such suspension it shall not be lawful for any Chinese laborer to come, or, having so come after the expiration of said ninety days, to remain with the United States.

Sec. 2. That the master of any vessel who shall knowingly bring within the United States on such vessel, and land or permit to be landed, any Chinese laborer, from any foreign port or place, shall be deemed guilty of a misdemeanor, and on conviction thereof shall be punished by a fine of not more than five hundred dollars for each and every such Chinese laborer so brought, and may be also imprisoned for a term not exceeding one year.

Sec. 3. That the two foregoing sections shall not apply to Chinese laborers who were in the United States on the seventeenth day of November, eighteen hundred and eighty, or who shall have come into the same before the expiration of ninety days next after the passage of this act, and who shall produce to such master before going on board such vessel, and shall produce to the collector of the port in the United States at which such vessel shall arrive, the evidence hereinafter in this act required of his being one of the laborers in this section mentioned; nor shall the two foregoing sections apply to the case of any master whose vessel, being bound to a port not within the United States, shall come within the jurisdiction of the United States by reason of being in distress or in stress of weather, or touching at any port of the United States on its voyage to any foreign port or place: *Provided,* That all Chinese laborers brought on such vessel shall depart with the vessel on leaving port.

Sec 4. That for the purpose of properly identifying Chinese laborers who were in the United States on the seventeenth day of November, eighteen hundred and eighty, or who shall have come into the same before the expiration of ninety days next after the passage of this act, and in order to furnish them with the proper evidence of their right to go from and come to the United States of their free will and accord, as provided by the treaty between the United States and China dated November seventeenth, eighteen hundred and eighty, the collector of customs of the district from which any such Chinese laborer shall depart from the United States shall, in person or by deputy, go on board each vessel having on board any such Chinese laborer and cleared or about to sail from his district for a foreign port, and on such vessel make a list of all such Chinese laborers, which shall be entered in registry-books to be kept for that purpose, in which shall be stated the name, age, occupation, last place of residence, physical marks or peculiarities, and all facts necessary for the identification of each of such Chinese laborers which books shall be safely kept in the custom-house; and every such Chinese laborer so departing from the United States shall be entitled to, and shall receive, free of any charge or cost upon application therefor, from the collector or his deputy, at the same such list is taken, a certificate, signed by the collector or his deputy and attested by his seal of office, in such form as the Secretary of the Treasury shall prescribe, which certificate shall contain a statement of the name, age, occupation, last place of residence, personal description, and facts of identification of the Chinese laborer to whom the certificate is issued, corresponding with the said list and registry in all particulars. In case any Chinese laborer after having received such certificate shall leave such vessel before her departure he shall deliver his certificate to the master of the vessel, and if such Chinese laborer shall fail to return to such vessel before her departure from port the certificate shall be delivered by the master to the collector of customs for cancellation. The certificate herein provided for shall entitle the Chinese laborer to whom the same is issued to return to and re-enter the United States upon producing and delivering the same to the collector of customs of the district at which such Chinese laborer shall seek to re-enter; and upon delivery of such certificate by such Chinese laborer to the collector of customs at the time of re-entry in the United States, said collector shall cause the same to be filed in the custom-house and duly canceled.

Sec. 5. That any Chinese laborer mentioned in section four of this act being in the United States, and desiring to depart from the United States by land, shall have the right to demand and receive, free of charge or cost, a certificate of identification similar to that provided for in section four of this act to be issued to such Chinese laborers as may desire to leave the United States by water; and it is hereby made the duty of the collector of customs of the district next adjoining the foreign country to which said Chinese laborer desires to go to issue such certificate, free of charge or cost, upon application by such Chinese laborer, and to enter the same upon registry-books to be kept by him for the purpose, as provided for in section four of this act.

Sec. 6. That in order to the faithful execution of articles one and two of the treaty in this act before mentioned, every Chinese person other than a laborer who may be entitled by said treaty and this act to come within the United States, and who shall be about to come to the United States, shall be identified as so entitled by the Chinese Government in each case, such identity to be evidenced by a certificate issued under the authority of said government, which certificate shall be in the English language or (if not in the English language) accompanied by a translation into English, stating such right to come, and which certificate shall state the name, title, or official rank, if any, the age, height, and all physical peculiarities, former and present occupation or profession, and place of residence in China of the person to whom the certificate is issued and that such person is entitled conformably to the treaty in this act mentioned to come within the United States. Such certificate shall be prima-facie evidence of the fact set forth therein, and shall be produced to the collector of customs, or his deputy, of the port in the district in the United States at which the person named therein shall arrive.

Sec. 7. That any person who shall knowingly and falsely alter or substitute any name for the name written in such certificate or forge any such certificate, or knowingly utter any forged or fraudulent certificate, or falsely personate any person named in any such certificate, shall be deemed guilty of a misdemeanor; and upon conviction thereof shall be fined in a sum not exceeding one thousand dollars, and imprisoned in a penitentiary for a term of not more than five years.

Sec. 8. That the master of any vessel arriving in the United States from any foreign port or place shall, at the same time he delivers a manifest of the cargo, and if there be no cargo, then at the time of making a report of the entry of the vessel pursuant to law, in addition to the other matter required to be reported, and before landing, or permitting to land, any Chinese passengers, deliver and report to the collector of customs of the district in which such vessels shall have arrived a separate list of all Chinese passengers taken on board his vessel at any foreign port or place, and all such passengers on board the vessel at that time. Such list shall show the names of such passengers (and if accredited officers of the Chinese Government traveling on the business of that government, or their servants, with a note of such facts), and the names and other particulars, as shown by their respective certificates; and such list shall be sworn to by the master in the manner required by law in relation to the manifest of the cargo. Any willful refusal or neglect of any such master to comply with the provisions of this section shall incur the same penalties and forfeiture as are provided for a refusal or neglect to report and deliver a manifest of the cargo.

Sec. 9. That before any Chinese passengers are landed from any such vessel, the collector, or his deputy, shall proceed to examine such passengers, comparing the certificates with the list and with the passengers; and no passenger shall be allowed to land in the United States from such vessel in violation of law.

Sec. 10. That every vessel whose master shall knowingly violate any of the provisions of this act shall be deemed forfeited to the United States, and shall be liable to seizure and condemnation in any district of the United States into which such vessel may enter or in which she may be found.

Sec. 11. That any person who shall knowingly bring into or cause to be brought into the United States by land, or who shall knowingly aid or abet the same, or aid or abet the landing in the United States from any vessel of any Chinese person not lawfully entitled to enter the United States, shall be deemed guilty of a misdemeanor, and shall, on conviction thereof, be fined in a sum not exceeding one thousand dollars, and imprisoned for a term not exceeding one year.

Sec. 12. That no Chinese person shall be permitted to enter the United States by land without producing to the proper officer of customs the certificate in this act required of Chinese persons seeking to land from a vessel. And any Chinese person found unlawfully within the United States shall be caused to be removed therefrom to the country from whence he came, by direction of the President of the United States, and at the cost of the United States, after being brought before some justice, judge, or commissioner of a court of the United States and found to be one not lawfully entitled to be or remain in the United States.

Sec. 13. That this act shall not apply to diplomatic and other officers of the Chinese Government traveling upon the business of that government, whose credentials shall be taken as equivalent to the certificate in this act mentioned, and shall exempt them and their body and household servants from the provisions of this act as to other Chinese persons.

Sec. 14. That hereafter no State court or court of the United States shall admit Chinese to citizenship; and all laws in conflict with this act are hereby repealed.

Sec. 15. That the words "Chinese laborers", wherever used in this act, shall be construed to mean both skilled and unskilled laborers and Chinese employed in mining.

Approved, May 6, 1882.

CHAP. 60.—An Act to Prohibit the Coming of Chinese Persons into the United States

Be it enacted by the Senate and House of Representatives of the United States of America in Congress assembled, That all laws now in force prohibiting and regulating the coming into this country of Chinese persons and persons of Chinese descent are hereby continued in force for a period of ten years from the passage of this act.

Sec. 2. That any Chinese person or person of Chinese descent, when convicted and adjudged under any of said laws to be not lawfully entitled to be or remain in the United States, shall be removed from the United States to China, unless he or they shall make it appear to the justice, judge, or commissioner before whom he or they are tried that he or they are subjects or citizens of some other country, in which case he or they shall be removed from the United States to such country: *Provided,* That in any case where such other country of which such Chinese person shall claim to be a citizen or subject shall demand any tax as a condition of the removal of such person to that country, he or she shall be removed to China.

Sec. 3. That any Chinese person or person of Chinese descent arrested under the provisions of this act or the acts hereby extended shall be adjudged to be unlawfully within the United States unless such person shall establish, by affirmative proof, to the satisfaction of such justice, judge, or commissioner, his lawful right to remain in the United States.

Sec. 4. That any such Chinese person or person of Chinese descent convicted and adjudged to be not lawfully entitled to be or remain in the United States shall be imprisoned at hard labor for a period of not exceeding one year and thereafter removed from the United States, as hereinbefore provided.

Sec. 5. That after the passage of this act on an application to any judge or court of the United States in the first instance for a writ of habeas corpus, by a Chinese person seeking to land in the United States, to whom that privilege has been denied, no bail shall be allowed, and such application shall be heard and determined promptly without unnecessary delay.

Sec. 6. And it shall be the duty of all Chinese laborers within the limits of the United States, at the time of the passage of this act, and who are entitled to remain in the United States, to apply to the collector of internal revenue of their respective districts, within one year after the passage of this act, for a certificate of residence, and any Chinese laborer, within the limits of the United States, who shall neglect, fail, or refuse to comply with the provisions of this act, or who, after one year from the passage hereof, shall be found within the jurisdiction of the United States without such certificate of residence, shall be deemed and adjudged to be unlawfully within the United States, and may be arrested, by any United States customs official, collector of internal revenue or his deputies, United States marshal or his deputies, and taken before a United States judge, whose duty it shall be to order that he be deported from the United States as hereinbefore provided, unless he shall establish clearly to the satisfaction of said judge, that by reason of accident, sickness or other unavoidable cause, he has been unable to procure his certificate, and to the satisfaction of the court, and by at least one credible white witness, that he was a resident of the United States at the time of the passage of this act; and if upon the hearing, it shall appear that he is so entitled to a certificate, it shall be granted upon his paying the cost. Should it appear that said Chinaman had procured a certificate which has been lost or destroyed, he shall be detained and judgment suspended a reasonable time to enable him to procure a duplicate from the officer granting it, and in such cases, the cost of said arrest and trial shall be in the discretion of the court. And any Chinese person other than a Chinese laborer, having a right to be and remain in the United States, desiring such certificate as evidence of such right may apply for and receive the same without charge.

Sec. 7. That immediately after the passage of this act, the Secretary of the Treasury shall make such rules and regulations as may be necessary for the efficient execution of this act, and shall prescribe the necessary forms and furnish the necessary blanks to enable collectors of internal revenue to issue the certificates required hereby, and make such provisions that certificates may be procured in localities convenient to the applicants, such certificates shall be issued without charge to the applicant, and shall contain the name, age, local residence and occupation of the applicant, and such other description of the applicant as shall be prescribed by the Secretary of the Treasury, and a duplicate thereof shall be filed in the office of the collector of internal revenue for the district within which such Chinaman makes application.

Sec. 8. That any person who shall knowingly and falsely alter or substitute any name for the name written in such certificate or forge such certificate, or knowingly utter any forged or fraudulent certificate, or falsely personate any person named in such certificate, shall be guilty of a misdemeanor, and upon conviction thereof shall be fined in a sum not exceeding one thousand dollars or imprisoned in the penitentiary for a term of not more than five years.

Sec. 9. The Secretary of the Treasury may authorize the payment of such compensation in the nature of fees to the collectors of internal revenue, for services performed under the provisions of this act in addition to salaries now allowed by law, as he shall deem necessary, not exceeding the sum of one dollar for each certificate issued.

Approved, May 5, 1892.

Responses to
Anti-Asian Sentiment

Part 5. Responses to Anti-Asian Sentiment

5.1.   Lai Chun-Chuen. Remarks of the Chinese Merchants of San Francisco upon Governor Bigler's Address, 1855

5.2.   Norman Asing. "To His Excellency Governor Bigler"

5.3.   Reverend William Speer. Plea in Behalf of the Immigrants from China

5.4.   A Reply to the Charges Against the Chinese

5.5.   Joel Franks. Chinese Shoemaker Protest in 19th Century San Francisco

A number of individuals, organizations, and groups did speak out against the anti-Chinese attitudes of the times. Reverend William Speer in defending the Chinese in the 1850s perpetuates stereotypes of the Chinese as a "heathen" and strange. Speer argues that the Chinese are a godsend in being an available force for the development of the West Coast and a people who will work at meager wages.

San Francisco Chinese merchants challenged California politicians generalizations, such as that of Governor Bigler's, that the Chinese were "coolies." The Chinese merchants voicing their objections of the violence and prejudice which had been directed against the Chinese asked for a definite date for the exclusion of Chinese exclusion so that adequate preparations could be made. Also, Chinese immigrants such as Noman Asing were outspoken in challenging the prevailing stereotypes of the Chinese, asserting that China has had a rich civilization which far preceded that of America's.

Reverend Speer addresses the attempt by the State of California to regulate or limit Chinese miners. In doing so, he argues that because California is advantageously situated to exploit the trade in Asia and because the Chinese can be a source of cheap labor to be utilized in growing cotton in California, the Chinese should be encouraged rather than discouraged in immigrating to California. Speer points out that there are Chinese who fit the stereotype of being lowly and degraded, but there are others who have the highest moral character and are an economic benefit to the state.

An interesting statement was prepared by representatives of the Chinese Six Companies, "The Other Side of the Chinese Question in California: Or A Reply to the Charges Against the Chinese," to send to President Ulysses S. Grant. The statement addressed widely held attitudes of the Chinese: that the Chinese will become a numerical majority; that Chinese laborers are "unfair" competition for jobs with white workers; that the Chinese work but do not contribute to the economy by spending their money in the United States; that the Chinese are "coolie" labor; and that the Chinese are "heathens." The statement protests the continual violation of the civil rights of the Chinese. The statement is an appeal to President Grant to take leadership in resolving the racial conflict on the West Coast since existing treaties between China and the United States protects the rights of the Chinese in America.

Joel Frank's selection on the Chinese Shoemaker Protest addresses active protest and resistance to adverse working conditions.

5.1

Lai Chun-Chuen

Remarks of the Chinese Merchants of San Francisco upon Governor Bigler's Address, 1855

Notice

The ensuing "Remarks upon Gov. Bigler's Message," was written in his own language by LAI CHUN CHUEN, a Chinese merchant of this city, connected with the respectable firm of CHAI LUNG. It was prepared in behalf of the subscribers to the *Hak-sheung Ui-kun,* or "Chinese Merchants Exchange," with which are connected their most influential and intelligent men. It has been rendered into English, paragraph for paragraph, and sentence for sentence, in the same order, and with no more variation from the style and idiom of the original, than the rules of good translation require.

The articles on the Companies have been prepared from facts carefully collected from responsible men connected with them, for the purpose of explaining to the American people their true nature. The mistaken notions, that they are commercial associations, that they have been engaged in the importation of laborers, and that the majority of the Chinese are "coolies," by which is meant a sort of peons or slaves of a degraded caste, working for the benefit of others, have done more than all others causes to bring these immigrants into disrepute, and to involve them in difficulties in the mining sections. Three years ago, in the famous two letters to Gov. Bigler, which excited both mirth and sympathy all over the land, the Chinese said "We assure you solemnly that we do not believe that there are any Chinese coolies in this country, who have bound themselves to serve for fixed wages, and who have given their families as pledges to their employers that they would fulfil their contracts. The Chinese in this country are not serfs or slaves of any description, but are working for themselves." This statement we believe to be true.

For the facts gathered in these articles we ask a candid consideration.

5.2
Norman Asing
"To His Excellency Governor Bigler"

Remarks on Gov. Bigler's Message

To His Excellency Gov. Bigler, and to the Legislature, and the People, of the State of California.

The committee of the Chinese Merchants of San Francisco desire to present, for your consideration, the following respectful representation:—

We have read the message of the Governor.

Firstly—It is stated that "too large a number of the men of the Flowery Kingdom have emigrated to this country, and that they have come alone, without their families." We may state among the reasons for this that the wives and families of the better families of China have generally compressed feet; they live in the utmost privacy; they are unused to winds and waves; and it is exceedingly difficult to bring families upon distant journeys over great oceans. Yet a few have come; nor are they all. And further, there have been several injunctions warning the people of the Flowery land not to come here, which have fostered doubts; nor have our hearts found peace in regard to bringing families. Suppose you say, "we will restrain only those who work in the mines; we would not forbid merchants," it is replied, that the merchandize imported by Chinese merchants chiefly depends upon Chinese consumption. If there be no Chinese miners allowed, what business can we have to do? The occupations are mutually dependent, like tooth and lip; neither can spare the other.

It is, we are assured, the principle of your honorable country to protect the people; and it has benevolence to mankind at heart. Now, the natives of China, or of any strange country, have one nature. All consider that good and evil cannot be in unison. All nations are really the same. Confucius says: "Though a city had but ten houses, there must be some in it honest and true." Suppose then we see it declared that "the people of the Flowery land are altogether without good," we can not but fear that the rulers do not exercise a liberal public spirit, and that they defer their own knowledge of right to an undue desire to please men.

It is said, that "of the Chinese who understand your language and laws, the number is very small; and that we have no community of feeling with you." Now those who trade in our native cities with your honorable merchants did understand your language, and were acquainted with your customs. But suppose villagers, from everywhere, emigrate, most of whom do not know your speech; and that pleasant intercourse should thus be as it were intercepted; that though the heart desires, the expressions will not flow; that though the teeth be unclosed, still the proper words are not released; ought either the one or the other nation to take offence?

If it be observed that the "number of our merchants in your honorable State is not great," we reply, that nevertheless the amount of merchandize arriving here is not small, embracing imports by men of all other nations, as well as the business of our own traders. And this mutual general traffic fills the coffers of thousands, and involves the interests of myriads of people. But the miner in the mountain, and the workman in the shop, do no less than the merchant, pay respect to your customs.

It is objected against us that vagabonds "gather in places and live by gambling." But these collection of gamblers, as well as the dens of infamous women, are forbidden by the laws of China. These are offences that admit of a clear definition. Our mercantile class have a universal contempt for such. But obnoxious as they are, we have no power to drive them away; and we have often wished these things were prevented but we have no influence that can reach them. We hope and pray that your honorable country would enact vigorous laws, by which these brothels and gambling places may be broken up; and thus worthless fellows will be compelled to follow some honest employment; gamblers to change their calling; and your policemen and petty officials also be deprived of opportunities of trickery and extortion. Harmony and prosperity would then prevail; and the days would await us when each man could find peace in his own sphere of duty. Such is the earnest desire of the merchants who present this.

It is said "that the Chinese go at once to the mines; that they have no other employment; that they come to this State only with the desire of obtaining wealth; and that having attained this object, they return home." We remember the times when the reports went abroad of the great excellence of your honorable State and its inhabitants. The people of the Flowery land were received like guests. An article left upon the road was not taken. Each was at liberty to traffic or to mine. In consequence, with the hope and desire of enjoying a residence where the customs were so admirable and just, we came. In those early times we were greeted with favor. Each treated the other with politeness. From far and near we came and were pleased. Days and months but added to our satisfaction. The ships gathered like clouds.—Merchants paid freely their customs and taxes; and miners their licenses. But from the commencement to the present time, the profits upon the imports to this State have not paid the shipping and other expenses; and many of us have brought various commodities, the whole sum of which we have lost. Must there be added to this the insults and ridicule of the little and the mean? Look at the mines. There openly they have planned, and in secret they have wrought us injury. They have destroyed life, and plundered property. Wagoners have extorted from us; boatmen vexed and done us violence. To these barbarities we dared not reply; we must submit to the degradation.

We are told we "are no profit to your honorable State." Truly, it has been of none to the people of China. We had secretly thought, as your honorable State is a newly opened country, as it is a broad land, as merchants from the four quarters of the world are gathered here, and in order early to obtain a virtuous and intelligent population, that men would be treated with politeness; and thus your population would become one worthy of honor and admiration, and hence should proceed a race exhibiting extraordinary virtues. Surely a fountain so opened would not cease to flow. But suppose one to stare rudely in the face of a visitor, and insult him at the door, the man who respected himself must be fettered from advancing further. And upon this subject it must be remarked again, that though the land we live in is certainly the same, yet the employments of the Chinese and Americans differ, and our places of habitation are not everywhere together.

Some have remarked that "emigrants from other countries bring their families; that their homes are distributed over the State; that some engage in manual employments, and amass wealth; that thus mutual interests are created, mutual civilities extended, and common sympathies excited; that while in every respect they adopt your customs, on the contrary the Chinese do not." To this we rejoin, that the manners and customs of China and of foreign countries are not alike. This is an ancient principle, and is prevalent now. What if other countries do differ somewhat from your honorable nation in hats, and clothes, and letters, and other things, while there is much that is common! In China itself, the people differ. In China, there are some dissimilarities in the inhabitants of various provinces, or departments, or countries, or townships, or even villages. Their dialects, their manners, their sentiments, do not wholly accord. Their articles of use are not all made by one rule. Their common customs all differ. One line cannot be drawn for all. And just so it must be in all parts of the world. It would certainly appear unreasonable, when the officers and the merchants of your honorable country come to our Middle Kingdom, were they rebuked for not knowing our language, or for not being acquainted with our affairs.

But there are things of greater consequence to be considered in connection with this matter. We Chinese and your honorable nation are possessed of a common nature. All must thank High Heaven for natures disposed to love the right and hate the wrong; and IT has ordered also the matter of hats, and clothes, and forms of ceremony. Therefore our Most Gracious Emperors have cherished and showed kindness to those from afar. No distinction has been made between subject and foreigner. They have set their minds and hearts to that subject, for the reason that in former times there has been much discord with other people. Our Emperors of the present Ta-tsing Dynasty have issued commands to officers, both civil and military, and to the people, to exercise perfect faithfulness in their duties to the officers, and the merchants, of your honorable country, declaring that they would not suffer one hair's violation of them. Kindness and politeness, therefore, were reciprocated; and high and low felt that they were one. All under heaven know this.

But of late days your honorable people have established a new practice. They have come to the conclusion that we Chinese are the same as Indians and Negroes, and your courts will not allow us to bear witness. And yet these Indians know nothing about the relations of society; they know no mutual respect; they wear neither clothes nor shoes; they live in wild places and in caves. When we reflect upon the honorable position that China has maintained for many thousands of years; upon the wisdom transmitted by her philosophers; upon her array of civil and of military powers; upon the fame of her civilization; upon the wealth and the populousness of her possessions; upon the cordial tenderness with which successive dynasties of Emperors have treated strangers; deeming native or foreigner all as one; and then behold the people of other nations heap ridicule upon us as if we were the same as Indians—we ask, is it possible that this is in accordance with the will of Heaven?—is it possible that this is the mind of the officers, and the people of your honorable country?—can it be possible that we are classed as equals with this uncivilized race of men? We think you must be wholly unacquainted with the amicable feelings which have hitherto existed between our two nations. We doubt whether such be the decision of enlightened intelligence, and enlarged liberality.

Finally. It is said that "henceforth you would prevent the emigration of people of the Flowery land." Hitherto our people have been imbued with your sacred doctrines; we have tried to exercise modesty and reason. If we can henceforth be treated with mutual courtesy, then we shall be glad to dwell within your honorable boundaries. But if the rabble are to harass us, we wish to return to our former homes. We will speedily send and arrest the embarkation of any that have not yet come. And now we, who are here, do earnestly request that a definite time may be fixed, by which we may be governed, within which we can return our merchandize, and make any necessary arrangements. We trust that in that case the friendly intercourse of previous days will not be interrupted; and that your honorable nation may maintain its principles in tenderly cherishing the strangers from afar. If there be no definite regulation upon this subject, but only these incessant rumors about forbidding the Chinese emigration, we fear the result will be that the class who know nothing, of every nation, will be ever seeking occasions to make trouble; that our Chinese people in the mines will be subjected to much concealed violence, to robbery of their property, and quarrels about their claims. Thus there will be unlimited trouble; and where will be the end of it? Further, if there be no definite date and regular method fixed for our return to Canton, where can we make preparations in San Francisco for the accommodation of several tends of thousands of the Chinese? We most earnestly request the officers of the government early to issue a definite enactment. Such a course will be the best for the interests of our nation. It will be the best for the Chinese here.

SIGNED BY THE COMMITTEE OF MERCHANTS.

CHINESE MERCHANT'S EXCHANGE.

San Francisco, Cal., Jan. 30, 1855.

The Chinese Companies

I. Their Members, Numbers and Property

As the reader has walked, upon some balmy morning, along the southern side of Telegraph Hill, his attention has been attracted by a large frame structure, evidently of Chinese architecture, yet different in its appearance from the Chinese dwellings. The front is painted light blue, and projects an airy portico. A pair of lions, carved in wood, guard the wide doorway; above and on either side of which are gilded tablets, with an inscription upon each of several large Chinese characters. It has often been referred to as "a temple." But its object is not religious. The building is an "*Ui-kun*" or company's house. The tablet over the door tells, if English sounds be employed for the Chinese characters, the name of the company,

"YEUNG-WO UI-KUN."

The two perpendicular inscriptions on either side are poetical lines. They read,

TSEUNG KWONG HAM MAN LI,
SUI HI P'O T'UNG YAN.

"May the prosperous light fill a thousand leagues; May the auspicious air pervade mankind."

The two smaller lines on either board inform us that they were "Set up on a fortunate day of the 8th month, 2nd year of the Emperor Hienfung"—"Carved by Fan I."

Upon entering the house by the side door an uncovered area is seen, in accordance with the Chinese custom, in the middle; from which rooms open toward the front and rear, and stairs ascend on either side to the second story. The smaller apartments below are occupied by the agents and servants of the company. The largest room or hall is pasted over with sheets of red paper covered with writing. These contain a record of the names and residence of every member of the company, and the amount of his subscription to the general fund. The upper story, and the attic, with the out-building on the upper side are, it may be, filled with lodgers; nearly all of whom are staying but temporarily, on a visit from the mines, or on their way to or from China. A few sick persons lie on their pallets around, and a group here and there discuss a bowl of rice, or smoke and chat together. In the rear is the kitchen.

Such is the Yeung-wo company's house. It is a fair specimen of similar edifices. Let us enquire what is their design?

For the information of the American community a series of questions was drawn up, and a copy forwarded to each of the five companies. The answer of the Sze-yap company is translated in full. The replies of the others are given for the sake of brevity only upon points where they differed. They are compiled from the records of the several companies by their agents, and I have reason to think are to be relied upon. The most trustworthy Chinese in the city vouch for their correctness. The numbers are not given to units by any company except the Ning-yeung, as the additional labor to the clerks would have been considerable. They are near enough for our object.

Sze-Yap Company

"Our house is built throughout of brick. It is surrounded also by a brick wall. It is situated in San Francisco, Pine Street, No. —. We have also a frame house in Sacramento. The company was originally composed of people from the four districts of San ning, San-ui, Hoi-ping, Yan-ping; hence the name, Sze Yap, [which means "Four districts."] Afterwards, men from the two districts of Hok-shan and Sze-ui also entered. We did not, however, change our name on this account.

In China it is common to have councils, and in foreign countries Ui-kuns (or assembly halls). Their object is to improve the practices of their members, and to instruct them in principles of benevolence. They are somewhat like American churches! The buildings furnish beds, fuel, and water to guests who remain for but a short period; also a lodging place and medicines for the infirm, aged or sick. Means are bestowed upon such to enable them to return to China.

There are three agents employed by the company; also a servant who sweeps the house.

The number of our members that have arrived in this port, according to the record made at their landing, from the first until Dec. 31, 1854, has been about 16,500. Of these have returned, perhaps, 3,700. In April of last year above 3,400 separated, and formed the Ningyeung Company. More than 300 have died. There are at present in California altogether about 9,200. We do not know the number who have left this for other countries.

Except the buildings used by the company, we have no other property. This has been purchased by the members; who have subscribed of their free will, some twenty, some fifteen, some ten dollars. A portion has been paid in; some will be paid when they are ready to return home. This is a perfectly voluntary matter; there has been no coercion used. Nor is any money required from the disabled, the sick, the aged, or from those making a second voyage to this country.

The objects to which the subscriptions to the company have been devoted are a follows: 1. The purchase of ground and erection of the buildings used by us; 2. The salaries of agents and servants; 3. For fuel, water, candles and oil; 4. To assist the sick to return; 5. For the bestowment of medicines; 6. For coffins and funeral expenses for the poor; 7. For the repairs of tombs; 8. Expenses of lawsuits; 9. Taxes upon our frame house at Sacramento; 10. Drayage, and other outlay, for passengers landing or departing, by ships. The unpaid subscriptions amount to $35,000; the names of others who have not yet stated the amount they intend giving will be good for perhaps $6,700 more.

The agents of the company are elected. At the election all the districts must have a voice. If from any one no members are present, they must be heard from. The agents must be men of tried honesty; and are required to furnish security before they enter upon their office. Their election is for the term of six months; of the expiration of which they must give notice, and call a new election. But if they be found faithful to their duties they are eligible to reelection.

Our company has never employed men to work in the mines for their own profit; nor have they ever purchased any slaves or used them here.

The present agents of the company are Chu Wingtin, Yu Fuseung, and Cheung Akong.''

Yeung-Wo Company

"The three districts of Heung-shan, Tung-kun, and Tsang-shing, are embraced in this company. The house built here is for their accommodation in coming and going.

The total number of men from these districts since the commencement of the emigration is about 16,900; there have died about 400, and returned 2,500. The number of those now in the country is in the neighborhood of 14,000.

Three agents are employed by the company: Tong K. Achick, Chu Yat, and Li Tsz-kun. There is a branch at Sacramento, and the Heung-shan people have a house in Stockton; but there is no regular agent employed in either city. The houses are mere lodging-places. The entire property of the company may be valued at above $20,000. There is perhaps $100,000 of subscriptions, which they have not received."

Canton Company

"We have a frame house in San Francisco, on Clay Street; and two frame houses, one in Sacramento, and one in Stockton. Its Chinese name "Sam Yap," [that is; "three districts"] is obtained from its originally including people from the districts of Nam-hoi, Pun-yu, and Shun-tak, in Canton province. Men from two others, Sam-shui and Tsing-yuen, have joined, however, since our organization.

Two agents are employed at present, Tam Yik-pui, and Chan Pat-cheung; also a porter to take charge of the house.

The entire number of Chinese who have come to San Francisco in connection with this company, according to the record of the ship-agent, is over 8,400. Returned to China, above 1,300. Dead, so far as record has been made of burials, over 300. Remaining in California, about 6,800. Some have gone to other countries and been otherwise lost sight of.

The term for which agents hold office is one year, at the close of which the agent gives notice, and a new election is called. If he has been found to be a trustworthy man, his security is renewed, and a new election is not entered into.

The amount of entrance fees and subscriptions not paid is about $22,000. That expected from individuals who have not yet put down their manes is perhaps $4,700."

King-Yeung Company

"This company's house is situated in San Francisco, No. 47 Broadway, near Kearny street. Its front is, however, toward the South. The house is of wood; it has an enclosed yard; and a brick kitchen attached. The company consists of the people of San-ning, who separated from the Sze-yap company.

It has two agents, Li Leung-nam, and Mui Tsin-sui; and a person who is cook and porter. They are elected for the term of six months.

When the company separated from the Sze-yap it contained about 3,450 men; this was in April, 1853. Since then till Dec. 31, 1854, there have arrived 4,899. Returned to China, 1,269. There have died 173. There are now connected with us 6,907 persons. There may be individuals dead, or departed to other regions, of whom we have no record.

Of money subscribed, but not paid in, there is due over $20,000. Of what will be paid by others there is about $4,000."

Yan-Wo Company

"The only house we own is in Happy Valley, San Francisco. The entire value of our property is $6,000. Not paid in, $15,000. Our entrance fee is $16.

There have come to California, in connection with this company, 2,100 persons. About 160 have gone back and about the same number have died in various parts of the State. The number now in connection with us is 1,780. They are from the two districts of San-on and Kwai-shin. A few are from Ka-ying Chau.

"Our agents are elected for the term of one year. There are at present two: Kong Kwok-yeung, and Fan Ui."

In our next number we propose to make further explanations respecting the general design and operations of the companies; and shall furnish a translation of some of their rules. We close for the present with presenting in a tabular form their computations of the total number of Chinese that have arrived in California; that have returned hence to their native land; that have died here; and finally, their estimate of the number at present in the State. We can from this table ascertain more nearly than by any other method the Chinese population of California. There are probably not a thousand men who have not connected themselves with one or the other of these five companies.

Table

Names	Arrivals	Departures	Deceased	Present
Yeung-wo Co.	16,900	2,500	400	14,000
Canton Co.	8,400	1,300	300	6,800
Yan-wo Co.	2,100	160	160	1,780
Sze-yap Co.	16,650	3,700	300	9,200
3550 of the Sze-yap separated, which are to be subtracted from their present and added to first column of the				
Ning-yeung Co.	4,809	1,269	173	6,907
Total,	48,889	8,929	1,333	38,687

II. Their Internal Organization

The sea-coast of Southern China presents a rugged, dun, treeless front to the voyager, not unlike ours in California. Its river gaps, however, invite, and fully recompense him, by spreading before the eye beautiful and populous savannas, planted with rice, sugarcane, and gardens. Only here and there a clump of trees is seen; perhaps the laichi, or the orange, or an ornamental tuft of bamboos near a village, or the banyan by a temple. The gorgeous crimson tropical sun-set is relieved by serrated lines of distant hills, that hedge the horizon.

In this region lies the province of Canton. In this portion of China foreign nations have traded since near the commencement of the Christian era. Its inhabitants are better acquainted with other countries than any other portion of the Chinese. They, and the people of Fuh-kien, the next province on the east, trade in great numbers to all the lands westward of them, to Coshinchina, Siam, Cambodia, Burmah, to all the islands of vast Indian Archipelago, and even to India; and they stretch away northward in their unwieldly junks to Formosa, Loo-choo, Corea, and Tartary. They are the boldest, rudest, and richest people of the Empire. When the news of the discovery of gold on the opposite shores of the "Great Eastern Ocean" reached them, it was natural that they, above all other Chinese, should rush to California. And we find that, with the exception of a few hundred scattering individuals, the entire body of Chinese emigrants to California has been obtained from the one province of Canton, and merely from the districts along its coast. They are the same people who for two hundred years past have trafficked along the Asiatic shores, and been thus fitted for this final and longer flight across the ocean.

This province is usually estimated to contain about 80,000 square miles, and a population of a little over twenty-seven millions; that is about the same as the British Islands, which are somewhat greater in extent. It contains fifteen Departments, which are subdivided into ninety-one districts. The most populous department is that of Kwang-chauiu, in which is the city of Canton, the capital of the province, and the great seat of foreign trade. This department embraces fifteen districts. It lies around a fine bay, studded with tall islands, and the mouths of three large rivers come together near the city. It is about one hundred and twenty miles long, and perhaps as broad. With the exception of a few thousand of the Sze-yap Company nearly all the immigrants in California are from the department of Kwang-chau-fu.

One great result of this emigration from the same department is that the dialect of all is nearly the same; while the few from, Shanghai, in the province of Cheh-kiang and from the province of Fuh-kieu, are nearly strangers to their own countrymen. They cannot understand each other in conversation.

We observe secondly, from this, that the predictions of a vast inundation of tens of hundreds of Chinese, from all parts of the Empire, are absurd. Several hundreds of the first immigrants here were Shanghai people, but there have been none thence for several years.

A third remark upon this is, that we may hence trace the root of many of the quarrels between bodies of Chinese from neighboring cities or towns, who have been unfriendly at home; which are just like those so famous among our own Scotch, and Irish, and English ancestry.

A fourth consequence of this feature of Chinese immigration is, the increased facilities which it affords for the missionary work, for preaching, teaching, and intercourse with them. In an assembly, nearly all can understand a public address.

When the Chinese visit any other province of their country in considerable numbers, it is their custom to have a common quarters, or rendezvous, which they style an *ui-kun,* that is, a gathering-place or company's house. It is like a club-house, in being supported wholly by voluntary contributions, and in the provision of food and lodging at their cost. And so, when they voluntarily emigrate to any foreign country, in Asia or America, they at once contribute to erect a house. Agents or superintendents are elected, who register the members and manage its concerns. Servants are employed to take care of the building, cook the food, and attend the sick. Provision is made for the interment of the dead, repairs of tombs, and the semi-annual worship of the spirits. And, beyond all this, rules are agreed upon for the government of this club, or company; and these are adopted or repealed at pleasure in the most democratic manner.

The subject of the rules, government and influence of these companies we propose to consider at another time. Their external organization has been now and in the previous article shown as clearly as possible. We shall dismiss it by some general observations.

The first is, that our people may see in the explanations we have given, how erroneous the ideas which have gained currency in regard to the nature of these companies. The members are no more "slaves" than the members of an American fire-company, or any other voluntary association, governed by rules established by the majority, and electing their own officers at regular periods.

Secondly. They have all declared that they have never owned, imported, or employed any slaves. There is slavery, or peonage, of a certain kind, in China, but it is very different from the bondage of Africans in the United States. It is said there are a few, not a hundred individuals, of that class here; but they never have been employed by the companies, and work probably on their own account. Americans, we are assured, have nothing to fear from that source.

Thirdly. The funds of the companies are not used for mercantile purposes, or to obtain revenue, and indeed are paid out nearly as fast as they come in. The treasuries of several of these companies are now empty, or in debt. Many of their people never pay the fees, and are on the other hand sources of great expense. The salaries of the agents and clerks is usually $80 to $100 per month; of the servants, perhaps, $60. The only property held by the companies is just what is absolutely necessary to accomplish their objects; such as a lot of ground, house and furniture, in San Francisco; and a house perhaps, at Sacramento, or Stockton.

A final observation is, that the statistics we have furnished in relation to the number of Chinese in California show how exaggerated are some of the estimates of our own people. The wild and baseless guesses of the Committee of the last Senate, and of the Governor of the State, have excited much unnecessary alarm. The formal statements of the agents of the companies show that about 48,940 Chinese have arrived in California, so far as their books have registered; 8,929 have returned; 1,333 have died; and there remain in connection with them at present, 38,687. The arrivals of women are not recorded by the companies. We think there are not more than two thousand in the State; and probably considerably less. At some future time we may be able to ascertain nearly the number. In order to verify the accounts of the agents, we have looked at the lists in some of the companies' houses, and made inquiries of some of the most respectable and truthful men in the city. We think that the statements given are not far from correct. To that number we may add probably a thousand for those that have not chosen to join any company; and we see that there are probably, in all, about 40,000 Chinese men in California.

III. Their Internal Order

An association of Americans, for commercial, political, literary or benevolent purposes, generally establishes its rules, or by-laws, for the government of its members. A military company, a society in a college, or a temperance or odd-fellow's lodge, have each their appropriate laws and penalties. So with a train of immigrants crossing the plains to Oregon or California, or a party of miners upon a remote prospecting expedition. These rules are established for the ends of mutual assistance, the promotion of order, and the punishment of the unruly. Yet it is understood that in all of them the laws of the country are acknowledged to be fundamental. What may be constituted by any association are but supplementary to the common laws, for purposes which they could not reach or particularize.

The Chinese companies in California are voluntary associations established upon the same principles, to a considerable extent. The

Chinese find themselves here a race of strangers, more completely so than any other people. The companies have several objects.

First. They afford conveniences for lodging, the storage of baggage, and a head-quarters or friends and acquaintances from the same locality; just as if the citizens of Massachusetts, New York, Pennsylvania, or Louisiana, had separate club-houses in San Francisco, which were places of general rendezvous for the people of those states. These companies are a great saving of expense and trouble to the Chinese, and are a remarkable illustration of their practical wisdom.

Second. They can thus make provision for the care of their sick, and the burial of their dead.

Third. Great facilities are afforded for the collection of debts. Accounts are sent, if there be any doubt about their payment, to the agents at San Francisco. Here the people are constantly going and coming; debtors can be more easily reached; their circumstances are known; if they refuse to pay, complaint is made to our courts of law, they are arrested, and the claim obtained.

Fourth. Disputes between miners and others can be settled without the expense, delay, and trouble, of a resort to our courts of law. A friendly arbitration is held before a meeting of their company, or before the five companies, where the case is more difficult, or where persons of different districts are involved. The proceedings on these occasions are generally calm, judicious, and satisfactory to the disputants. In former days, encouraged by the examples of lynching among our own people, the companies sometimes took the law in their own hands so far as to inflict corporal punishment upon offenders in their houses, but such practices are now disclaimed by them. The days of Normal Assing are past; offenders are handed over by them to our courts, in cases which their counsels cannot adjust. Thus far these associations have been of great benefit to the Chinese. They are entirely democratic in their nature. Without them our State could not have been so exempt from Chinese crime, beggary, and strifes. Yet on the other hand there are some weighty objections to them, and when our own population shall have become more settled and orderly, it is probable that the complete Americanization of the Chinese residents may be promoted by their dissolution.

Fifth. It need scarcely be remarked to any one who reads the accounts of the companies, which we have carefully prepared from original documents, that their whole economy is social, and not commercial, in its character. We do sincerely hope that the statements given, on as good authority as can be obtained, will hush the groundless clamor about their importation of coolies, their working the mines for the benefit of wealthy capitalists, and their power over their countrymen. These *clubs* have no such objects in view.

In order to place the whole subject of the nature of these companies in the clearest and most satisfactory light, we have obtained from one of them a copy of a constitution which was lately drawn up. The others have no documents so full and explicit as this; which has been lithographed and distributed among its members in the mines. We give the general substance, and often the exact translation of the paper.

New Rules of the Yeung-Wo Ui-Kun

Since it is necessary for the government of the people and the promotion of the common good that rules should be drawn up, we members of the Yeung-wo Company now dwelling in a foreign country have established the following. As successive emigrations have become less substantial in their character, and troubles have sprung up like thorns, we deem it necessary to draw up those which formerly existed in a general form in a new and definite shape, and to publish them to all men. They are in conformity with the customs of the foreign country in which we are sojourning. We trust they may be exactly observed, by common consent. They were adopted in the following order on a prosperous day in the ninth moon of the year *Kap-yan* (1954).

General Regulations

People of the three districts of Heung-shan, Tung-yuen and Tsang-shing are required to report themselves at the company's room;— otherwise the company will exercise no care for them in their concerns. The entrance fee shall be ten dollars; if not paid within six months interest will be expected. These fees may be paid to collectors sent for the purpose into the Northern and Southern Mines, in the fourth and tenth month of each year. No fees will be required from those proved to be invalids, or transient persons.—Receipts for payment of fees must be entered on the books, and bear the company's seal. Disputes will not be settled between persons who have not paid the entrance fee. Members purposing to return to China must make the fact know to the agents, when their accounts will be examined and measures will be taken to prevent it if the entrance fee or other debts remain unpaid. Strangers to the agents of the company must obtain security who will be responsible for their character and debts. Members leaving clandestinely shall be liable to a fine of fifty dollars; and the security for a debt for helping him thus to abscond shall be fined one hundred dollars.

In the company's house there must be no concealment of stolen goods; no strangers brought to lodge; no gunpowder or other combustible material; no gambling; no drunkenness; no cooking (except in the proper quarters); no burning of sacrificial papers; no accumulation of baggage; no filth; no bathing; no filching oil; no heaps of rags and trash; no wrangling and noise; no injury of the property of the company, no goods belonging to thieves; no slops of victuals. For the heavier of these offenses complaint shall be made to the police of the city; for the lighter, persons shall be expelled from the company. Baggage not allowed to remain longer than three years when it must be removed; nor more than one chest to each person. Invalids that cannot labor, are poor and without relatives, may be returned to China at the expense of the company for their passage money; but provisions and fuel and other expenses must be obtained by contributions. Coffins may be furnished for the poor, but of such a careful record shall be kept.

Quarrels and troubles about claims in the mines should be referred to the company, where they shall be duly considered. If any should refuse to abide by the decision of the company, it will nevertheless assist the injured and defend them from violence. If when foreigners do injury—a complaint is made, and the company exerts itself to have justice done without avail, it ought to be submitted to. Whatever is referred for settlement to the assembly of the five companies conjointly, cannot again be brought before this company alone.

Where a man is killed, a reward shall be offered by the company for his apprehension and trial, the money being paid only when he has been seized: the members of the company shall subscribe each according to what is just. If more than the anticipated amount is required, the friends of the deceased shall make up the deficiency. Complaint shall be made of offenders to the court, and proclamations for their arrest shall be placarded in the principal towns; but any one found guilty of concealing them, shall pay all the expenses to which the company has been put. Difficulties with members of other companies shall be reported to the agents of company, and if justice demand shall be referred for the judgment of the five companies conjointly. Offences committed upon shipboard, on the seas, shall be referred to the five companies conjointly. Difficulties brought upon men by their own vices and follies will not receive attention. Thievery and receiving of stolen goods will not be protected; nor will troubles in bawdy houses; nor those in gambling houses; nor debts to such; nor extortions of secret associations; nor the quarrels of such associations; nor those who are injured in consequence of refusal to pay their licenses; nor smuggling; nor any violation of American laws. The company will not consider complaints from a distance by letter, of a doubtful character, or without sufficient proof. No reply will be made to anonymous letters or those without date and a specification of the true origin and nature of difficulties. Names must be carefully given in all complaints from the interior. No payments of money will be made in the settlement of cases where the rules of the company are not complied with. Where the conduct of an individual is such as to bring disgrace on the company and upon his countrymen, he shall be expelled, and a notice to that effect be placarded in each of the five companies' houses; nor will the company be responsible for any of his subsequent villainies, or even make any investigation should he meet with any violent death. Costs connected with the settlement of disputes shall be borne by the one decided to be in the wrong. In difficulties of a pressing and important character in the mines a messenger shall be sent thence, and a judicious person shall at once accompany him to the place. In any quarrel where men are killed or wounded the person who originated it shall be held accountable. Any defensive weapons belonging to the company shall be given to individuals only after joint consultation, and the register of their names. Those requiring such weapons for defense shall give security for their return, if any shall take them on their own responsibility they shall be held accountable for any consequences. Any one using the seal or addressing a letter in behalf of the company, unauthorized, shall be severely censured if the matter be unimportant; if a serious offence, he shall be handed over to the court of law. The parties and witnesses in cases shall be examined under oath. Representatives from the people of different countries and townships shall be notified by the agents of the company of the time of any meeting; and when assembled they shall not leave till the business is dispatched. Notices of meetings upon urgent business shall be marked with the words "urgent case;" the representatives so informed shall be fined ten dollars if not present within an hour of the time. In arbitrations, the agents of the company, the representatives, and the witnesses, shall all be put on oath.

Collection of Debts
Claims for debts, to avoid mistakes, must particularize the true name, surname, town, and department of the debtor. The agent of the company shall give the claimant a bill of the debt, which will be received again when the money is paid. No claim can be presented of less than ten dollars. Claims presented through the company must, when afterwards paid, be receipted by the company; else the debtor will not be allowed to return to China. Persons making false claims against an individual shall recompense him for any expenses to which he shall be put in consequence thereof. Accounts must be acknowledged by the debtor to be correct, before collection. A person appointed as collector for another must endorse the account. A creditor in returning to China must name an agent who will receive the payment of any claims made by him. Accounts sent from China for collection shall be admitted by the company. The agent will not pay over collections except upon the presentation of the bill of acknowledgement he has previously given. Part payments must bear the receipt of the company. In cases of dispute about debt, the debtor may return to China if the representative of his district is willing to

become his security. Debtors shall not be hindered returning to China on their pleading poverty, or chronic sickness. In losses occasioned by oversight of the agent, he shall be held responsible for the amount, unless he declare them upon oath to have been unintentional. Claims for debt, if unpaid, must be again put on record at the expiration of three years. Claims presented by a member of another company shall be certified by the agent of that company, and when recorded shall be subject to a fee of twenty-five cents.

Duties of Officers

This company shall elect three agents, one to attend to the internal affairs, one to business with Americans; and one as treasurer; and these shall mutually assist one another. A faithful servant shall be hired as a house-servant and porter. There shall be also elected a committee of four, as counsellors, who shall receive five dollars a month for tea-money. The monthly accounts of the company shall be counted till the last Sunday of the month, on which day the committee shall audit, and publish them by a placard. The treasurer shall never retain more than four hundred dollars in his own hands at one time, and his deposits in the treasury and payments from it shall be under the supervision of the committee of four. The treasury shall have four different locks, and each of the committee one key. The treasurer must always be present when money is taken out. Should the committee employ collectors who have not been duly elected by the company, they shall be held responsible for them. The account of the company shall be closed with each month, that there be no private or wasteful employment of its funds; and in cases of fraud, a meeting shall be called and the offender expelled. When inadvertent mistakes are made in accounts, the committee shall state them to be so on oath, and the correction shall then be entered. Agents or committee men whose accounts are not clear shall be censured. None but the agents shall have common access to the account books. Payments in behalf of the company shall, when made at their house, be endorsed by the committee, but in the interior they may be made by the agent alone. The office of the agents shall be kept open daily from eight o'clock in the morning till five in the afternoon. The doors shall be closed at New-years for three days. Agents shall not use offensive language against each other; but any differences shall be settled by a meeting of the company. If lodgers at the company's house do not comply with the regulations and respect the authority of the agents, they shall be expelled by a meeting of the company. Agents who are remiss in attending at the office shall be mulcted to twice the amount of their salary for the time lost.

What Are Coolies?

The Chinese in California are supposed by not a few Americans to belong to a debased caste of their countrymen, recognized by the generic name of "Coolies." Questions upon this point are among those most commonly presented to individuals who have been acquainted with them at home.

The mistaken ideas which prevail on this subject have arisen from confounding the Chinese people and customs with those of India, where the entire social system is widely different. The British traders in Canton attached Indian appellations to many articles of solely Chinese produce or use. The Hindustanti word "coo-lie" was by them inflicted upon the Chinese, in whose language it has no equivalent, and who have no caste or class whom it represents.

What is the Indian "coolie"? He is, we reply, the representative of a degraded class of the Hindus. The system of "caste" prevalent in that country is familiar to all. It is known that there are four distinct and fixed divisions of society. Of these castes, the highest, the *Brahmans*, came originally from the head of the supreme creator, Brahm.—The *Vishya*, or *Bias*, sprang from his body—constituting the agriculturists and capitalists. From his arms issued the *Kshatriya*, or military caste. The *Sudras*, or laborers, sprang from his feet. They are the most degraded of all, performing only servile duties. They are used in tilling the soil, and in menial occupations. The Vedas, or sacred books, are closed against their perusal. Under these four great divisions, there are a multitude of inferior distinctions.

The word "coolie" originated from a singular race of people, of which there are several tribes, together calling themselves *Kuli*, or *Koli*—a word which signifies "clansman." They are the aborigines of India; apparently much more ancient than the Mohammedan and other races who have successively conquered the country. Some are still wild inhabitants of the mountains and jungle. Other tribes have embraced Hinduism; of these, most near the coast and large rivers are fishermen, while the residents of the interior are generally employed in farming, as village watchmen, or as servants. They are a strong, robust people of a light copper color, and use freely animal food, which the superior castes abhor. The kulis of Bombay are the only inhabitants subject to a regular poll-tax, which is over six rupees each. Their habits, food and persons are unclean, and their own countrymen despise and oppress them.

Such is the debased class of Hindus to which the name kulis or "coolies" appropriately belongs. Europeans in India often apply the epithet to other servile laborers and employees, of a low caste. But it is this people alone to whom it should be rightfully given. And it is these kulis of the hills that have of late emigrated in large numbers to the Mauritius and the West India Islands.

The Europeans and Americans resident in China, never, so far as our observation extends, employ this word, as in India, to signify wild races, fishermen, laborers, watchmen, or particular debased classes. The coolie in Canton is the house-servant, the bearer of the sedan chair or the porter of the tea or silk warehouse; a class subject to no cincture of contempt, one from which some of the wealthiest and most influential merchants have sprung, and embracing occupations sometimes accepted by their sons for the sake of learning the language and customs of foreigners trading there.

Now, with the Hindu kuli, the object of our apprehensions, compare the emigrants to our shores from the empire of China. First— One in the least acquainted with the social system of that nation need not be reminded that there *no caste* exists. Its whole apparatus of caste he flings away, as something uncomfortable and unnecessary. And so the social and political system built upon this pantheistic base. There are no fixed divisions in the body politic; no employments necessarily hereditary; no essential superiority of nature; no permanence of rank; few offices beyond the reach of the humblest individuals gifted with talent and energy. Strange as the declaration may seem to many, who regard them with blind prejudice, it is yet true that few nations hold opinions, on many points in politics, more democratic than the Chinese.

What are the Chinese we see swarming in our streets and crowding our mines? They are just what any other people are: laborers, cooks, boatmen, farmers, carpenters, stone-masons, brick-makers and bricklayers, shop-keepers, book-binders, weavers, tea-packers, gardeners, and just what an equal number from any other land might be expected to present in the variety of their occupations. Some, that speak English best, have been scholars in missionary schools, or employees about foreign *hongs*. Here and there is a literary man, though rarely seen, and his accomplishments lost upon this air. Then, there is an abundance of the vilest classes—the gambler, the infamous female, and others, who prey upon the fortunate, the unwary, or the wanton.

How did they get here? Just as any others. Some had means of their own. Some borrowed. Some sold their small possessions to join in the rush for "The Golden Hills," They were imported by no capitalists—Chinese, English, or American. They are owned or held in slavery by no one, save in the bondage of obligation to pay one's honest debts.

From an extensive acquaintance with them and their employments, and after inquiry into the points we have been considering, I am assured that the prejudices existing against the Chinese generally in this State, as a kind of slaves or bondsmen, is the result of want of information. Prejudice against them upon such grounds is unfounded. When this is fully understood, their condition, as poor, friendless, inoffensive, foreigners—many of them willing to do the best they can, and to learn to do better—will ensure them sympathy, instruction and protection from many by whom they are now avoided and condemned.

To His Excellency Gov. Bigler

Sir: I am a Chinaman, a republican, and a lover of free institutions; am much attached to the principles of the government of the United States, and therefore take the liberty of addressing you as the chief of the government of this State. . . . The effect of your late message has been thus far to prejudice the public mind against my people, to enable those who wait the opportunity to hunt them down, and rob them of the rewards of their toil. . . .

I am not much acquainted with your logic, that by excluding population from this State you enhance its wealth. I have always considered that population was wealth; particularly a population of producers, of men who by the labor of their hands or intellect, enrich the warehouses or the granaries of the country with the products of nature and art. You are deeply convinced you say "that to enhance the prosperity and preserve the tranquility of this State, Asiatic immigration must be checked." This, your Excellency, is but one step towards a retrograde movement of the government. . . . It was one of the principal causes of quarrel between you (when colonies) and England; when the latter pressed laws against emigration, you looked for immigration; it came, and immigration made *you what you are*—your nation what it is. It transferred you at once from childhood to manhood and made you great and respectable throughout the nations of the earth. I am sure your Excellency cannot, if you would, prevent your being called the descendant of an immigrant, for I am sure you do not boast of being a descendant of the red man. But your further logic is more reprehensible. You argue that this is a republic of a particular race—that the Constitution of the United States admits of no asylum to any other than the pale face. This proposition is false in the extreme, and you know it. The declaration of your independence, and all the acts of your government, your people, and your history are all against you.

It is true, you have degraded the Negro because of your holding him in involuntary servitude, and because for the sake of union in some of your states such was tolerated, and amongst this class you would endeavor to place us; and no doubt it would be pleasing to some would-be freemen to mark the brand of servitude upon us. But we would beg to remind you that when your nation was a wilderness, and the nation from which you sprung *barbarous,* we exercised most of the arts and virtues of civilized life; that we are possessed of a

The following letter was published in the *Daily Alta California* of May 5, 1855. Governor Bigler of California was the first governmental official to advocate the exclusion of the Chinese.

*"To His Excellency Gov. Bigler," in *Daily Alta California* (San Francisco: May 5, 1855).

language and a literature, and that men skilled in science and the arts are numerous among us; that the productions of our manufactories, our sail, and workshops, form no small share of the commerce of the world; and that for centuries, colleges, schools, charitable institutions, asylums, and hospitals, have been as common as in your own land. . . . And we beg to remark, that so far as the history of our race in California goes, it stamps with the test of truth the fact that we are not the degraded race you would make us. We came amongst you as mechanics or traders, and following every honorable business of life. You do not find us pursuing occupations of degrading character, except you consider labor degrading, which I am sure you do not; and if our countrymen save the proceeds of their industry from the tavern and the gambling house to spend it on farms or town lots or on their families, surely you will admit that even these are virtues. You say "you desire to see no change in the generous policy of this government as far as regards Europeans." It is out of your power to say, however, in what way or to whom the doctrines of the Constitution shall apply. You have no more right to propose a measure for checking immigration, than you have the right of sending a message to the Legislature on the subject. As far as regards the color and complexion of our race, we are perfectly aware that our population have been a little more tan than yours.

Your Excellency will discover, however, that we are as much allied to the African race and the red man as you are yourself, and that as far as the aristocracy of *skin* is concerned, ours might compare with many of the European races; nor do we consider that your Excellency, as a Democrat, will make us believe that the framers of your declaration of rights ever suggested the propriety of establishing an aristocracy of *skin*. I am a naturalized citizen, your Excellency, of Charleston, South Carolina, and a Christian, too; and so hope you will stand corrected in your assertion "that none of the Asiatic class" as you are pleased to term them, have applied for benefits under our naturalization act. I could point out to you numbers of citizens, all over the whole continent, who have taken advantage of your hospitality and citizenship, and I defy you to say that our race have ever abused that hospitality or forfeited their claim on this or any of the governments of South America, by an infringement on the laws of the countries into which they pass. You find us peculiarly peaceable and orderly. It does not cost your state much for our criminal prosecution. We apply less to your courts for redress, and so far as I know, there are none who are a charge upon the state, as paupers.

You say that "gold, with its talismanic power, has overcome those natural habits of non-intercourse we have exhibited." I ask you, has not gold had the same effect upon your people, and the people of other countries, who have migrated hither? Why, it was gold that filled your country (formerly a desert) with people, filled your harbors with ships and opened our much-coveted trade to the enterprise of your merchants.

You cannot, in the face of facts that stare you in the face, assert that the cupidity of which you speak is ours alone; so that your Excellency will perceive that in this age a change of cupidity would not tell. Thousands of your own citizens come here to dig gold, with the idea of returning as speedily as they can.

We think you are in error, however, in this respect, as many of us, and many more, will acquire a domicile amongst you.

But, for the present, I shall take leave of your Excellency, and shall resume this question upon another occasion which I hope you will take into consideration in a spirit of candor. Your predecessor pursued a different line of conduct towards us, as will appear by reference to his message.

I have the honor to be your Excellency's very obedient servant.

Noman Asing

5.3
Reverend William Speer
Plea in Behalf of the Immigrants from China

Addressed to the Legislature of California, in behalf of the Immigrants from the Empire of China to This State.

To the Honorable Senate and Assembly of the State of California:

In despotic countries the humblest individual is allowed, at times, to approach the sovereign. The sceptre is extended to him, and he touches it and lives. And there are places also where he may stand and wait, with his private or public supplication, and cast the paper at the royal feet, and it is taken up and considered. A representative government grants its meanest citizen an equal privilege. Just so far as it is a *common-wealth,* aiming to act for the general good, and not by divine right, or for the benefit of a few, does it secure, and respect, and solicit an expression of reasonable opinion. There are circumstances which move the writer to open his mouth, he trusts, without presumption. His sympathies and principles as a Christian minister, his patriotism, and his convictions, stir him. And not less his deep and heartfelt compassion for a race of strangers, most strangers in this land where we all are strangers; a race on whom we have unthinkingly and unkindly set the heel. In their difficult and troubled condition, he feels a gratification in their resorting to him as their "friend." In attempting to simply do them justice, he distinctly states that he leans on no party, that he represents no one interest, that he would aggrandize or injure no district; but seeks plainly, sincerely and earnestly to set forth the truth, believing that candid and earnest men will likewise hear, and will give to the facts and reasons presented all that attention the intrinsic weight of the subject deserves.

And this *particular question* is one that above all others needs a manly, sincere and liberal spirit to investigate it. Races long and widely separated become peculiar, arrogant, and offensive. The Chinese and ourselves, both in their country and ours, find in each other's manners and conduct much to ridicule and hate. It will be observed that a large class on either hand of those who visit the other's country are the most bitter enemies of those among whom they lived.

They have seen among them nothing to esteem, to imitate, or to adopt. But let us, boasting and possessing a real superiority in genuine civilization, in every species of power, in the truest refinement of human nature, and in the knowledge of a Heaven-descended charity and hope of salvation—let us, gentlemen, who do not only believe, but know, that we are superiors—put off the temper of meanness, and spite, and selfishness, and bigotry. I appeal to you as Representatives of an intelligent, whole-souled, progressive people. I appeal to men that can conceive the motives, and enjoy the expanded hopes, of the glorious religion of the Lord Jesus Christ. You are in slavery to no man, to no doctrine, to no limited interest of time and place. If I am wrong in any of the views I shall offer, I desire nothing so much as a truthful and charitable correction of them. And I confidently expect that with a Legislature characterized by so much intelligence and moral principle as the present, what conclusions are palpably fair and just may be received with the honesty and candor with which they are respectfully submitted.

The Questions at Issue

Two questions come before your Honorable body for discussion: first, the terms, and second, the extent, according to which mining by Chinese should be permitted. The first is involved in petitions that the rate of license for Chinese miners shall be again reduced to the sum of $4 per month, the same as for other foreigners; the second, in petitions that the capitation tax of $50 each on landing be diminished to $5 each. A simple repeal of two separate acts of the last Legislature is asked, and the restoration of the laws previously existing on these points. The two questions, it may be noticed, are entirely distinct. The granting of the first class of petitions alone allows a continuance of the privilege of mining to the Chinese in the State, but debars further immigration. This is the most important desideratum. The granting of both classes of petitions would restore the privileges of the miners, and also permit further immigration, for which many in the agricultural districts, particularly in Southern California, and interested in cultivating the swamp lands, are solicitous. It is quite possible some members may prefer action on the first alone, with the present light, leaving the rate of the capitation tax unchanged. To grant the second class of petitions alone appears to be a matter of no consequence at present, as the Chinese would continue to leave the State as far as possible, and discourage the immigration of their friends; nor, indeed, on the other hand, would an increase of even the present capitation tax be a matter of any importance to those unfriendly to them, since the sum of fifty dollars accomplishes their object as effectually as would any larger sum, if the law be enforced.

The general view to be represented is this: that the interests of California forbid a policy calculated to exclude or debase Chinese immigration here.

This subject has never yet been thoroughly discussed. It will be my aim to lay before you such statements as appear to approximate the truth. If any of these are incorrect, they will probably be found in regard to facts and opinions, underestimated. And I trust they may be scrutinized, and corrections be made of any that lean in the other direction.

Who are the Chinese?—not Coolies

To obtain a satisfactory view of the Chinese as we find them in California, it will be necessary first to ask, who are these people? and how did they come here?

It has been said they are *coolies*. By this it is meant they belong to a general degraded caste in their native country. The word "coolie" is sometimes applied to Chinese laboring men, inferior servants, and farm hands, by Europeans. But there is *no caste* in China, any more than in the United States. The mistaken ideas which prevail on this subject have arisen from the confounding the Chinese people and customs with those of India, where the entire social system is widely different. The English newspapers, familiar with Indian usages, and viewing all the nations of the East through the medium of the press in their great colonial presidencies of Bengal, Bombay and Madras, have originated in Great Britain and America gross mistakes in regard to the other countries of whose trade the East India Company held also a long monopoly. The Hindustani word "coolie" is one of those inflicted upon the Chinese, in whose language it has no equivalent, and who have no caste or class whom it represents. It would be justly held degrading to style an English laborer of whatever occupation, in China, a "coolie," and it is not right to attach to Chinese the odium of a social debasement which is peculiar to another country, to other institutions, and to another and most dissimilar people. Their emigrants here are just what any other people are: laborers, cooks, boatmen, farmers, carpenters, stone masons, brick-layers, shop-keepers, book-binders, weavers, tea-packers, gardeners, and just what an equal number from any other land might be expected to present in the variety of their occupations. Some, that speak English best, have been scholars in missionary schools, or employees about foreign *hongs*. Here and there is a literary man, though rarely seen, and his accomplishments unappreciated. Then, there is an abundance of the vilest classes—the gambler, the infamous female, and others, who prey upon the fortunate, the unwary, or the wanton of their own countrymen.

Not Slaves—Their Companies

Again, they were *not brought here by capitalists,* either Chinese or others. The very mistaken notions of our own people in respect to this subject arose from not understanding, as was natural enough, the nature of their "Companies." This was explained by me in a series of articles in the *Oriental* newspaper, last spring. The following extract will suffice at present for any who still labor under such erroneous ideas:

> When the Chinese visit any other province of their country in considerable numbers, it is their custom to have a common quarters, or rendezvous, which they style *ui-kun,* that is, a gathering-place or company's house. It is like a club-house, in being supported wholly by voluntary contributions, and in the provision of food and lodging at their cost. And so, when they voluntarily emigrate to any foreign country, in Asia or America, they at once contribute to erect a house. Agents or superintendents are elected, who register the members and manage its concerns. Servants are employed to take care of the building, cook the food, and attend the sick. Provision is made for the interment of the dead, repairs or tombs, and the semi-annual worship of the spirits. And, beyond all this, rules are agreed upon for the government of this club, or company; and these are adopted or repealed at pleasure in the most democratic manner. The members are no more 'slaves' than the members of an American fire-company, or any other voluntary association, governed by rules established by the majority, and electing their own officers at regular periods. They have all declared that they have never owned, imported, or employed any slaves. There is slavery, or peonage, of a certain kind, in China, but it is very different from the bondage of Africans in the United States. It is said there are a few, not a hundred individuals, of that class here; but they never have been employed by the companies, and work probably on their own account. Americans, we are assured, have nothing to fear from that source. The funds of the companies are not used for mercantile purposes, or to obtain revenue, and indeed are paid out nearly as fast as they come in.

Interest of Our Shipping

At the ports of Whampoa, Mucao, Hong Kong, and Shanghai, these strangers come in contact with American and European commerce. Their unwieldy bulks, fashioned after antediluvian models, cannot navigate the broad Pacific beyond their own familiar coasts. The Chinese greatly prefer American clipper ships, on account of their superior speed, cleanliness, safety, and less liability to detention on entering our ports.

The *Shipping List* in 1852 remarked:

"The trade between this place and China was at the outset, from a variety of causes, much larger in proportion to the population of California, than it now is. Aside from the natural tendencies to extravagance which sudden wealth induces, making an extraordinary demand for the fancy articles of our Celestial neighbors, many of the early miners were Lower Californians, Mexicans, and Chilenos, who, in many cases, invested the product at the mines in Chinese goods; and being in most cases of a class unacquainted with their value, they paid far more for them than they could be bought for near their homes, offering of course no inducement for a second adventure. They were also bought by traders at the different towns along the coast, which at the outset was a fair business; but since the yield at the mines has been less to individuals, their business has also become of less value. A very perceptible difference was made in the demand when the law imposing the foreign miners' tax went into operation, as the foreign miners were the only purchasers in that section of the country."

The variety of the commodities open to *our* export and import is but partially represented by the Custom House entries of the incipient intercourse of the past few years. A reference to the tabular statements of articles subject to tariff, as specified in treaties at the close of the Opium War, will exhibit a range for the employment of unlimited capital.

It is not California alone but the countries and people lying along the whole American coast from Alaska to Chili that are interested in the establishment of a regular and reliable commerce with Asia. Four years ago a commercial newspaper of this State looked forward to the necessities of such an intercourse, and made the following judicious remarks:

"The trade in silk goods and articles of Chinese manufacture could be indefinitely increased, could traders from the south coast be certain of always finding stocks from which to select goods suitable to their wants; but this will not, cannot be, until houses regularly established keep up constant supplies, for up to this time no traffic has been pursued with less system; and shipments have been so often made at random, by parties on the other side, too often containing large amounts of goods entirely unsuited to the wants of the market, causing serious loss to the shippers, that it is not likely these experiments will be again repeated to much extent. In a word, this trade will not be developed until capitalists have taken the matter in hand, pursuing it steadily and systematically; and not until then a rich reward awaits them.''

The exports from California have been necessarily small to China as to all the rest of the world. They have consisted chiefly of gold, silver, quicksilver, cinnabar, and a few manufactures. Our harvest has hitherto not been golden corn, but gold itself; not precious grain, cut from the sunny face of the hills, and winnowed with the wind, but more precious grains, dug from their dark interior or from deep ravines, and washed in the cold rushing streams. But the time is coming when we shall have agricultural and manufactured products to return. Until the present time a much larger number of vessels have crossed the ocean to Asia than from there. Our clippers have pursued their course westward after landing their cargoes from the Atlantic States and Europe; from the same cause the farmer and manufacturer in California will always have the advantage of merely nominal freights. And further, the tendency must be to throw the trade into the hands of American vessels. Thus the gigantic marine which has advanced with such amazing progress must by the aid of California, more than any other influence, control more and more the commerce of the whole Eastern world.

Agricultural and Manufacturing Interests

By far the most desirable class of occupations for the employment of the Chinese laborers in California is in connection with the development of agriculture and the preparation of its proceeds for use by ourselves, and the nations of the East.

First in interest stands cotton. ''Cotton is king,'' in many most important senses. The dress of the lower class in China is universally, in summer and winter, cotton. In summer, it is but a short glazed frock; in winter the number of these increases in the same proportion that the degrees of the thermometer diminish.

The favorite cotton region of China is the alluvial valley of the great Yang-tsze-kiang River, like the Sacramento in its moist, fat soil, and frequent inundations. However, it is also cultivated in Canton province. I have made inquiries and find there are some in California who are acquainted with the process. Yet this is a department of agriculture which can only be encouraged by liberal inducements, as by grants of the tule lands, and by a legislation that shall encourage the Chinese to make their homes among us, and impart a sense of security and a hope of permanent advantage. Their past experience has inclined them to only come, rush to our mines, and hasten home with a meager prize, or in angry disappointment.

Cotton here comes back to its original cultivators. It was taken from Eastern Asia to Persia and Arabia. The common names of some of its tissues are derived from the Chinese. Naukeen, the ancient capital, is the region from whence the most substantial web has been obtained.

Now let any one reflect upon the circuitous and expensive routes which American cotton must pursue, from the swamps of Georgia, by rivers, railways and oceans, through Lowell or Manchester, to the Hindoo and Chinese "go-downs;" zigzagging all around the globe; taxed, and tolled, and tariffed; insured against the storms of the Antarctic capes and the typhoons of the tropics. The cotton bale in its journey, like sheep among thickets, leaves its fleece to warm the nests of a hundred different birds. Despite all arguments or theories, it seems self-evident, that by some means or other, this most universal and most valuable of all the figments wherewith the human race hide their nakedness, or shield them from the elements, must, in the course of time, be to a large extent grown and manufactured in California. Whether we hinder or prosper the issue, whether it be delayed even till we are laid in our graves, this may be foretold.

Chinese, our merchants report, favor the American article, and its importation is likely to gradually increase. Cotton is a product for which the soil and climate of California appear peculiarly adapted. Three years ago, Major P. B. Reading, if memory serves, made some satisfactory experiments in its culture, upon his farm near Shasta. Within a few weeks past a sample of some grown here was sent to Mobile, for examination. The judgment was most "flattering." It was pronounced "beautiful."

There are other great agricultural interests concerned in the treatment of the Chinese in California, though none comparable in national and supreme importance to that of cotton.

The numerous alimentary gifts in the power of the ancient Oriental world to confer upon our agriculture and horticulture the present opportunity will now allow me even to name. Rice is one of the most important—which supplies the principle nourishment and beverages of two-thirds of the inhabitants of the globe. The cultivation of this article, and of sugar, have been abundantly urged in our public print.

Transported Interest

The Chinese on landing in San Francisco usually remain there but a few days. The permanent residents in the city do not number above a few hundreds. They then proceed by the steamers to Sacramento, Stockton, Marysville, and other points on the Sacramento and San Joaquin Rivers. They are guided very much by the information and opinions of those who have been in the country longest, and had most experience here in the mines. And it may be remarked that their deference to those in whom they find they can confide is one of the most remarkable traits in their character.

The amount of pecuniary benefit derived by steamers, sailing vessels, stages, wagons, and such conveyances of passengers and goods by land and water, can scarce be computed. On the river steamers they have travelled by hundreds on a single vessel, particularly during the periods when their direct immigration has been most large. Allowing each individual in the fifty-three thousand arrivals and twelve thousand departures but a single trip at seven dollars, and each of these here one downward and upward trip during their residence till now, which will not seem too great on the whole, since many of them make repeated journeys in a single year, and we see this interest during the past few years benefitted over a million of dollars in passage money. The imported from their own land, and the American groceries, clothing, and other merchandize, consumed by them annually would pay towards the sailing and steam vessels, in freight, fully in proportion to their comparative population. The drayage in cities and towns has come in for its share of support.

A Marysville merchant estimates the number of teams employed there, not alone by Chinese freights, but also in merchandize for their use, as at least "twenty-five to thirty a week." This, for twenty-five a week, would amount, at the rate given above, to fifty thousand dollars a year. These facts afford some ground of conjecture as to the amounts that reach this hard-working class, whose employment brings them to all parts of the mining region. And there are some, we are informed, who have become rich through the profits derived from Chinese customers.

Interest of Mining and Laboring Population

We will now suppose the Chinese immigrants to have made their way into the interior towns, up into the gulches, and to occupation in mining and labor of various kinds. As far as we have considered the question, most persons would agree with the truth of what has been said;—but here there spring up some objections. These we would treat with respect. Some have made them in the mere spirit of captiousness and bad temper. But it is natural that our novel and most peculiar state of society; their twanging and guttural sounds, without the remotest analogy to the sonorous and flexible language that rolls from our throats; their shy and timid habits; their industry, even when all others were lying by; and the offensiveness of their vices, should create impressions unfavorable to them and dislike to their presence, even among some of the best men. The wiser would of course reflect that there must be a commixture of good people and bad ones among them; that evil as well as good must come from their presence; that the evils would be first manifested, and that the advantages would be more slow; that they must be understood to be fairly judged; that they could not be expected to be patterns of morality, where they were surrounded by so many temptations and examples to the contrary. And, again, the Christian would look upon them with a pitiful heart. But still, it was not strange that the multitude were against them.

The objections may be classed under two heads:—First, that these strangers are of no pecuniary benefit to California; that they interfere with American labor; and that they carry nearly all they make out of the country. Second, that their vices make them dangerous to our people, and to our posterity.

Now, let us meet these difficulties fairly; and first, as to their profitableness, not alone to the commercial interest, in their transit, and to the agriculturist prospectively, but *in their present employments, and as they are.*

It is assumed that there are about forty thousand men, and a couple of thousand women, in the State. It is assumed that full three-fourths of the men are miners, and no allowance will be made for the necessary outlays of the women.

Foreign Miners' Licenses

The income from the Chinese about which most has been said in our newspapers is that from "foreign miners' licenses." The report of the Comptroller of State, for the fiscal year ending June 30, 1855, estimated the half coming to the State treasury during the next year, at $150,000. The last report estimates that for the year ending June, 1856, at $160,000. The Hon. Messrs. Crenshaw and Norman, in a committee report to the last Legislature, stated that "the whole number of foreign miners' licenses issued to the mining counties in this State for the year 1854, was 103,140, worth $412,560." It is needless to attempt an estimate of the aggregate income to the various treasuries from a variety of taxes, licenses and assessments, the sum of which is considerable, and helps to that extent to sustain the local officers and aid public improvements.

Interest of Landed Property

The amount paid for rents, and for mining claims, is an immense sum; higher, in proportion to the value of the property obtained, than by any other people. It is beyond more than a vague conclusion. The following estimate, from the best evidence I can obtain, affords some basis for calculation. There are in

San Francisco, about	30 houses, averaging $120 per month, in all,	$3,600
San Francisco, about	40 houses, averaging $100 per month, in all,	4,000
San Francisco, about	60 houses, averaging $60 per month, in all,	3,600
San Francisco, storage, say		2,000
	Total	$13,200
Sacramento,	50 houses, averaging $60 per month, in all,	3,000
Marysville,	20 houses, averaging 50 per month, in all,	1,000
Stockton,	8 houses, averaging 40 per month, in all,	320
Auburn,	30 houses, averaging 40 per month, in all,	1,200
Jackson,	20 houses, averaging 30 per month, in all,	600
	Monthly total,	$19,320
	Annual total in the six places,	$231,840

There are many towns and camps through the country, where three, five or ten houses, it would be found on inquiry, are rented, for various sums, to Chinese. At first mention it may seem questionable, yet possibly the entire income from rents and leases, in all parts of the State, might prove to be half a million a year. This must be acknowledged, however, to be only a conjecture.

Mining Claims and Implements

In addressing gentlemen, many of whom are from the mining districts, it is needless to say that their superior knowledge will find some of the estimates under the following heads, placed too high, others too low. Yet, I will endeavor to follow such light as I have been able to obtain from personal visits, conversations, and the newspapers of the State.

To get an idea of the ordinary expenditures, let us notice, first, the amount of money invested in claims. We may hear of as much as $1,500, or more, having been paid by a company of Chinamen, though such instances are rare; but $300, or $500, is often given for ground that is worked out in a few weeks. It has been considered not an exaggerated estimate, that twenty thousand, or two-thirds of the mines, would pay four dollars a month, the same amount as the license, on this score. Yet this would make an aggregate of eight thousand dollars a month, when we count up all that are scattered over the State. However, lest even this be objected to, let us include under that head the outlays for water, which is rated often at two dollars a day. Add for mining tools, sheet-iron, lumber, canvas for tents, leather, and other expenses connected with mining and shelter, six dollars a month. These items, in some respects the most important connected with their labor, amount to two million, four hundred thousand dollars in the year. Some of the most experienced American miners say that the Chinese lay out as much money for these articles as themselves; and that amount would, in this case, certainly not seem a large estimate.

Boarding and Provisions

In the towns the Chinese indulge in a greater variety of food; while in the mountains many articles are more expensive. They think three dollars a week, say twelve dollars a month, a low calculation. This is a hundred and forty-four dollars a year for the whole number. A large share of this goes to butchers and farmers in the mines, and to our own traders.

Clothing and Bedding

The immigrants bring always a chest of clothes and a bundle of bedding. But the amount of these articles is small, so that in a year or so you may notice American pants, then shirts, then coats and caps or hats. Servants, and a few merchants, dress in good broadcloth—some quite handsomely. Many purchase watches, and a less number rings, fanciful studs or buttons, and other jewelry. Allow, however, for pantaloons, shirts, coats, and caps or hats, thirteen dollars in the year. For blankets and other articles of household use, say seven dollars a year.

Boots and Shoes

But the first thing our friend John mounts, is a pair of the largest boots he can find. Working in the water, they sometimes knock out a pair in a month. These cost them three to five dollars the pair. They complain of this outlay as one of the heaviest to which they are subject. Put down boots at a lower figure than some of them sanction, and say, for boots, and also shoes, which are worn about the camp slipshod, twenty dollars a year.

Eight dollars a year would certainly not cover miscellaneous expenses.

Reckon up these items, connected with mountain life and labor, and we may be surprized to find the result. And yet that result might be shown by more complete information to be much below the truth. It is—

For mining claims, implements and water,	$2,400,000
For boarding	5,760,000
For clothing	800,000
For boots and shoes	800,000
For miscellaneous items	320,000
Total ordinary outlays	$10,080,000

Their Small Profits

It is the opinion of some of our citizens that the Chinese spend but little here, and carry the larger part of the proceeds of their labors home to China. But after the fullest inquiry among themselves and our people I am satisfied this is not correct. Their claims are the poorest, and there are many draughts upon them for licenses, taxes, assistance of their poor countrymen, their companies, charitable purposes, &c.; they meet with many losses from robberies, ignorance, and in other ways, so that but few send or carry back any large amounts.

They Spend Freely

It is the testimony of the most reliable merchants in the country, that no idea concerning the Chinese is more incorrect than that they live on the meanest diet, and that almost wholly imported from China. They are very economical, and are sharp traders; yet the statement is repeatedly made, in the mines, with an air of truth, that the Chinese live even better than any other people; that they yield more to animal gratifications; and indulge in feasts, some of them celebrations of religious or national holidays, others mere convivial occasions with friends. And when these occur they appear wholly regardless of expense, paying several dollars for a single fowl. They are fond of neat and rich, but not gaudy dress, and not a few sport costly gold watches and ornaments.

Exployed by Miners

The practical miners are not only profited by the purchases of claims, and the sums paid to their hydraulic companies, but also by the employment of the Chinese to work as hands. In some portions of the State, the Chinese are exclusively employed in this, preferring to work at reasonable steady rates rather than be subjected to the expenses, uncertainty, and difficulties connected with holding claims of their own.

"In El Dorado county, says the *Mountain Democrat,* they rarely interfere with the miners. They generally work in old deserted claims, where they cannot realize more than from two to three dollars a day, and seldom this much. When they get a good claim they buy it and pay liberally for it. Business in some of the small mining camps in our county would be wholly suspended during the summer months were it not for them. They are content to work laboriously for two dollars a day, and work claims which no others would. They make good hands, and are frequently hired by the miners. We have heard but little complaint against them by the miners, and the feeling which at first existed against them, and which was greatly exaggerated, is fast wearing away. They are a sober, quiet, industrious, inoffensive class of men, and, in our opinion, are a great benefit to our county. They pay annually into our treasury, for licenses alone, from sixty to eighty thousand dollars—a sum we cannot afford to lose. They pay our merchants promptly for every article they buy. They attend to their own business, and are rarely engaged in brawls. The mines they work would be unproductive were it not for them, being too poor to pay others for working them. Where is the miner in our county who would toil from 'early morn till dewy eve' for two dollars a day, with no prospect of obtaining more? A Chinaman will do it cheerfully, but other miners will not. For the last year but few of them have worked on their own account, being principally hired by miners.''

Corroboration of These General Statements

To place this branch of the subject in the clearest light possible, I have obtained the opinions of intelligent friends, resident in the mountains, or having extensive dealings and intercourse with the Chinese there.

The first is a letter from a gentleman whose employment leads him to travel through the length and breadth of the State, and to become acquainted with all classes of men. He says:

''At your request I present you in brief my views respecting the Chinese in our country, that most unfortunate and least appreciated class of foreigners, with whom we are here brought into contact. Now, in the cities are seen the very worst specimens of them; but in my travels through the different parts of the mining regions of California since '49, and especially during the past nine months, in frequent journeys extending from the head waters of the Feather to the Merced, I can say decidedly I believe, that among the American mining population there is no other class of foreign miners who do not speak our language, who sustain as high a character for industry, honesty, and direct patronage of American productions and enterprise. I have often enquired of merchants as to their business with the Chinese, and almost always been answered that their trade was very extensive and important; that while they consume large quantities of imported provisions from China, yet that they purchase much that is American, often even that which is most expensive, even luxuries such as chickens, eggs, fresh meats in cans, pork, even when it might be twice as dear as beef, melons, fruit, &c.; that the Chinese would purchase when the expense was such as to deter Americans, for the Chinese would have what they wanted, cost what it may. They are generally free from drunkenness, quarrels, and lazy habits which characterize many others in the mines, and labor faithfully, satisfied when none others will work. I have just called upon an agent of the California Stage Company in this place, and was told by him that, to the best of his judgment, taking all their stage routes together, full one-quarter of their passengers during the last year had been Chinese; that they patronize public conveyances in proportion to their numbers more than Americans. I find, also, that the Chinese are often employed as cooks, and are very well spoken of as such, as also in other kindred occupations. They seem almost to be universally respected among the mining and laboring portion of the inhabitants. I can say decidedly, I believe, that among the working classes in the mountains, they are truly considered as worthy of much regard, and the strong feeling is that they ought not be taxed as high as they are; that they ought to have legal protection from those who rob and steal from them, even to murdering them, for they have no redress unless an American is witness to the deed, and comes in with the law to their relief; and that their oath ought to be allowed in legal tribunals, at least so far that a jury or court might, if it judged best, receive their testimony.

The following is a letter from an influential merchant in the city of Marysville:

"It is impossible for me to give an accurate estimate of the amount of goods sold in this city to Chinamen. I have conversed with several of the mountain merchants, and they give it as their opinion that more than three-fourths of their sales to Chinamen are for American products. Almost every merchant in the mines has more or less Chinese trade, and a good many of them are dependent almost entirely on them for their business. The following are the kind of goods, provisions, &c., they consume the most of: potatoes, cabbage, pork, chickens, flour, and almost every article of vegetables raised in this State— they buy clothing, shoes, boots, blankets, American brandy, whiskey, gin, hams, beans, lard, codfish, lobsters, and almost every article of American production to some extent. As they become Americanized, the demand for American products increases with them. Their trade is valuable, being almost entirely cash. They are generally prompt in meeting their contracts. They are shrewd and close dealers, but spend their money freely for luxuries and comfort—it is said when a Chinaman does not live well it is because he has not the money to procure such as he would like. The Chinamen say that the estimate is made that they spend in the country seven-tenths on an average of all the money they make. Dealers with them in the mines are of the opinion their estimate is nearly correct: that is, of those I have conversed with. There are about twelve or fifteen teams on an average per week leaving this city with loads for Chinese merchants in the mines. This I should think is about correct, but the amount taken out by American merchants to supply their Chinese trade is a great deal more. To say the amount is equal, it would give employment to twenty-five or thirty teams per week, which I think is under the actual number. Look at our public conveyances, and you will see them generally crowded with Chinamen—for a Chinaman was never known to walk when there was any chance to ride. Many of the stage routes could not be sustained were it not for them. They are fond of travelling, and do not remain long in one place. From these hints you can draw your own estimates. I am pleased to learn that some steps are about to be taken to endeavor to get the exorbitant and unjust tax reduced; and have no doubt, could the people vote on the subject, a large majority would decide against the present tax."

Mr. S———, a butcher in the Southern mines, says: "I often sell as much as four hundred weight of beef a day to the Chinamen, and charge them sixteen to twenty cents a pound. They hardly ever ask for it for less if they are treated fairly and get good weight. I liked them very much as a people, and used to befriend them in many of their troubles, in which they used to always come to me.

They preferred pork, even at twenty-five cents a pound. I have sold in one day as high as fourteen hogs, averaging seventy-five pounds each. They will pay as high as a dollar a pound for nice dried sausage. They are very fond of fowls, and buy a great many. For a large one they pay two dollars, the general price now is about a dollar and a half. But I have sold a fat chicken at three dollars and a half, for a feast. They like fish too, whenever they can be got, and use dried or salt fish daily.

As for the clothes they buy, I would rather have a trade with them than with white people. Small stocks will do, and they are not so particular about fits. It is a great advantage to men that have not much capital to trade with. The profits are greater than on finer goods. They use most of the articles we do, and like to dress well on particular occasions. They wear not only flannel shirts, but check also, and a good many French prints.

The general articles they use are profitable. There is as much made on liquors sold them as almost anything else. Men put on them shameful mean stuff; and they always keep liquor in the camp, and they use it at their meals. They like a milder tobacco,—get a considerable amount of American tobacco, and shave it down, to smoke, and make little cigaritas. They have just as good tents, every bit, as other people, and use a great deal of drilling and canvas for hose.

The Chinamen are the best customers the stages have. They never ask for passage free, and pay down without trouble. Nearly every good citizen in this country would vote to keep them here, and in fact takes their part when they get into difficulty. They are among the quietest and best we have.''

We have the following testimony that the Chinese use all kinds of American groceries and merchandize, from a gentleman engaged in heavy business:

"The principal articles purchased by the Chinese population, in my line of business, take a very wide range, embracing nearly all those in use amongst our general population. I have found the Chinese particularly prompt in fulfilling their engagements with me, both in sales and purchases, and I have transacted a comparatively large amount of business with them. I find, on reference to my book, that the articles most permanent in my sales are, salt fish, pork, lard, salt, liquors, flour, tea, sardines, preserved meats, raisins, olive oil, macaroni and vermicelli, paper and matches, together with a variety of other articles that are either the product of American industry, or pay a large profit in the way of trade.''

An auctioneer in San Francisco, who sells daily to Chinese customers, writes that "butter" is the only article, to his knowledge, that they do not buy.

"Being engaged in the provision trade in the city of San Francisco since 1850, we say with pleasure, that we have had a fair proportion of the Chinese trade. They use the luxuries, or we may say dainties of life, in a greater profusion than our own countrymen, being, as a general thing, extremely fond of good living, and sparing no expense to attain it. They are consumers of every variety of merchandize, with one exception. Butter is an article not used by them, but no doubt will be as they become used to our manners and customs.''

Domestic Interest

Our wives and families have a very deep interest in the presence and labors of the Chinese. In a country where females are yet few, and the cares of large households exhausting to their feeble strength, the aid of these patient, busy, economical people, many of whom have had a previous training in various departments of domestic drudgery in the houses of American, English, and other foreign residents at various ports along the Chinese coast, has been felt to be a boon. And the best influence that has been exerted upon these strangers has been by the intelligent and gentle women of America. The grateful pleasure cannot be uttered which one feels in observing their unostentatious kindness, the patient efforts to instruct in the rudiments of our tongue and our knowledge, and the silent but powerful impressions for good thus made. Women, true to the character of their sex, are the best ministry that philanthropy and the gospel can employ in elevating and ennobling the wanderers from a land of gloom.

Miscellaneous Advantages

This subject is one so expanded and comprehensive, that with the barest glance at only its chief features, a number of interesting points must still remain unnoticed. The development of the marine treasures of our coast is one of these. Valuable species of fish, precious shells, and other products of the ocean's shoals and shores, must lie always ungathered unless we can employ the gleaners and divers from the Asiatic side. And so there are other occupations that await them, that which time alone can fit them for, and fully display to us.

But I cannot dwell further on the numerous points of advantage spread before us in the immigration to this new American territory of a race who were civilized long previous to ourselves, and who, though now surpassed in some departments of national improvement, yet in some others are not so much behind us as our superiority to a great portion of those poorer specimens that have emigrated here, and the ignorance of the language and character of the rest, and as our pride, would permit us to acknowledge. This much has been shown, from a great variety of facts and arguments, that the *general emolument to this State, resulting from the Chinese immigration, cannot be counted within millions of dollars; that every interest that is important to us as a people is deeply involved in their various labors, in humane treatment of them, and in prudent and equitable legislation on matters affecting them.*

Morals of the Chinese

The second general class of objections made in California to the presence of the Chinese is, the evil *influence of their morals.* On this score, no defence is attempted. The writer sees all the pollution, and all the baseness, that must characterize mankind where there is no Divine revelation to instruct and reform. He knows what exists among the Chinese, abhors it, and is often made most deeply sensible of their moral inferiority to the specimens of purity and excellence produced by genuine Christianity. But these considerations he may offer in palliation. First, they are immeasurably superior to any other unchristianized people whom he has seen, or of whom he has read; and we must either seclude our nation from the rest of the world, or else we must rise above the influences that stream upon us for evil, from every other kind of immigration as well as from this. Secondly, that they are not likely to be allowed to immigrate to such an extent as to resist influences for their transformation; and their vices should be restrained and punished by the arm of the law. Thirdly, they have been brought here, if the providence of God is read aright, that they may see Christianity, and come in closer contact with its influences. Fourthly, that the power of our civilization and our religion have subdued other races far more numerous in our midst. The negro is the most debased form of humanity; yet the number of negroes converted to Christianity is greater, proportionably, than of whites, and some of the most sincere Christians in the land have a black skin. The Indian, also, is slowly yielding, wild as beast of the forest though he is originally. The Indian tribes are abandoning the religion of their forefathers; and, better still, numbers of them are exemplary members of evangelical sects, whose missionaries labor among them. The Cherokees, for instance, are equal to some of the whites.

Honor in Paying Debts

The remarkable honor in paying just debts, so often noticed by our merchants, is, in one sense, a national characteristic. In their native land, every man is expected to have his accounts settled, or be declared bankrupt, at the close of the year; and it is one leading object of their association into their voluntary companies, to have agents at San Francisco who shall prevent the return to their native land of any in debt, either to Americans or to each other. An instance is mentioned of a Chinaman who called at a store to settle a bill of half a dollar, incurred months before by a friend. Thousands of dollars worth of merchandize have been trusted to the miners in particular neighborhoods, with small or no loss. In conversation with merchants in the mountains, the frequent testimony was that their pay is the best pay, and their trade the best trade in the mines.

The difference between the Chinese miner and the pale-faced miner, is this: the former manages to live always within his means; the latter, too often, beyond. So that the profit the storekeeper derives from his Chinese customer is apt to be lost by crediting the French, Irish and Americans.

Almost the only crime for which they are brought before our Courts, is that of petty theft, committed by a few of the most poor and miserable creatures among them. They timidity—their disguised pride—their industry, and the harshness exercised towards them, prevents ordinary crimes, which they might otherwise commit. No people are so scrupulous, for the same reasons, in paying their debts. They allow no poor, though there are enough of them, to go wandering round as beggars. Nor do they ever permit themselves to be seen drunk in the streets. Can such testimony be borne in behalf of any other people in California, that they have so *few beggars, so few drunkards, and so few criminals?*

They may safely be compared, in these respects, with any Continental immigration to the United States. There are no complaints of hordes of paupers in almshouses and hospitals, and criminals filling the prisons. The few that do apply at our hospitals find difficulty in obtaining entrance or an effectual cure. Yet the European immigration has advantages that overbalance its evils, and we therefore welcome it. Shall we expect any Asiatic immigration to which we shall not also find great objections? Certainly none less objectionable than the Chinese.

The Legislation Needed

Justice to this subject, which is as important to the United States bordering on the Pacific ocean as intercourse with Europe is to the United States bordering on the Atlantic, and its ramifications into every interest of our people, and into the great future, demands, then, intelligent, wise, and judicious legislation. The Chinese are a people unaccustomed to our mode of government. Their laws are old, few, and, on the whole, in principle at least, just. Frequent and special legislative interferences gall them. Changes distress them. They become anxious, bitter, and petulant. And, beside, special legislation in reference to any class in a community tends to degrade that class. It creates dangerous and unwise distinctions. And it throws stones in the way of improvement.

If the views presented in this Plea commend themselves, gentlemen of the Legislature, to your judgment as reasonable, your knowledge of the modes in which they may be applied to the present state of affairs doubtless leaves little more for me to say. When we ask the sphere of legislation, four points may be indicated as requiring their attention. 1. The *number* allowed to immigrate to this country should not be too great. We may not be prepared to afford them useful employment. They may come in excess, and not settle down, and assimilate to our institutions and wants.

It is therefore the preference of many judicious men, and not unreasonable, to allow for the present the law which fixes a capitation tax to remain, provided it is so administered as not to interfere with commerce, and the passage to and fro of those engaged in regular business. And judgment can only indicate future duty from observation of

its results, or in compliance with the future wants and desires of our
own people.

2. The amount of the license required from miners deserves consideration. The amount fixed by the present law is oppressive. Few are
possessed of good claims. It beggars them. It drives them to the
mountains and thickets like wild beasts. It fills them with hunger,
sickness and despair. It turns them, what their honorable character
with our trading population in the country shows is not necessary,
into cheats and liars. It will in time fill our prisons. And makes them
loathe and hate us as a people, and our name, our country, our government and the Christian religion, which they understand we profess.
If put to the former standard of four dollars per month, the sum affords a handsome State and County revenue, and they appear willing
to pay it. If put lower, as some have proposed, there is danger of new
legislation, in two or three years, to increase it again.

There are some humane and right-minded men engaged in the collecting of the licenses. To them we would render all praise, and indeed peculiar praise. But the conduct of others, that are monsters in
human form, is not unknown to you; their unjust and unauthorized
modes of extorting the barren gleanings, so hardly scratched out from
the rocks by these poor men; their barbarity to those who resist or
hesitate—often, if the case were understood, for sufficient reasons;
and again their downright robbery, though clad with the honorable
authority of officers of the State, by demanding payments for previous
periods, by forcing an individual in a camp to be paymaster for the
rest, who may be as irresponsible to him as Patagonians; by distraining, and instantly bidding off to some miscreant of our own color,
their necessary tools, and their very bed-clothing, and the garments
not on their back. You have heard of all these things, so that your
teeth involuntarily gritted, and your face flushed with anger and
shame.

4. Better *protection* must be extended to Chinese residents generally. Some means should be devised by which the statements of Chinese should be received in regard to crimes affecting their lives, persons, and property. They do not perhaps understand sufficiently the
nature of an oath to be admitted in our courts to enjoy an equal privilege with those acquainted with the sanctions of Christianity. But no
other means probably than receiving their affirmation, allowing it the
credence that according to internal evidence and the accompanying
circumstances it seems fairly to deserve, will prevent degraded and
outlawed creatures from robbing, bruising, cheating or killing a Chinaman, when no white witness is near.

The *protection* of the Chinese miners from marauders is vital to
their quiet, and to their usefulness to ourselves. They can have no
heart for industry, and no respect for laws, where they are plundered

by night and by day, by infamous wretches, who boldly rob a camp in the face of a hundred, if no whites are present, and who have no compunctions in murdering even the unresisting. There have been hundreds of such cases.

Relations of the Subject

Gentlemen of the Legislature: This plea has laid before you a few of the facts relating to this great subject, and a few of its bearings upon ourselves, and yet a very few, and only in a brief and merely suggestive form.

To you as *statesmen* its intelligent and serious consideration is a matter of great importance. A few years ago the Union was divided into the North and the South. Now it is divided into the North, the South, and the West. Though those two portions of the Atlantic States can scarcely realize that ten years have put the several States on the Pacific coast in a position of influence which it required them ten scores of years, generations of men, and rivers of blood, and stupendous labors and expenditures, to occupy; yet it is none the less true. The gold of California has sustained the commercial credit of the Union. It has saved shaking fortunes; it has comforted millions of pining eyes and hoary heads; it has filled the world with fleet and hurrying ships. Yellow gold, the crop of this soil, is as essential now to the prosperity of the Union as the wheat of the North, and as the cotton of the South; and we'll balance our bars against either the sheaf or the bale.

We find now the Atlantic and Pacific at length united at several points in Central America. And five different lines have been surveyed, and a national railroad virtually determined upon, which shall, throughout its whole length in republican territory, and in a straight line, and the shortest, connect the great commercial interests of the two Oceans.

Humboldt says, "*The problem of the communication between the two seas* is important to all civilized Europe. At a time when the new continent, profiting by the misfortunes and perpetual dissensions of Europe, advances rapidly towards civilization, and when the commerce of China, and the Northwest coast of America, becomes of greater importance, this subject is of the *greatest interest* for the *balance of commerce* and the *political preponderancy of nations*." "Should a canal communication be opened between the two oceans, the productions of Nootka Sound, (fur, oils, &c.) and of China, will be brought more than two thousand leagues nearer to Europe and the United States. Then only can any *great change* be effected *in the political state of Eastern Asia:* for this neck of land, the barrier against the waves of the Atlantic ocean, has been for many ages the bulwark of the independence of China and Japan.

And I cannot but here advert to the political fatuity of some who describe, in glowing language, the results of the gigantic plans which are to link the sides of the continent, and then connect these opposite continents, by steam and talk of the "riches of the Indies;" and who yet spurn and crush the first ambassadors which the Indies send us, even though, like the Gibeonites, they have "old shoes and clouted upon their feet, and old garments upon them, and all the bread of their provision was dry and mouldy,"—men who see that in a sense we shall possess the earth, and have come to make a league with us, and lay their possessions at our feet. The Chinese are a reading, thinking people; who tell, and who put on record what they know. Some may despise the influence of those who come to California. But even now among the men nearest the Imperial throne, are those who are sought on account of their previous intercourse with foreigners. Poor boys educated at missionary schools have been taken into the confidence of the minsters of state. It is folly, it is insanity, to think, however men may reason or protest to the contrary, that the impressions of American received here will not, to a large degree, shape the whole future intercourse of the nations who are now for the first time saluting each other.

Several Chinese commenced plantations for the cultivation of sugar. These employ Chinese overseers and operators, who boil the sugar, and perform the more difficult parts of the labor. But they prefer natives for other work, as they can be employed more cheaply. But a few years must pass before the former soft and thriftless people shall have wholly disappeared, and their places be filled by the hardier and more valuable race from the continent of Asia. And so shall it be with all the Islands of the Pacific. The races that inhabited them for a time are dying, like the aborigines of this continent. We cannot populate them. Europe cannot, and will not be allowed to populate them. Who shall till their garden soils, and pluck their luscious fruits, and dive for their pearls, and hew their spicy woods, and make them hospitable caravansaries of the sea? No answer need be given to those who have observed how the people of China are now settling every group, and how the few whites are anxiously inviting them to come.

5.4
A Reply to the Charges Against the Chinese

Facts Upon the Other Side of the Chinese Question: With a Memorial to the President of the U.S. from Representative Chinamen in America.

A reply to the charges against the Chinese as embodied in the resolutions adopted at the Anti-Chinese Mass meeting, held April 5th, 1876, in San Francisco. Respectfully submitted to the unbiased judgment of the American People, President, and Congress, by the Friends of right, justice, and humanity.

Preamble

Being fully aware that the subject in controversy, namely, *The Chinese Immigration to this Country,* is one of paramount importance to both State and Nation;

That it is a debatable question, of which thus far but one side has had a full bearing;

That it is the constitutional right and privilege of every citizen in this Free Republic to write, publish, and speak candidly his own sentiments on any public subject, whether popular or unpopular.

And, moreover, believing that several charges against the Chinese, which are embodied in the Address and Resolutions of the Citizens' Anti-Chinese Committee, adopted at the Mass Meeting held in San Francisco, April 5th, are untrue, or exaggerated;

The Friends of Right, Justice, and Humanity, While entertaining the highest respect for said Committee and the vast assembly which honored their Address and Resolutions with their approval, they are compelled to dissent from them, and to accept the challenge contained in the above mentioned resolutions, "to successfully refute the charges they have made against the Chinese."

In submitting this Reply to the intelligent and unbiased judgment of the American people, President, and Congress, the Friends of Right, Justice, and Humanity fondly hope that it will receive the consideration it deserves, notwithstanding it proceeds from a minority—since a question of a national interest, like this of "Chinese Immigration," should be decided from reason and fact and by the voice, not of one State alone, but of the majority of States.

The Committee open their address by declaring their intention to respect the provision of treaties, the decision of courts, and the higher considerations of humanity, in dealing with the Chinese who are domiciled in our midst.

The spirit of fairness and humanity toward a helpless class of human beings, and of submission to law and authority, thus shown by the Committee, is very commendable indeed.

Had, however, this fine declaration gone one step further, and included the Chinese that may come hereafter, and before the abrogation of the American treaty with China, it would be unexceptionable.

No reasonable man will say that their claim is not well grounded. But it is not exclusively theirs. All persons who thoroughly acquaint themselves with all the facts in the Chinese case, both *pro* and *con,* are able to form an intelligent and correct judgment on this subject.

And if the people and Congress, outside of California, are not competent to adjudicate this subject intelligently, why do the Committee invoke, with so much fervor, their decision?

Reply to the Charges Against the Chinese

First Charge—"The Chinese will soon outnumber our people."

The Committee estimate the Chinese population in California at 200,000, (about one-fourth of the entire population of the State,) of whom 75,000 reside in San Francisco, and constitute "one-fourth part of our people."

This estimate is grossly incorrect. In order to be fair on this point, we will give the statistics as they have been gathered from reliable sources, beginning with the statement of Chinese passengers arrived at and departed from the port of San Francisco since 1852, which was compiled from the Custom House records and published in the San Francisco *Evening Post.*

Year.	Arrived.	Departed.
1852	20,025	1,768
1853	4,270	4,421
1854	16,084	2,339
1855	3,329	3,473
1856	4,807	3,028
1857	5,925	1,938
1858	5,427	2,542
1859	3,175	2,450
1860	7,341	2,000
1861	8,490	3,580
1862	8,175	2,792
1863	6,432	2,404
1864	2,682	3,910
1865	3,005	2,295
1866	2,245	3,111
1867	4,290	4,475
1868	11,081	4,210
1869	14,091	4,835
1870	10,870	4,236
1871	5,540	3,260
1872	9,770	4,800
1873	17,075	6,805
1874	16,085	7,710
1875	18,021	6,302
First quarter of 1876	5,065	625
Total	214,126	99,089

"This gives an excess of arrivals over departures of 124,137. The number of Chinese in California before this record began to be kept is estimated at 10,000, so that the total of Chinese now in the country, without deducting the deaths, would be about 134,000. Deduct 24,000 for deaths, and we have the round number of 110,000 Mongolians now with us."—*S. F. Post,* April 20th, 1876.

Next we add the statement regarding the number of Chinese in America, as obtained by the Senate Sub-Committee on Chinese investigation from the Presidents of the six Chinese Companies, which is as follows:

Sam Yup Company	10,100
Young Wo Company	10,200
Kong Chow Company.	15,000
Wing Young Company	75,000
Hop Wo Company	34,000
Yan Wo Company	42,000
Total	148,600

"They estimated that there were 30,000 in San Francisco, and 30,000 in the State, outside of San Francisco."—*S. F. Bulletin,* April 20th. 1876.

If we accept the report of the Senate Sub-Committee authorized by the six Chinese Companies, which makes a more liberal estimate of the entire Chinese population in America than the Custom House statistics do, there are now 148,000 Chinese in the United States, of whom 60,000 reside in California, and of these 30,000 live in San Francisco, and 30,000 in the State at large.

If, therefore, the population of San Francisco now reaches, according to the generally accepted estimate, the number of 250,000, and that of the entire State is 800,000, the Chinese number in this State and City above given is *less than one-eighth* of the population of the City, and *less than one-thirteenth* of the population of the entire State.

Surely, the computation makes a great difference in the estimate made by the Committee, that "the Chinese in California constitute one-fourth of the population of the entire State, and the Chinese in San Francisco are one-fourth of its population."

But the Committee aver that, "considering the source from whence comes the Chinese immigration, viz: China, which contains 400,000,000 of inhabitants as against 40,000,000 who live in the United States, and considering that this is an age of cheap and quick transportation by reason of steam, etc., they feel alarmed at this increasing invasion (*i.e.* immigration) lest it may soon outnumber our Pacific Coast population, and imperil our best interests."

However, if the rate of Chinese immigration be in the future as it has been in the last twenty years, the Committee may as well allay their fears, since there is no reason why the gauge should not keep steady in the future as in the past.

The Chinese immigration to this coast comes only by sea, and about three or four times a month. White immigration comes in every day, both by sea and by land, and in very large numbers.

Finally, it must be remembered that China has been a secluded empire for ages, and the policy of the Imperial Government is sternly opposed to the expatriation of its subjects—hence it refuses to appoint any consular agent in our State for their protection, saying that "if they come here they must take the risk."

The vision, therefore, of 400,000,00 of Chinamen soon overrunning the land, and driving out the white man—notwithstanding the fact that after a period of twenty-five years of Asiatic immigration, but 148,000 of them are domiciled in our midst—is either a gross delusion of a diseased imagination, or a wicked imposition, practiced on the credulous by scheming demagogues.

Second Charge—"In the Labor Market the Chinese can underbid the white man or woman."

Our first answer to this accusation is, that if underbidding in the labor market were an offense punishable with banishment, many white laborers, both skilled and unskilled, would be compelled to leave the country. Certainly this offense is quite common to Europeans, Africans, Americans, as well as Asiatics. And under a penal statute prohibiting it, the inventors of machines, the builders of railroads, nay all who make use of steam or horse power on a large scale, should likewise quit the country, because all of them, like the Chinese, only in a greater measure, can underbid the white man or woman in the labor market.

But, is the charge true that Chinamen can under-labor the white man or woman?

The Committee support their assertion by another, that "the Chinese can subsist more cheaply, and consequently work for lower wages than the white laborer, man or woman."

Supposing, for the present, that Chinese labor is cheap—which is not the fact—we dismiss as not pertinent to this discussion the reason why it is so, whether it be in consequence of their frugal mode of living, or from any other individual cause; holding that the right of living in a most economical manner was never disputed to individuals even in the most despotic countries.

We therefore ask, in what labor market can the Chinaman underbid the white laborer? Is it in the scientific, artistic, or mechanic field of labor?

The Chinese cannot, evidently, compete with the white race in scientific labor, such as of law, divinity, physics, mathematics, engineering, chemistry, etc., etc., all of which branches furnish employment to a very large multitude, because the oriental instruction of the Chinese is vastly different from the modern western education, and they are not sufficiently versed in the western languages, both modern and ancient.

For the same reason, they cannot compete with the white race in most of the liberal, polite or finer arts, perfected by western civilization; hence they cannot compete with our school teachers, professors of belles-lettres, musicians, painters, sculptors, actors, and a thousand other artists.

In what labor market can then the Chinese underbid the white man or woman?

It is in the market of purely mechanic labor, but only in a small measure. It is in that part of the field which is open indiscriminately to the European, African, American, and Asiatic laborer. As, for instance, in the manual work of factories, shops, fields, or gardens; in the domestic service particularly of the menial kind.

However, even in this restricted part of the labor market, it is not true that the Chinese can underbid at pleasure the white man or woman. They cannot compete for instance with the white laborer, when higher wages are offered to the latter than to the Chinaman for the same kind of work, as is commonly the case.

They cannot compete when the work is accomplished by the white laborer with the aid of machines propelled by steam or horse power, or other mechanical appliances which the Chinaman, on account of his poverty, cannot have. The effect of these machines is to increase the production of manufactures or the amount of work, and thus to reduce the price of labor. It is in this manner that some laundries in San Francisco, with the aid of machinery, can reduce the price of washing to less than half a cent per piece, and thus undersell the Chinaman who works by hand.

The charge, therefore, that ''in the labor market the Chinese can underbid the white man or woman,'' is not altogether true, either in a general or particular sense.

Third Charge:—''The Chinese do not here invest their money; do not buy, but import from China most of the clothes they wear and the food they consume; send to China the proceeds of their labor, and provide for the return of their dead bodies.''

Supposing these to be facts, what inference do the Committee draw from them? That the Chinese are not useful to the State?

However, it has been shown already, that they have aided and are now aiding to develop the natural resources of the country, to multiply industries, to widen the field of labor and to increase our wealth. And is not this a sufficient proof of their usefulness?

Was ever the obligation imposed on either capital or labor, to spend the money fairly earned in the same place where it is earned? Do white capitalist or laborers recognize such a law anywhere? If so, then the wealth of the Bonanza mines would have to remain in Nevada and in Virginia City, instead of San Francisco. By universal consent, each individual is free to invest his own money in the manner and place he deems most advantageous to himself. This species of liberty is one of ''the inalienable rights with which all men are endowed by their Creator,'' according to the declaration of our Independence.

However, the above charge does not hold good with regard to the Chinese, some of whom have bought thousands of acres of land which they have put under cultivation, and others have acquired real

estate property in San Francisco, the value of which, according to As-
sessor Badlam's statement before the Senate Committee, last year,
was over $100,000.

Nor is it true that "the Chinese do not use or consume our products, and that they altogether remit to China the proceeds of their
labor." We can do no better than repeat the answer made on this
same point to the Jesuit Buchard, in a lecture delivered at Platt's Hall,
March 14th, 1873, by the Rev. O. Gibson, a Protestant missionary for
ten years in China, and long resident of San Francisco, having charge
of the Chinese mission on this coast:

"It is about time that the fallacy was taken out of this kind of talk.
Many Chinamen wear garments made out of our cloth, they wear our
boots and our hats; they are fond of watches, and jewelry, and sewing
machines; they ride in our cars and steamers; they eat our fish, and
beef, and potatoes, and exhaust our pork market. Take the one item of
pork alone, and the Chinamen of this coast pay to our producers on
this coast half a million of dollars annually. If we would itemize the
various products which they consume, we should find that they do not
send home over ten per cent of their earnings."

To form an idea of the amount of money which the Chinese pay
annually to the people and Government of the State and Nation, let us
make the following modest computation:

If we reckon that each Chinaman pays yearly to the business community of the State for the articles of life he uses and the food he
consumes, such as fresh meat and groceries, and for his conveyance
in street cars, railroads, and steamers, only $20 a year, or less than $2
per month, upon the estimate we have before made of only 60,000
Chinese sojourning in California, the amount of money thus paid here
by them amounts to $1,200,000 annually.

Our opponents say that the Chinese have scarcely any real estate
property; if so, they must, and do, pay high rents for their dwellings.
In San Francisco alone, their rental in the quarter they inhabit, which
comprises about eight blocks, cannot be less than $150,000 per
month, which, being added to the rental paid by the Chinese wash-
houses and cigar stores throughout the city, it will swell to $200,000
monthly, or $2,400,000 yearly. Assuming that the 30,000 Chinese in
cities and towns throughout the State, outside of San Francisco, pay
no less than $500,000 for house rent, and that the annual insurance
paid by Chinese merchants is no less than $100,000, we have a total
of $3,000,000 paid annually by the Chinese to real estate owners in
this State.

Add now the poll tax, which is for them $120,000; also the license
tax for mining, washing, etc., which can be no less than $50,000 a
year, and behold a grand total of the amount of money disbursed annually by the Chinese population in the State of California, for the

benefit of the Government, merchants, real estate owners, railroad and steamer companies, equal to $4,370,000.

This vast sum, however, does not comprise the Custom duties which the Chinese pay for the articles they import to the United States. Rev. O. Gibson has estimated the duties on their imports to be no less than $2,000,000 each year. Certainly the figures of Chinese imports for 1874 and 1875, as gathered from the Custom House, seem to warrant this statement:

Imports 1874 and 1875.

	1874.	1875.
Tea,	$1,096,400	$ 518,926
Rice,	812,261	1,141,462
Opium,	226,632	757,640
Sugar,	481,273	183,656
Silk,	626,424	209,336
Coffee,	151,585	162,823
Other articles,	1,374,422	1,741,739
Totals,	$4,688,797	$4,715,582
Grand total,		$9,404,379

Now do not these figures effectively contradict the statement which has so much prejudiced the popular mind against the Chinese, that they spend no money in this State, but "remit to China the proceeds of their labor?"

Fourth Charge: "The majority of Chinamen have been imported under servile-labor contracts, and the women for lewd purposes, against the spirit and letter of our law."

This charge is indeed serious; for it asserts that Chinamen and China-women are slaves, and slavery of any kind is prohibited by the Constitution and laws of the United States.

There is no question, therefore, as to the nature of the offense; the only question is as to its existence. Therefore we ask, where is the proof? Have any considerable number of Chinamen and Chinawomen been interrogated as they should, with regard to their condition of life, and whether they have come to this country of their own free will and accord? We have not learned that any considerable body of Chinese have yet been examined on this particular, and that they have uniformly sustained the charge.

But who are the parties that have made these contracts and are holding Chinamen and Chinawomen in bondage? This is equally unknown.

The Anti-Chinese Committee speak of secret companies that hold them in servitude and enforce the labor contracts under severe penalties, which our laws cannot prevent.

. . . to think that the so-called Six Chinese companies import both men and women for service, against their own free will, and that they exercise coercive authority over them, we desire to sum up the facts relative to the character of said companies and of the Chinese in general, as elicited by the investigation lately held by the Senate Committee.

1st. Rev. O. Gibson, for ten years missionary in China, testified that "in China there is no slavery of men."—S. F. *Bulletin,* April 12th.

2d. Ching Fung Chow, President of the Yan Wo Co.: "Chinamen never sell their wives at home."—S. F. *Alta,* April 20th.

3d. Rev. Dr. Loomis, formerly missionary in China: "In social relations the Chinese are commendable; man and wife are faithful."— S. F. *Bulletin,* April 20th.

4th. Ex-Governor F. F. Low, formerly Minister to China: "Most of the Chinese women who emigrate are loose in their morals, but there is not much immorality among the females in China, as it is punished severely there."—S. F. *Chronicle,* April 12th. "He did not believe any Chinese were brought here against their wills.—*Chronicle, ib.*

5th. Rev. O. Gibson: "Was of opinion, that a majority of the Chinese who come to the United States were free and untrammeled, being bound by no contract whatever. He did not think that the Six Companies had any power over their members other than a persuasive power."

"The Six Companies were an association formed for the purpose of protecting the interests of its members, and there were no contacts, so far as he knew, between the companies and any Chinaman who comes to this country."—S. F. *Chronicle,* April 13th.

The Presidents of the Six Chinese Companies supported Dr. Gibson's statement, adding, that one of their objects is to take care of the sick; that they discourage prostitution, gambling, and Chinese immorality, an do not import either males or females, nor advance any money for their passage.

6th. A. Altmayer, a member of the firm of Einstein Bros., (manufacturers of boots and shoes, who have, until late, employed Chinamen of the Hop Wo Co.) testified that "He did not think that the men were the slaves of the Company, for *they threw up their contract when they chose and left without opposition.''*—S. F. *Chronicle*, April 15th.

Even if this evidence should conflict with contrary evidence, and its high authority be disregarded, it will most certainly establish one thing, namely, that the Anti-Chinese Committee have not yet found positive proof for sustaining the sweeping charge which they have made against the Chinese, namely, that "they are slaves imported to this country for servile labor or lewd purposes against the spirit and letter of our Constitution and law."

There may be undoubtedly some persons who make a traffic of Chinese females for immoral purposes and restrict their liberty; but it is questionable, even with regard to them, whether they have been imported against their wills.

Certainly, the law of Congress provides that our Consuls in Chinese ports shall duly investigate both the object of their emigration and their voluntary departure, and if they find that they are taken against their will, or for lewd purposes, they are required to refuse them the certificate of emigration which all masters of vessels must require of emigrants bound to the United States; and the law of Congress to Regulate Chinese Immigration, passed in December, 1869, requires, moreover, that no Chinese female shall be permitted to emigrate to the United States who is not accompanied by either her father or her husband.

Therefore, if the law has been violated in this respect, not the Chinese Companies, but our Consuls at the Chinese ports are to blame, and the appeal to Congress should be on our part to see that the law is enforced.

Sundry Charges and Conclusion

We dismiss as unworthy of consideration the charges that *"The Chinese are pagans; are not a homogeneous race, do not adopt our manners, our food, our style of dress, etc."*

It will be a sad day, indeed, for this great Republic, when it shall prescribe personal qualities of this kind of conditions to immigration. America will again become a wild then, and her great boast as "The Land of the Free" will be no more. Such qualifications for simple residents as recommended by the Anti-Chinese Committee are unknown even in the most despotic countries.

The Chinese are accused of being *filthy, diseased, immoral,* and *vicious* people, who fill our prisons and crowd our hospitals.

The Report of the Board of Directors of the California State Prison, for 1875, gives the total number of prisoners as 1,083, of whom only 187 are Chinese, notwithstanding they find but little mercy in our courts. The County Hospital Report shows also but a small proportion of Chinese patients. The City Record of mortality among them is very small, and Dr. Toland has testified that they are personally clean.

But if these evils exist, why do not the Municipal Authorities remedy them? Legislation is not exhausted as it is alleged, only faithful police officers who do not accept bribes are required, as shown by the investigation.

Again, if these charges be true, how does it happen that the Chinese have "*monopolized*," as you say, a great portion of the domestic and commercial service, and in the very best houses, for nearly twenty years? Can it be that our wealthy and honored citizens will confide their households to filthy, diseased, immoral and criminal servants? Either our citizens are not what they seem or it is not true what you say in regard to the Chinese.

But it is enough. This Anti-Chinese Crusade, started by sectarian fanaticism, encouraged by personal prejudice and ambition for political capital, has already culminated in personal attack abuse, and incendiarism against the inoffensive Chinese. Anti-Coolie Clubs are now arming and preparing to follow the late example of the people of Antioch, who have banished the Chinese and burned their quarters.

It is high time that the Municipal, State, and National authorities, in common with law abiding citizens, should awake to the imminent danger that threatens to break the peace and to disgrace both State and Nation. They must assert their authority in defense of our treaty obligations with China, for the protection of Chinese emigrants and in behalf of law and order.

5.5
Joel Franks
Chinese Shoemaker Protest in 19th Century San Francisco

Topical Introduction

One of the things which Euroamerican workers and employers agreed upon in post-Civil War America was that Chinese immigrants possessed an uncommon respect for authority. For workers, this indicated that the Chinese in America lacked the freedom-loving manliness that they believed fashioned the American republic into a citadel of liberty. For employers, this indicated that the Chinese in America made disciplined factory operatives, who would contentedly ignore the trade union movement. Even now, over one hundred years later, people of Asian descent are praised and condemned for ignoring the demands of democracy and social justice. However, as the following discussion adapted from Joel S. Franks', "Boot and Shoemakers in Nineteenth Century San Francisco, 1860–1892,: A Study in Class, Culture, Ethnicity, and Popular Protest in an Industrializing Community," unpublished dissertation, University of California, Irvine, suggests, people of Asian descent have been fully capable of combatting what they perceive as injustice.

The widespread belief that Chinese workers were "tools of Monopolists" was maintained in spite of what should have been seen as contrary evidence. For example, Chinese shoemakers in industrializing San Francisco demonstrated that neither a trade union tradition nor labor militancy were foreign to their experiences.

Shoemaker guilds existed in nineteenth century China. Like their better known European counterparts, these guilds regulated working hours, apprenticeships, payment, and strikes. Apparently, Chinese shoemaker protest was rare, but usually fiercely conducted. In Canton, the introduction of machines for sewing shoes provoked such hostility from shoemakers that authorities feared a general uprising. Eventually, the machinery was quietly dispatched to Hong Kong.

In San Francisco, Chinese shoemakers were enrolled in a guild like association, which, unlike modern labor unions, included bosses, as well as wage workers. This organization was presumably called Li-Sheng T'Ang, which means "Hall for Treading the New." Generally, the issue which aroused Chinese shoemakers to protest in the 1870s revolved around whether Chinese merchants and Euroamerican employers understood and respected the rules governing the shoemaker's work. These shoemakers, in some respects, exhibited what English historian, E. P. Thompson, describes as "a consistent, traditional view of social norms and obligations, of the proper economic functions within the community, which taken together constitute the moral economy of the poor." While, perhaps, we can't describe this moral economy as political in a contemporary sense, Thompson argues, "it cannot be described as unpolitical." It rests, that is, on "definite and passionately held, notions of the commonwealth—notions which, indeed, found some support in the paternalist tradition of the authorities; notions which the people reechoed so loudly in their turn that the authorities were, in some measure, the prisoners of the people." (Thompson: 1971)

Social relationships between the people and authorities in premodern, precapitalist societies such as nineteenth century China assumed mutual obligation between elite and non-elite groups. As long as the authorities fulfilled their obligations, they were deemed worthy of respect. Once they let such matters as profit and power distract them from their obligations to the poor, then they might well encounter popular protest and insurrection.

Chinese immigrant shoemakers, like other immigrant workers in the United States, brought with them a sense of what was just and unjust and were perfectly capable of protesting unfair treatment, as well as adapting their collective behavior to the changing American environment. One observer of San Francisco's early industrial scene declared that the best remedy against strikes was a mixed labor force of Chinese and Euroamericans. Employing only Chinese workers could prove unrewarding, because, he lamented, "they will combine." He argued that "they have the power of combination if you do not happen to get along with them and have a difficulty with one, the whole lot of them will stand up for each other, and as a general thing to go out together."

It was not just that a Euroamerican employer had to recognize that a wrong done to one Chinese worker was perceived by his Chinese employees as a wrong done to them all. He also should have understood that his Chinese work force often consisted of kin members, as well as people from the same village or region. Familial and community ties might bind Chinese workers, as they did other immigrant workers, in such a manner that the values of the market place were not alien to them, but, at the same time, possessed remarkably little importance to them in comparison to Euroamerican employers.

In the early 1870s, Euroamerican boot and shoe manufacturers probably became more suspicious that the Chinese workers was not as servile as they had assumed. On the one hand, many Chinese shoemakers were leaving white run firms to start their own businesses or cooperatives. On the other hand, they were participating increasingly in strikes against Euroamerican manufacturers and their Chinese merchant allies.

In 1876, Chinese shoemakers staged a brief, but violent, uprising in San Francisco. Before this display of popular wrath took place, a Chinese trading company and labor contractor had agreed to place 750 Chinese workers in two Euroamerican firms. The white manufacturers successfully attained a sizable deposit from the contractors, who, in turn, demanded an equal amount from the workers. Once employed in their new jobs, the Chinese shoemakers found their white bosses to be less than honest in their dealings with them. They went on strike and sought repayment of the money they had given the contractor. The Six Companies proved incapable of soothing the shoemakers' anger when the contractor refused to return their money. Consequently, fifty shoemakers attacked the trading company of Yee Chung and Company. The outcome was a bloody melee, in which many were reportedly injured.

Euroamerican manufacturers were known to have put Chinese shoemakers in quarters apart from their main factories. One reason was that publicly employing Chinese workers during the midst of a highly popular anti-Chinese movement was not always good for business. In any event, these secret work sites were often unsafely crowded with workers and poorly ventilated. That San Francisco city authorities were inspired to take action against these work sites is not so surprising as who they blamed in the matter. In 1882, for example, Chinese shoemakers employed by the firm of Buckingham and Hechts' were arrested for violating a cubic-air ordinance; that is, an ordinance presumably aimed at eliminating crowded working conditions. The Chinese shoemakers, then, refused to work until the firm paid their fines.

The rest of the 1880s saw continued strike activity among Chinese shoemakers. At this time, however, they seem to turn more from traditional notions of justice—the moral economy—to greater privileges as modern, industrial workers. In the summer of 1887, 300 Chinese shoemakers initiated a work stoppage in many Chinese run firms for a pay raise of $1.15 to $1.40 daily. All the involved firms were determined to defeat the strike. One firm, Hop Kee and Co., even brought in some white workers to replace their striking Chinese employees.

The strikers just as stubbornly resisted their bosses. The full nature of their demands was revealed as they held nightly meetings. What they wanted was a combination of the modern and the premodern. First, they objected to living in the factories in which they worked. They wanted their full wages without being compelled to pay board to their employers. Second, one hundred men working at Hue-Kai and Co. wanted $2.25 daily or at least an end to night work. Third, some workers objected to the practice of having to make a certain number of shoes daily or pay a fine of twenty-five cents per unmade shoe. Finally, some issued a premodern based protest against working with others who possessed different kin, village, and regional backgrounds. A compromise was eventually arranged. Yet the employers seem to have won more than they lost. The strikers were allowed to board themselves, but they received no wage increase and continued to labor in "mixed" work forces.

Clearly, however, those who counted upon Chinese shoemakers' docility miscalculated. These workers were, indeed, products of a premodern, precapitalist society that was significantly based upon paternalistic social, cultural, and economic arrangements. Still, Chinese shoemakers proved similar to laboring people in other premodern, precapitalist societies in that they were willing to draw a line of resistance beyond which those higher up in the social hierarchy dare not go without risking the collective protest of the poor. Additionally, like other preindustrial immigrants to the United States in the 19th and 20th centuries, their experiences with industrial capitalism quickened their ability to adopt methods of insurgency and objectives more in turn to their new and changing environment.

References

E. P. Thompson, "The Moral Economy of the English Crowd," *Past and Present*, no. 50 (1971), 76–136.

PP. 31, 145-149
53-59
67-85, 111-117, 131-145, 151-161,
189, 213-215, 229-231, 235-308